D0801780

"GET ME ELLIS RUBIN!"

"GET ME ELLIS RUBIN!"

The Life, Times, and Cases
of a Maverick Lawyer

ELLIS RUBIN

AND

DARY MATERA

ST. MARTIN'S PRESS

NEW YORK

Design by Robert Bull Design

Library of Congress Cataloging-in-Publication Data

Rubin, Ellis.
    Get me Ellis Rubin! / Ellis Rubin and Dary Matera.
       p.   cm.
    ISBN 0-312-03352-4
    1. Trials—Florida.   I. Matera, Dary. 1945–   . II. Title.
KF220.R825 1989
345.73'0092—dc20
[347.305092]
                                        89-32753
                                         CIP

First Edition

10 9 8 7 6 5 4 3 2 1

To the two Irenes who made my life,
and this book, possible—my mother and my wife.

CONTENTS

PREFACE   ix

ACKNOWLEDGMENTS   xvii

INTRODUCTION   xix

1 FIVE NICKELS, PART I   1

2 FIVE NICKELS, PART II: *The Trials*   15

3 PROGRAMMED TO KILL, PART I   23

4 PROGRAMMED TO KILL, PART II: *Trial on
     Television, Television on Trial*   41

5 THE SHEIK, PART I: *Lifestyles of the Incredibly
     Rich and Obnoxious*   67

6 THE SHEIK, PART II: *The Billion-Dollar Babies*   79

7 THE DEATH OF A DEBUTANTE, PART I   97

8 THE DEATH OF A DEBUTANTE, PART II:
    The Driver   113

9 THE JAILING, PART I   123

10 PRENTICE RASHEED AND THE TUTTI-FRUTTI
    DEFENSE, PART I   127

11 PRENTICE RASHEED AND THE TUTTI-FRUTTI
    DEFENSE, PART II: *The Not-So-Grand Jury*   135

12 THE JAILING, PART II   147

13 LOCKJAW   155

14 BUSTING THE BLACKOUTS, PART I:
    Don Quixote and King Alvin I   167

15 BUSTING THE BLACKOUTS, PART II:
    Tricky Dick and the Redskins   177

16 THE JAILING, PART III: *Dark Thoughts
    from a Black Cell*   189

17 THE CONDO MURDER, PART I   195

18 THE CONDO MURDER, PART II:
    The Depositions   213

19 THE CONDO MURDER, PART III: *The Defense*   229

20 A NIGHTMARE IN DELAWARE, PART I   241

21 A NIGHTMARE IN DELAWARE, PART II:
    Advil, Asthma, and Autoeroticism   253

22 VISUAL OBSERVATIONS   271

AFTERWORD   281

UPDATE   285

INDEX   287

PREFACE

IT OFTEN appears that every time South Florida becomes embroiled in some raging national controversy, Ellis Rubin is at the heart of it. Sometimes, if one sneaks a look behind the curtain, the renowned Miami defense attorney can be spotted merrily working the controls of the tempest like a modern-day Wizard of Oz. With Rubin, though, it's no illusion. He is both the controller and a flesh-and-blood legal wizard. "Both are great guys."

Even Rubin's most fervent enemies are forced to admit, however grudgingly, that he has performed in the courts like no attorney before him. He has shocked and startled. He's made jurors weep and spectators scream in protest. His peers have showered him with praise and lashed out at him in anger. He's inspired editorial writers to jump on his bandwagon and moved them to reach for their most acidic ink.

Rubin's controversial trailblazing has resulted in a string of legal precedents that have burned his name into judicial history.

And he's accomplished this by providing a powerful voice for the forgotten "little people" in danger of being crushed by a society that continues to struggle against racism, elitism, chauvinism, and oppression.

As a former South Florida journalist, I've long been fascinated with the sixty-four-year-old attorney and his turbulent career. On slow news days, while waiting for the inevitable murder and mayhem to erupt somewhere in Miami, I often wandered into the newspaper's library to kill time by perusing Rubin's clip files. I found hundreds of stories recorded on microfilm from the 1950s and 1960s, along with mountains of yellowing clippings from the 1970s and 1980s. The trail of fresh newsprint usually led right up to the previous day's editions, a factor that remains true today.

Studying the attorney's clips was like a crash course in the history of our nation over the past forty years. Amid the screaming headlines from the big murder and kidnapping cases, I discovered everything from Bay of Pigs and Watergate burglars to the seeds of the Iran-Contra scandal.

A more recent trip through Rubin's past took me on a journey that included one of the first airline hijackings, a ring of crooked cops ripping off cocaine dealers, a landmark sexual-abuse case, a billionaire Arab oil sheik, a gentle vigilante, theological malpractice, the National Football League, a reverse twist on the Scopes Monkey Trial, a serial murderer, religious cults, topless dancers, topless doughnut-shop waitresses, artificial heart transplants, desegregation of church schools, the bitter air traffic controllers' strike, and hundreds of others.

The names that popped up along with Rubin's were abundant and familiar: Jimmy Hoffa, Jackie Gleason, Marilyn Monroe, Carol Channing, Pete Rozelle, President Richard Nixon, Governor Claude Kirk, Connie Francis, Johnny Carson, Phillip Michael Thomas, Anita Bryant, Jackie Mason, Frank Sinatra, Hedy Lamarr, Larry King, Dr. Ferdie Pacheco. They joined hundreds of names readily familiar to Floridians.

One case took an entire file—the famous "television intoxication" trial. Although it happened in 1977, the debate over that volatile issue continues to this day (Chapters 3 and 4).

As much as the clips told me, they were nothing compared to the excitement generated by studying Rubin up close.

Rubin's office, a converted house off Biscayne Boulevard near downtown Miami, is a whirlwind of activity. At any given time his lobby would be packed with troubled faces straight from that morning's front page. There were celebrities of various repute, bandit cops, youth gang members, Guardian Angels, and wailing babies with famous bloodlines. On some occasions there was even Yahweh Ben Yahweh, a white-robed, turbaned black man who professes to be the son of God and claims eight thousand similarly dressed followers.

After two years of shadowing Rubin, I was able to penetrate the thick husk that covers the public figure and courtroom genius. Inside, much to my surprise, was an entirely different person.

The meticulously dressed lawyer seen locally in the courtroom and nationally on such television programs as "60 Minutes," "Donahue," "Oprah," "Larry King Live," "Nightline," "Today," and "Good Morning America" is the polar opposite of the private citizen who prefers to lounge around his bayside condominium in jogging shorts and sneakers. To quote from newspaper clips, the high-powered attorney that the public sees is "forceful," "flamboyant," "charismatic," "controversial," "renowned," "illustrious," "celebrated," "notorious," "eloquent," "loquacious," "garrulous," and "acclaimed."

When the jury goes home and the television minicams pack up, Rubin transforms into a soft-spoken family man who exhibits an unmistakable shyness.

Charles Fishman, a writer for the *Orlando Sentinel*, described the perplexing duality this way:

> The Ellis Rubin of the TV news and the talk shows and the newspaper headlines is almost the alterego of the real Ellis Rubin. It's a little like a ventriloquism act: The private Ellis Rubin creates and operates the public Ellis Rubin, and the act has been on the road so long—since 1951—that it's often hard to tell who's onstage.

Socially, Rubin's life is a similar paradox. One day he dons a tuxedo and dines with Miami's high society in the finest four-star restaurants. The next day he can be found gulping down a burger and fries in a fast-food joint in a dangerous ghetto. I've accompanied him in both settings, and he appears more comfortable in the latter.

Studying the man, I began to see the two sides come together.

The passion and anger boils out of his public persona. The kindness and caring for those in need simmers underneath, from the private side.

For those who believe in such things, Rubin is a Gemini. In astrology, Gemini is the sign of "the twins."

"There are definitely two of him," says Irene, his wife of thirty-three years. "Both are great guys."

And both are intriguing.

It took a long time, but I was finally able to unlock the mystery of his quizzical shyness and conflicting personalities. It was a startling revelation that began with a small boy and ended up being as heartrending as any of the two thousand stories I've written. I had to convince him to open up about his personal battle to overcome a debilitating handicap, and to allow me to include the inspirational story in this book (Chapter 13). The result is a chapter that, in its own way, is as moving as the intense courtroom dramas that fill the rest of the pages.

When it came time to write about Rubin's continuing career, my task was to sift through nearly forty years of cases to focus upon a dozen or so that held the most significance. It was an extremely difficult assignment—recalling one single day in Rubin's life dramatizes just how difficult. It started with a trip to the Florida Supreme Court in Tallahassee. Rubin argued against the death penalty in two separate, back-to-back cases. One involved a man, the other a woman. (Rubin had not been their original lawyer and wasn't responsible for their convictions.) Rubin was allotted a half hour each to persuade the state's seven justices that two human beings shouldn't be strapped into an electric chair and jolted to death. To his left on the podium was a row of small lights. The lights changed from green to white to red, to warn him when his time was up. When the light flashed red, that was it. End of discussion.

It was the ultimate, life-or-death race against the clock.

Rubin beat the red light, and the death sentences, in both cases.

We paused briefly for lunch at the airport, then caught a noon flight back to Miami. Arriving at Rubin's office ninety minutes later, we were notified of an urgent message from Judy Amar, the infamous "Bandit of Boca del Mar." Amar had donned designer gowns and driven luxury cars to burglarize Palm Beach mansions in style. She was finally captured and forced to trade in her chic dresses for a drab prison uniform. Amar wanted to consult with Rubin about her scheduled appearance the following morning on Oprah Winfrey's talk show. We rushed over to the jail so that Rubin could dispense some advice on what Amar should and should not say during the nationally televised interview.

Returning to the office, there was another in a continuing series of meetings with a secret Drug Enforcement Agency witness who had firsthand knowledge of the cocaine smuggling operation of a top foreign military leader. Subsequent meetings would be at various locations, including aboard the yacht *Zein,* a multimillion-dollar floating palace that had once served as the honeymoon suite for Prince Rainier and Princess Grace of Monaco. (The vessel was docked near Rubin's home, and he and Irene had become friends of the captain.)

This particular meeting was called to discuss the informant's appearance before the Senate Subcommittee on Narcotics and Terrorism.

In the midst of this tense discussion concerning security arrangements for a man with a half-million-dollar price on his head, the receptionist buzzed that singer Connie Francis was on the line. Rubin said he would call her back. A half hour later, the receptionist buzzed again. This time Hedy Lamarr was on line one, and Tanena Love, the mother of Johnny Carson's only grandchild, was on line two. (I was later dispatched to Francis's apartment to help her with a writing project.)

After assuring the nervous drug informant that things were under control, Rubin was handed a stack of messages. Included were requests to call the *Miami Herald,* the *Miami News,* the *Fort Lauderdale News/Sun-Sentinel,* the *Palm Beach Post, The Wall Street Journal, The New York Times,* the *Washington Times,* and several television stations. The reporters wanted to interview Rubin about five different cases.

A secretary came in with additional telephone messages. These were from political operatives across the state who were trying to push Rubin to run for the U.S. Senate.

We slowed down for a half hour to have dinner at Rubin's favorite restaurant, the S&S Diner. The small, art deco, countertop eatery offers two vegetables with each main course and a staff of motherly waitresses to make sure you eat them. Rubin ordered the $4.95 beef stew special and chose apple sauce and beets as his vegetables. Minutes after Rubin spooned in his last scoop of apple sauce, we were off again. We dashed to Yahweh Ben Yahweh's fortresslike Temple of Love so Rubin could discuss legal matters with the unconventional religious leader. Some Yahwehs had been accused in the newspapers of chopping off the heads of nonbelievers. The wild accusations came from a former member and admitted murderer. We stuck around to catch one of Yahweh Ben's rousing sermons, offered before a sea of white-robed, white-turbaned worshippers who danced, chanted, and sang out their leader's name.

"Slow day," Rubin cracked as we left the Temple of Love shortly after 10:00 P.M.

The next morning, Rubin was up at 6:00 A.M. to shower and prepare for Judy Amar's "Oprah" taping. He was at the jail by eight to help steady his client during the show.

That was too much for me. I slept in.

Looking back, I realize I could compile all the stories I was forced to leave out of this book into a riveting collection. Lost in the winnowing process were such high-voltage cases as Rubin's involvement with Watergate burglars Frank Sturgis and E. Howard Hunt; a subsequent lawsuit based upon an accusation that Hunt had taken part in the assassination of President John F. Kennedy; a suit brought by the Watergate wives; the shocking "River Cops" cocaine rip-off trial; the terrifying saga of Tampa serial killer Bobby Joe Long; a gossipy scandal involving a Catholic priest who married a woman and performed his own wedding ceremony; comedian Jackie Mason's battle with Frank Sinatra; Jackie Gleason's battle with his wife, Beverly; Jimmy Hoffa's battle with a splinter Teamster group; the fight against censorship of cable television; the battle to get a dying firefighter a Jarvik artificial heart; the "Bromo-Seltzer" murders; and literally hundreds of others.

Rubin could also very easily be the focus of a television miniseries tracing the chronology of the fight against the spread of communism into the Caribbean and Central and South America. Rubin's involvement began with legal cases rising out of the unrest in Cuba in the early 1950s. It continued with Castro's revolution, the bearded dictator's turn toward communism, and the resulting mass exodus of Cubans fleeing to Miami. That was followed by Rubin's association with the Bay of Pigs Brigade, President John F. Kennedy's unfulfilled promise of a free Cuba, and the emergence of Cuban anticommunist organizations. The clips become repetitive with the fall of Nicaragua and the growth of the Nicaraguan Contra forces in the Florida Everglades.

There just wasn't enough space.

But this should tell you something about the cases that were selected for this book.

Despite Rubin's accomplishments, his life hasn't been a cake-walk. Mavericks in any profession are often subjected to the relentless wrath of their peers. With Rubin, this has proven true to a harrowing degree. His legal and political enemies have tried numerous times to still his voice. Blindsiding attempts were made to disbar him. Each time, the higher courts ended up chastising the accusers.

Rubin was jailed four times, once briefly as the result of a false accusation, and three times for the same mind-boggling "offense" of refusing to represent a murderer who tortured and killed a young woman (Chapters 7 and 8). Instead of being broken, Rubin came out of jail tougher, smarter, and more determined than ever to obey his own higher ethical and moral standards.

And the experience hasn't slowed him down a step. Whether he's being forced to defend himself, or whether he's rushing to the rescue of someone else, the sparks of controversy continue to rocket off Ellis Rubin like a Fourth of July sparkler.

I suspect they always will.

D. M.

ACKNOWLEDGMENTS

There is no way that I can express my complete gratitude to the men and women of the Rubin clan for their contributions to this book. Mark and Guy Rubin "held down the fort" and ran the office while I was busy with Mr. Matera and the many, many files, transcripts, newspaper and TV clips, and interviews necessary to record the truth. They even planned and supervised, along with my son in law, Lee Newman, the construction of our new office building during this hectic period of our careers. Daughters Peri and Kimberly also contributed—Peri by managing and administering the office over the past ten years and then giving birth to my first granddaughter, Sydnee Jayne Newman, and Kimberly by heading up our newest division, that of public relations. Of course, the office would not even be in existence without my trusted right arm and partner—adviser over the past thirty-five years, my dearest Irene.

Thanks to the following from the law office of Rubin, Rubin & Fuqua, P.A.: Harry Matthew Fuqua, Kelley Finn, Hinda Klein, Robert I. Barrar, Jr., Jeff Morse, Laritza Orozco, Estela M. Tapanes, Bonnie MacFarlane—and our associate attorneys, Frank Quintero, Jr., Rene Palomino, Andrew Richard III, James S. Benjamin, and Dan R. Aaronson.

Special thanks for the extensive editorial assistance provided by

Fran Matera, Ph.D.,
School of Communication,
University of Miami and
The Walter Cronkite School of Journalism and
Telecommunication, Arizona State University.

And to: my sister, Jeanne and husband Ellis Tarsches, Laurette and Lloyd Arnel, Teddy Goldstein and his Peggy and Betty; Natalie and Mike Weitzman, Rose and Sam Kestenbaum; Red Terry, Bill Behan, Buddy Koffman, Hilly Rosen, Don Bronsky, Dick Frankel and all the other YMCA Camp Arrowhead Boys; Eileen and Jamey Haley, Norm Gold, Len and Gene Crowley, Shelly Horowitch, Allen Cave, Joey Taylor, Roger Schumacher, Robert Lott, Mr. Kavanaugh and Rita Eisenberg; and Lee (Jim) Cary, Glen Sanborn and Elmer Shafer of First Company, Second

Platoon, Holy Cross' V-12 Unit; Paul Gross, Bob McClosky, Irving Cypen, Stanley Stein, Smokey Stover, Al Hutchinson, Ben-Bob and Mary Rust, Keith Barish, Johnny Bowman, Boris and Becky Spaseff; Jerry O'Malley, Nelson Faerber, Jr., Corey Hoffman, Peter Dunbar, and Andrea Hillyer, Hon. Joe Boyd, James Atkins, Ray Hare, Mel Grossman and Shelby Highsmith; Lew Bickley, Phil and Harriet Mann, Jeanie and Charlie Cavalaris, Yolanda Quinones.

Plus: Julie Thornton, David Waksman, Charlie Monast, Ron Sladon, Robert Erlich, Micki Dahne, Melvin Belli, Marvin Mitchelson, Jack Kassewitz, Jr., Betty Scott, Marty Monroe, Kelly Hancock, Dan Insdorf, Prentice Rasheed, Les Share, Lisa Keller, Johnny Brown, Drs. Leonard Haber, Arthur Stillman, Marty Grossman, Robert Marlin, Jay Levine and Danny Stone.

From the City of Miami Police Department: Sgt. William O'Connor, Sgt. David Rivero, Sam Harlan, Det. John Spear, Det. Clarence Hall and Lt. Mike Gonzalez. From the Metro-Dade Police Department: Richard Hall and Capt. Kevin Hickey. From the City of Hollywood, Florida Police Department: Sgt. Jack Smith. From the Broward County Sheriff's Department: Dets. Philip Amabile and Richard Scheff.

And to the media: Gene Miller, Bob French, Robert Collier, Amy Dunn, Al Messerschmidt, Leo Suarez, Larry Keller, Renee Krause, Chris Murray, Molly Murray, Lynne Duke, Pat Curry, Christine Evans, Marcia Richardson, Milt Sosin, Cy Berning, Henry Reno, Charles Whited, Carl Hiaasen, James Martinez, Edna Buchanan, Joan Fleishman, Patti Magee, Andy Taylor, Jan Fisher, Barbara Storer, Mark Brender, Bob Zelnick, Larry King, Ted Koppel, Mark Worth, Wayne Hicks, Rick Buck, Meg Grant, Jeanne DeQuine, Steve Kane, Jack Ellery, Bernice and Allan Courtney, Tom Cawley, Bobby Groves, Barry Gray, John Broward, John Eastman, Craig Worthing, Gordon Shaw, Henry Barrow, Wayne Ferris, Brian Murphy, Richard Bard, Ike Flores, Fred Tasker, Joel Achenbach, Bernard Goldberg, Doug Young, Tammy Haddad, Harry Reasoner, Malcom Balfour, Jay Ducassi, Bob Sherman, Charlie Trainor, Bob East, Pete Cross and the many press photographers whose work grace this book.

A very special thanks to: Chris Dawson and the Student Legal Research Service of the University of Miami School of Law and to Navy CPO Plotnicki who "persuaded" a young midshipman to keep up with the rest of the battalion during those early morning four mile runs and one mile swims, which I am still doing thanks to the motivation of The Miami Runners Club and *Runners' World* magazine.

To the following universities for inviting me to lecture students and faculty: University of Tennessee; Nairobi University, Kenya, East Africa; New England College of Law; Florida International University; Nova University; Stetson University; and the University of Miami.

Contributions can be sent to and help can be obtained from:

The National Stuttering Project   Stuttering Resource Foundation
4601 Irving Street   and   123 Oxford Road
San Francisco, CA 94122-1020   New Rochelle, NY 10804

Finally, infinite thanks to our agent, Connie Clausen, for her wise advice and support; to our editor, Toni Lopopolo, for her skill and sensitivity; and to Maryanne Mazzola, Emi Battaglia, Tom Noonan, and Jeff Cope of St. Martin's Press.

—E. R. & D. M.

INTRODUCTION

WHEN I was thirteen years old, growing up in Binghamton, New York, I summoned the courage to go on a camping trip with my Boy Scout troop. I wasn't afraid of being out in the woods at night. It was the thought of being with a group of people that terrified me. I had a severe stammer, and kids sometimes made fun of me. I decided to go on this outing because I knew there'd be at least one person I could spend time with. He was my best friend and had never been put off by my handicap. His father owned a meat market a block away from where my father operated an army-navy store. We were about the same age and had been friends for years.

My friend was unusual in his own way. He had a strange and wonderful imagination. As we sat apart from the other campers, in the dark of the woods, alert to the spooky night sounds, my friend began telling stories. He spoke of life on other planets and had some delightful views on the types of beings he imagined would be found there. He talked about traveling to these worlds, time travel, ghosts, and the possibility of freezing time. He told me about extrasensory perception, dream interpretation, reincarnation, and the ability to read minds. My friend had an endless string of "what if" stories to tell, and I was spellbound.

He wanted to be a writer, and I was certain he would succeed.

My best friend's name was Rod Serling. He became the writer he dreamed of being, and more. As the creator of the television show "The Twilight Zone," Rod became one of the most influential mystery and science-fiction minds in history. I can't describe how it felt, and how it still feels, to turn on a television and see one of Rod's engrossing campfire stories come to life.

Back then, I was so certain that Rod would attain his dream that I was almost too embarrassed to tell him mine. I wanted to be a defense attorney like Clarence Darrow or Sam Leibowitz. I read everything I could get my hands on about them, including transcripts from their trials. I spent hundreds of hours alone at the library, imagining myself as a golden-tongued attorney pleading sensational cases before juries. But I was a stammerer. I could never be like Clarence Darrow or Sam Leibowitz until I overcame my speech impediment.

"You'll make it," Rod would say, never once laughing with the others or discouraging me. "Don't worry. The stammering will go away. You'll be a great lawyer one day."

When I was down about my inability to speak, Rod would cheer me up with a tale about an attorney defending a three-eyed creature from another planet. I'd laugh and feel better. His confidence gave me a boost.

Incredible as it sometimes seems, I did attain my dream of becoming a trial lawyer. It wasn't easy. I labored to overcome my stammering and stuttering and made great strides, but I still had the problem when I graduated law school. It was preposterous to think a stammerer could perform in a courtroom. I conceded as much and intended to return home, help my father run the army-navy store, and then branch into legal research or another area where I could hide behind a desk and silently make a living.

I was thoroughly depressed when I sank into my chair at the University of Miami Law School commencement in 1951. I had come so far, but ultimately had lost. When I looked up, I couldn't believe my eyes. There at the podium stood Sam Leibowitz! He was the commencement speaker. Leibowitz was the famous New York attorney who went to Alabama to save the lives of nine black men falsely accused of raping two white women in the classic case of the "Scottsboro Boys." I knew the transcript by heart.

Leibowitz gave an unforgettable speech that afternoon. Full of conviction, he told us that defense attorneys were the key to keeping America free. He said the protective ideals of the U.S. Constitution and the Bill of Rights were constantly under attack. The "authorities" were chipping away at the right to a fair trial, presumption of innocence, unreasonable search and seizure, and proof of guilt beyond a reasonable doubt. He warned us that the old guardians like himself were dying out, and that without a new generation to take up the fight, America would succumb to a re-emergence of robber barons and torture-chamber confessions. The average man and woman would be stripped of their dignity and liberty, and would be legally and economically enslaved. Leibowitz challenged us to take the torch he was passing, become defense attorneys, and protect America.

I felt he was speaking directly to me. I wanted to leap out of my seat, grab the flaming torch I imagined him holding, and charge into the first courtroom I could find.

Because of Leibowitz's speech, I decided to remain in Miami and become a defense attorney—stammer or no stammer.

Shortly afterward, I got my first case. A black man named Henry Larkin had shot and killed a man in the hallway of his apartment building. He was charged with murder. Larkin said the man had come after him with a knife. In those days there were no public defenders. Everyone was on his own. Groups of young attorneys used to mill around in court, laugh at the one criminal judge's jokes, volunteer for cases, and hope to be appointed. I was hanging around the courthouse when someone told me about Larkin. I went to the jail. He nearly cried when I offered to represent him.

The day before the trial, my first trial, I read in the *Miami Herald* that Leibowitz, then a New York judge, was back in town for another speech. I found out where he was staying and went to his hotel.

"Mr. Leibowitz," I said, stammering, standing paralyzed at his door, case file in hand. "I was in the audience when you gave the ca, ca, commencement address here. I became a defense attorney because of what you said. Now I'm facing mm, mm, my first case tomorrow. Can you give me some help?"

It was an incredible intrusion, and I must have been a pathetic sight. Leibowitz just smiled and invited me in. He then proceeded to outline my entire defense. He raised his eyebrows every time I tripped over a word, but never said a thing about my speech impediment.

The next day I stood before twelve people in a court of law. The life of Henry Larkin was in my hands, or more precisely, in my misfiring mouth. But instead of fear, a strange feeling came over me. I felt taller and stronger, and for the first time in my life I was confident. My own troubles vanished and were replaced by the far greater problems of Henry Larkin. He was a good, honest man who had never broken the law in his life. It was up to me to convince a jury that he had acted in self-defense and shouldn't be sent to the electric chair.

I talked for hours that day, remembering everything Sam Leibowitz taught me, and pleading, in every sense of the word, for the man's life. I was raw and unskilled, but enthusiastic and determined.

The jury was out three minutes. When they returned, the judge joked, "What took you so long?"

The foreman, a local newspaper columnist named Jack Bell, joked back, "We had to take a cigarette break to make it look good."

The verdict was not guilty.

Henry Larkin hugged me and broke down in tears. A newspaper reporter was in the courtroom and wrote a story the next day about the green young attorney saving the black man's life.

But there was one thing the story didn't mention. I hadn't stammered once during my entire argument.

I hardly ever did again.

I tried to call Sam Leibowitz, but he had left town. Needing to share my double victory with someone, I called Rod and told him about the "miracle" of my untangled tongue. He was elated. Then he grew serious.

"Ellis, it's a sign!" he proclaimed. "You've found your place in time. You were destined to speak for the innocent and oppressed. Never forget that!"

Rod was quick to see some unexplained universal phenomenon in practically everything. In his eyes, what happened to me could only have happened in "The Twilight Zone." Actually, stammerers and stutterers have been known to lose their handicaps in similar situations. Country singer Mel Tillis is but one example. Still, who can say? Some of us like to live in a world where everything has a clear-cut explanation. Others, the more romantic among us, prefer Rod Serling's landscape where anything is possible. As an attorney dealing with facts, figures, and documented proof, I should be steadfastly entrenched in the physical world. In reality, I often wander into that other, more interesting place.

For whatever reason, Rod's words have stayed with me throughout my life.

DURING THE past thirty-eight years I've been in more than three thousand trials, including 285 for first-degree murder. New cases come in every week. And I've discovered that truth can sometimes be stranger than even Rod Serling's fiction.

I've also tried to do my best to defend the "poor and defenseless," which Sam Leibowitz said was my primary function. Some people, including my wife, feel I've overdone it. I spend a great deal of time on what are known as *pro bono* cases. The term comes from the Latin *pro bono publico*, "for the public good." It's more commonly translated to mean "for free." A state prosecutor once stood in court and described my clients another way: "Rubin's riffraff."

Actually, I've had my share of wealthy clients, including celebrities, rich businessmen, doctors, and a billionaire Arab oil sheik. The "riffraff" waiting in my office don't seem to frighten them away. Some people say the problem is that I can't say no. That's part of it. Each time someone in deep trouble walks through my door, anguished, often crying, and always desperate, it's hard to turn him or her away.

Payment can come in many forms. A handshake. A hug. A baby's smile. A holiday card. A birthday card. A home-cooked meal. A friendly face in court. A picketer carrying a sign outside a jail.

Henry Larkin, my first client, came by every Friday for the rest of his life and handed me an envelope with a five-dollar bill in it. Never missed a week. Even when I told him to stop, he kept coming.

What my critics, and even my clients, don't realize is how much these people have given back to me. Over the years I've been fortunate enough to be a part of some major court proceedings. Precedents were set, lives were dramatically altered, and in a small way, history was changed.

It's been exciting. In the following pages I'll take you from the back of the courtroom to a seat beside me at the defense table. You'll experience the strategy sessions, the involvement of the media, and the mental combat of the trial. In a few cases we'll even pierce the sanctity of the judge's chambers and the jury room. Sometimes we'll go even further. We'll accompany the accused through the day or evening of the crime, trace the arrest, and visit him or her in jail.

As for the part I played in all these cases, I'd like to think that I've made my campfire buddy, Rod Serling, and my mentor, Sam Leibowitz, proud.

—E.R.
Hendersonville, N.C.
Summer 1989

"GET ME ELLIS RUBIN!"

1

FIVE NICKELS, PART I

CHARLES WESLEY JOHNSON had two great weaknesses: red wine and older women. He combined the two to lead a life of luxury and debauchery. Charlie was faithful to the wine and unfaithful to the women. That was his downfall.

But what a sensational fall it was. On Thursday, April 17, 1952, Charles Wesley Johnson pulled off one of the most memorable crimes in Florida history. The newspapers called it the work of a top-flight gang of criminal geniuses who had planned and carried out their scheme with split-second precision.

It was nothing of the sort. It was merely Charlie Johnson, five nickels, a bottle of wine, a public telephone, and a streak of blind luck.

I first saw Charlie standing in a line of prisoners at the twenty-five-story Dade County Courthouse. At the time, the courthouse was the tallest building south of Jacksonville, a city four hundred miles away. Charlie's cell was on the top floor, up where a family

1

of turkey buzzards from Hinckley, Ohio, had ominously taken up winter residence upon the gray stone building's stepped, pointed roof. (To this day, their descendants arrive from Hinckley each fall.)

Charlie was the only white man in the group that morning. Judge Ben Willard took special notice. Everyone took special notice of Charlie. He was thirty-three, six feet tall, about 145 pounds, deeply tanned, movie-star handsome, meticulously dressed, and had perfect manners. His hazel eyes and light brown, sun-streaked hair were set against a dignified patch of gray at his temples. Charlie also proved to be well read and articulate. He spoke with a peculiar accent similar to that of Cary Grant. Like Grant, he appeared to be an aristocratic foreigner from a land far more romantic and sophisticated than America.

Charlie had ended up in such an undignified place because he had grown tired of his latest romantic interest and wheeled out of her life in the woman's black Rolls-Royce. He didn't wander far. He went joy-riding around unhurried Miami, hitting all his favorite seaside bars, sipping wine under the thatched, sabal palm roofs and running up big tabs he couldn't pay, but could always talk his way around. He gave practically everyone in town a ride in the Rolls, shuttling groups back and forth from the inland bars clustered downtown, over a causeway lined with banyan trees and royal poincianas blooming fiery orange, to the beaches, which were then covered in waves of tall sea-oat grass instead of shoulder-to-shoulder hotels and condominiums. The fun lasted a week or so, until the Miami police caught up with him. They confiscated the car and gave Charlie a room with a great view and a chance to study the big, black scavenger birds up close.

"What brings you here?" Judge Willard asked.

"I stole a car," Charlie answered.

"How do you plead?"

"Guilty, I guess," Charlie said.

By now, Judge Willard was starting to take a shine to Charlie.

"Now wait a minute, Mr. Johnson," the judge lectured. "This is a serious crime. You could get ten years. Are you sure you want to plead guilty?"

"Okay, not guilty," Charlie said.

Judge Willard laughed. He then asked Charlie if he wanted to be tried by judge or jury.

"Your Honor," Charlie said, dripping with respect, "you appear to be a man of the utmost honesty. I would be happy to have you hear my case."

Judge Willard looked over at the gaggle of young attorneys hanging around the court, trying to get cases.

"Anybody want this one?"

I immediately stepped forward.

"Okay, lawyer," the judge said. "You go upstairs and talk with your client. The trial will begin at one-thirty."

Talk about speedy trials. It was a little after ten, and I would have to be in court, trying the case, in less than four hours. But that's the way it was in those days. Miami was more of a sleepy tourist town then, and, hard as it may be to imagine today, there wasn't much crime.

Charlie and I talked in the jail's unventilated visiting area. He told me he was a radio engineer and had been a radio operator in the merchant marine for five years during World War II. I was a naval reserve officer, so we had something in common. Charlie had wanted to join the navy, but he was color-blind and had been rejected—a handicap that I noticed didn't hinder the selection of his beautifully matched slacks, shirt, and sport jacket. Born in Spokane, Washington, he had attended the Jesuit's Gonzaga University and, according to him, had been a first cellist with the Spokane Symphony Orchestra. He had married and divorced twice, and had three children living with his second wife. Charlie's father was a wealthy dentist, and Charlie had attended medical school in Mexico, where he learned to speak Spanish fluently. A wanderer by nature, Charlie spent a year exploring Indochina, Burma, Malaya, and India before joining the merchant marine.

Charlie said he hadn't worked in years. He explained that his considerable needs had been provided through "the kindness of lonely widows." His territory was the aptly named Gold Coast of Florida, the real-estate-rich coastal area that extends down U.S. 1 from Palm Beach to Miami. Then, as today, the Gold Coast was teeming with rich widows left with the fortunes their husbands worked themselves to death to acquire. For Charlie, it was paradise.

Almost. After a few years he found that his tolerance for older women was waning, and the life of idle tropical luxury had grown boring. So he jumped into his latest keeper's chariot and set a course for wine and adventure.

"Call the car's owner," he told me, outlining his defense. "Tell her I'm sorry. Tell her I'll go back to her if she drops the charges."

He winked at me and said, "Be sure to tell her that I love her."

I called. A woman with a soft voice answered. I relayed what Charlie had said. I told her that he loved her. She was very happy. She didn't want Charlie to go to jail.

"I love Charles very much," she confessed. "Is he all right?"

"He is at the moment, but jail is a terrible place. Especially for a man like Charles," I said.

"Oh no! I'll be right down," she said.

She arrived within the hour. She was a lovely woman in her mid-fifties, draped in a flowing, ivory linen day dress topped by a blue, wide-brimmed hat that matched the silk sash around her waist. Her hair was dyed blond with not a dark root in sight. Her skin was kept as smooth as humanly possible by the best creams and facials money could buy. As she entered the musty jail, a wave of fifty-dollar-an-ounce perfume cut through the air and freshened the entire room.

Charlie had asked me to warn him when she arrived, so that he could return to his cell. As always, he knew what he was doing. The woman cried when she saw her poor Charles trapped behind the rows of black bars. She demanded his release into a conference room with an authority that jerked the jailer into action.

They had an emotional reunion.

We entered the court at one-thirty sharp. The woman informed Judge Willard she was dropping all charges. The judge asked her if she knew what she was doing. She responded with a look that frosted the judge's eyebrows. End of discussion.

I watched Charlie and his lady walk out of the courtroom hand-in-hand. They left in the black Rolls. Charlie was driving. He waved to me as he drove off.

All seemed right with the world.

The next time I saw Charlie Johnson was a few weeks later. I didn't exactly see *him.* I saw his picture. It was on the front page of the *Miami Herald* under a headline of a size and blackness I hadn't seen since World War II ended. The story described Charlie as the leader of a gang of kidnappers, who, in a masterful plot, had taken the son of one of Miami's richest and best-known families, then released him for a sizable ransom. The state attorney was on record promising that Charlie and his cerebral cohorts would be caught and sent as quickly as possible to the electric chair.

I was stunned. Good-Time Charlie was the leader of a gang of cutthroats?

The ink had barely dried on the newspaper when I heard on the radio that Charlie had been apprehended in Cuba, by the Cuban secret police. There were more headlines. When Charlie arrived at Miami International Airport nine days later, Channel 4, the only television station in Florida, sent its brand-new news crew out to capture the historic event. Fresh-faced reporter Ralph Renick was there with a crew carrying one of those bulky old cameras and a portable wire recorder. I didn't own a television set, so I rushed over to a department store, fought off the salesman, and waited for the news.

Sure enough, there was Charlie. Despite being handcuffed and surrounded by burly police officers, he looked as dapper and nonplussed as ever. Clad in a yellow shirt with big blue flowers, a light tan sport jacket, mustard-colored slacks, brown and white oxfords, and dark sunglasses, and with his tousled hair blowing in the light breeze, he photographed like a Hollywood star. Renick, who would later gain a few pounds and become the white-maned dean of Florida broadcasters, pushed his way in as close as he could get. Charlie walked over, looked into the camera, leaned toward the microphone, and said, in his best Cary Grant voice:

"Get me Ellis Rubin!"

I nearly fell over. Here was Public Enemy Number One, calling out my name for all the world to hear. I rushed to the courthouse and was immediately ushered in to see my client. The place was packed with police officers, prosecutors, FBI agents, and reporters. Charlie was under heavy guard. Everyone was tense. The guards no doubt expected that any second the rest of Charlie's gang was going to burst through the brass doors in a blaze of machine-gun fire.

Like the guards, I too was nervous. Only instead of a rescue squad, I feared that a lynch mob might be forming.

"Good to see you, Ellis," Charlie said, eyes twinkling brightly. "I see you got my message. I'm in a bit of a spot here."

I was amazed. Here he was, a few months away from a possible date with the electric chair, and he was as cool as ever. I escorted him into an interrogation room. Two guards tried to follow us inside, but I screamed out some legalese and shut the door on them.

"Charlie, what did you do?"

"I made a couple of phone calls."

"Where's your gang?"

He threw back his head and laughed.

"There's no gang, Ellis. The newspapermen exaggerate. It was just me."

"You? That's impossible."

"Quite possible, Ellis. Quite possible."

He proceeded to tell me his story.

When Charlie was in jail on the auto-theft charge, he and his three cellmates killed time by talking about what they each considered would be the "perfect crime." Charlie never said whether the eventual plan was his, a cellmate's, or a collaboration, but he left the jail that time with more than just his freedom. His mind was spinning with wild and dangerous thoughts. After a few weeks of wine and roses, he grew bored and once again escaped from his lover's palatial oceanfront estate.

As was his style, Charlie wandered the tropical town, befriending bartenders, charming the ladies, and running up tabs. He was also putting together his plan. It didn't take much. A week or so later he was ready.

On a humid Florida afternoon, Charlie Johnson entered a Greyhound bus station near Flagler Street, in the heart of downtown Miami. He walked to the pay phones and surveyed the surroundings. To his right was a wall of lockers, to his left, the ticket counter. Directly across from the phones was a candy and newspaper stand. Charlie entered the middle phone booth, closed the door, and spread out the tools that would enable him to commit "the perfect crime."

They were five nickels, a small piece of paper, and a bottle of wine. He stacked the nickels to the left of the phone. The bottle of his favorite vintage rosé was placed on the counter to the right. The paper, which contained four phone numbers, was set to the left of the wine.

Plunk. He dropped the first nickel into the slot and dialed the number at the top of the list—a cab company on Miami Beach. Although Charlie was quite drunk, he sobered up when he spoke. He asked for the manager of the cab depot.

"Hello, this is Dr. Henderson at Doctors Hospital in Coral Gables," Charlie said. "Mrs. Dan Richter has just had a serious accident and was brought here in critical condition. She may not survive. She has repeatedly asked to see her son, Ricky. Will you

small ones. After Richter left for the hotel, Miami police detectives Joel McNeill, Marshall Wiggins, and Earl Taunton arrived and set out after him.

Plunk. Nickel number five. Charlie consulted the last number on his list and dialed the front desk of the Ponce de Leon Hotel. A clerk answered, looked around the lobby, and spotted a man who fit the description given by the caller. He sent a bellboy to bring him over. Confirming that the man was Dan Richter, the clerk handed him the phone.

"Mr. Richter, I want you to go to the Greyhound station down the block," Charlie instructed. "Once you are inside, I would like you to walk to the candy counter and purchase a pack of gum. Take out two sticks and place them in your mouth and begin chewing. You will see a bank of lockers against the opposite wall. Please go to the lockers, choose one that is not in use, insert the rolled newspaper, place the correct change into the slot, and remove the key.

"By now you should have chewed the gum into a malleable condition. To your left you will see three telephone booths adjacent to one another. Choose the first one, walk inside, and close the door. Remove the gum from your mouth, mold it around the key, then adhere the key to the underside of the telephone counter. You are then to walk out of the bus station without looking back, and return to your store. Let me reiterate that we have people watching the entire route, so don't do anything irrational.

"You have seven minutes to complete your task. The stopwatch starts right now."

Click.

Charlie took a long swig of his wine, sat in the phone booth, and waited.

Dan Richter saw the Miami police detectives as he exited the hotel lobby. Detective McNeill decided to station detectives Wiggins and Taunton in front of the bus depot, and he would personally monitor the drop from inside. He rushed over and took his position.

A minute later, Dan Richter walked into the Greyhound station, bought the gum, chewed two sticks, placed the rolled newspaper containing the ransom into the locker, and attempted to enter the phone booth to his left. It had recently been painted and was locked. The booth in the center was occupied—by Charlie—so he chose the one on the right, put the gum on the key, and stuck the key to the underside of the counter. Richter exited the phone booth and walked out of the bus station. Charlie staggered out of his booth and into the other, took the key, walked to the locker, retrieved the newspaper, walked out of the bus station—and right into Friendly's Bar, half a block away.

He sat at the bar and, in clear view, spread open the newspaper. Inside was $200 in cash and a mountain of glittering jewels.

"Drinks are on me, everybody!" he announced.

A crowd quickly gathered.

"What the hell you got there, Charlie?" the bartender said, eyes bugging out.

"My aunt died and left me this," Charlie explained.

The bar crowd consoled Charlie on his aunt's misfortune and complimented him on his windfall. They toasted his aunt a half-dozen times and had a rousing party in her memory. Charlie paid off his tab and then handed the friendly bartender a small chunk of diamonds.

"Here, my good man, secure this as collateral against my future bar tabs."

Meanwhile, Detective Joel McNeill was catching hell from his superiors. Despite the simplicity of the drop, he had missed it! His eyes had been open too wide.

Detective McNeill had visited his ophthalmologist that morning as part of an annual police physical. The doctor had dropped in a solution that made his pupils dilate so that they could be checked for specific eye problems. Detective McNeill was told to wear sunglasses for the next twelve hours until the solution wore off and his pupils could function properly to protect against excessive light.

If there's one thing that Florida has, it's excessive light.

As Detective McNeill walked to the bus station, the bright Florida sunshine, which can be blinding to normal eyes, cut through his sunglasses and temporarily blinded him. While he was waiting for his eyes to adjust, Dan Richter made the drop and placed the key in the opposite booth. Charlie recovered it. When his eyes cleared, Detective McNeill focused them on the wrong booth. He either missed the pickup or ignored it. Without McNeill's identification, Charlie was able to stroll right past the detectives stationed outside.*

*Dan Richter recalls a different version of what happened to the detectives that day. He says that after he left the Ponce de Leon Hotel, his father, Joseph,

The eerie luck that shielded Charles Johnson that afternoon had struck again.

While Charlie was hoisting the first of his celebratory drinks, Bert Walowitz was dutifully driving down South Dixie Highway to Doctors Hospital in Coral Gables. The trip took less than an hour. Walowitz did his best to keep young Ricky calm, assuring him that everything was going to be fine. Actually, Ricky had not been told about his mother's "accident" and was delighted to get out of school early. Walowitz played tour guide and pointed out all the interesting sights along the way. Ricky was enjoying the adventure.

Waiting at Doctors Hospital were FBI agents and virtually the entire Coral Gables police force—armed and ready for some serious kidnapper butt-kicking. Walowitz pulled up, saw the officers, and figured something had happened. He never once imagined he might be part of it. When the officers saw the cab, then spotted Ricky, they pounced upon Walowitz like starving Dobermans on a piece of raw meat. Walowitz was yanked out of the car, slapped around, thrown on the hot hood, frisked, handcuffed, and heaved into a patrol car with bars separating the driver and the passenger.

"How could you do such a thing, Walowitz?" the detectives growled.

"Do what?" the absolutely mystified cabbie asked in reply.

Ricky, excited by the police cars and all the action, continued to have a ball. He never knew, nor was he ever told until years later, that he had been "kidnapped."

Walowitz was taken to the police station to be interrogated. Outside, his family was crying, the cab company officials were crying, everyone was crying at the terrible plight of Bert Walowitz.

Everybody except Charles Wesley Johnson. He was having the time of his life. Charlie left the bar after about an hour, ambled down the block, and ducked into Stone's Tavern. He repeated the previous scene, spreading out the cache on the counter, buying

---

became confused and told one detective that his son had been instructed to go to the jewelry store first, then to the bus station. That detective walked back to the store. Dan Richter says a second detective passed in front of him as he entered the bus station, so he felt everything was under control. However, according to Richter's version, the second detective was on the phone with the FBI when the drop and the pickup went down. Richter said the detectives regrouped at the bus station and watched the locker for fifteen minutes—but the pickup had already been made and Charlie was gone. The detectives were watching an empty locker.

drinks for the house, paying off his tab and leaving the bartender with a precious gem as security against future tabs.

He duplicated his celebration at two more bars, sharing his good fortune with his faithful friends and friendly bartenders. After partying at the fourth bar, he stumbled into his room at the fleabag Peerless Hotel, also on Flagler Street. Two unidentified friends put him to bed. The hotel's owner, Aurelien Roberge, checked up on Charlie and found his wallet sitting on the night table. Roberge rifled through it, counted $160 in twenties, one ten, and a few scattered ones, and brought it into the office for safekeeping.

Charlie awoke the next morning around nine. Sobriety and the stark surroundings combined to flash a brief moment of sanity into his brain. It occurred to him that someone out there might be looking for him. If not the police, then any of a dozen unsavory characters who had seen him display his bounty at the four bars.

"I think it is imperative that I make a hasty retreat from this country," he explained to the fuzzy image in the tarnished mirror.

The "hasty" part of his escape soon gave way to the more powerful draw of the beautiful tropical morning and the ample supply of wine waiting in the nearby bars. No need to rush. He was only the most wanted person in Florida, and the object of a massive manhunt. Charlie hit Friendly's again, and Stone's, and the Backstage Bar. At 11:10 P.M., he checked into the nearby Royalton Hotel. He checked out thirty-five minutes later, and checked into the Fort Knox Hotel, another block or so away.

Charlie instructed the hotel clerk to call the airport and make a plane reservation for the next flight to Havana. He also told the clerk to coordinate the flight departure time with a cab ride from the hotel to the airport. The clerk was asked to make the reservations in the name of "Kingsley Elliott," a radio handle Charlie had used while working as a disc jockey. The clerk made the arrangements and earned a nice tip. At 2:45 P.M., Charlie left for the airport. At 3:45 P.M., he was aboard Cubana Airlines flight 495 to Havana. He arrived around 4:30 P.M. and settled in at the Hotel Bellamar, on Cuba's unspoiled Marianao Beach.

While Charlie slept, all hell was breaking loose in Miami. Special editions of the newspapers screamed the latest information on the brilliant gang of kidnappers. There was little else being broadcast on the radio, as up-to-the-minute reports filled the airwaves. The attention was so widespread that it even penetrated the secluded world of Charlie's favorite bohemian saloons. Soon the bartenders and patrons were wringing their hands over what to do.

"Could it be Charlie? It has to be Charlie," they speculated. "No, it can't be Charlie. Should we call the police? But what if it is Charlie? He's such a great guy! What should we do?"

The patrons debated and drank, and drank and debated. Phones were picked up and slammed down. Arguments ensued. Little by little, the calls trickled in to the Miami police. From this bar and that bar, a pattern emerged. A call even came from one of Charlie's former cellmates from the car-theft arrest. The man, Antonio Feliz, told the police about the daydream session, and remarked how Charlie Johnson's version of "the perfect crime" was similar to what he had been reading about in the newspapers. In record time, the police had Charlie identified and had released pictures of him from his prior arrest.

The police, the FBI, and the state attorney's investigators fanned out across downtown Miami, following Charlie's wine-soaked trail. They tracked him through the bars and hotels, eventually climbing all over the poor clerk at the Fort Knox Hotel, snatching his tip, and learning that Charlie had left for Cuba.

They wired a full description, an arrest warrant, and a pickup order to the Cuban police.

The information never arrived.

Charlie Johnson would probably have spent the next few years wooing Havana señoritas and improving his tan, had it not been for the *Miami Herald.* Hot on the story, a reporter called the Cuban police the following day for an update on the search. When informed that the Cubans knew nothing about the dashing criminal in their midst, the *Herald* decided to relay the information. It was enough to send the Cuban secret police out searching the tropical island for one Kingsley Elliott, a.k.a. Charles Wesley Johnson.

The Cuban secret police mirrored the search of their Miami counterparts. They picked up Charlie's bilingual trail and traced him from bar to bar, from hotel to hotel, until they found him the next day, sleeping peacefully at Havana's flagship inn, the Hotel Nacional. They rousted him from his siesta and searched his room, but found nothing. They told him he would be extradited unless he led them to the jewels, which they promised to split. Charlie, always willing to share with new friends, led the officers to Marianao Beach, where he had stashed the diamonds under a mattress in the Hotel

Bellamar. The secret police confiscated the jewels and threw Charlie in jail. The Cuban police then called the *Miami Herald* and gloated that they had captured the dangerous felon. The *Herald* promptly ran a big story, boasting how the newspaper had helped capture the kidnapper. Somewhere amid all the gloating and boasting, the official lines of communication between the Cuban and Miami law enforcement agencies were magically unsnarled. Detectives were dispatched from Miami. Nine days later the Cuban president, Fulgencio Batista, ceremoniously signed a warrant ordering Charlie Johnson's return to the United States.

And that's when things really got crazy.

2

FIVE NICKELS, PART II:

The Trials

CHARLIE SHOWED up at his arraignment smartly dressed in a sparkling white T-shirt, a chocolate-colored sport jacket, tan pants, and the ever-present brown-and-white oxfords. Thirty years later, actor Don Johnson, who resembles Charlie, would sport a similar style on the television show "Miami Vice" and create an international fashion sensation.

The judge, unimpressed with Charlie's wardrobe, wanted to set the trial for June, a little more than a month away. I had naval reserve duty that month and had to go to sea. The judge moved the trial to July, giving me additional time to prepare.

During the days immediately following Charlie's arrest, the police and the FBI applied intense pressure for leads on the rest of Charlie's gang. They refused to believe, or to accept, that Charlie had acted alone. The state prosecutor remained intent upon keeping his promise to execute the conspirators side by side in a barber's row of electric chairs.

Only there wasn't any gang—unless you count Bert Walowitz. And Charlie steadfastly refused to implicate the cabdriver. The prosecutors offered to waive the death penalty in return for Walowitz's hide, but Charlie and I would have none of it.

"What, pray tell, is a Walowitz?" Charlie kept asking.

The cops, who suspected that poor Walowitz wasn't involved, finally let the cabbie go.

If there had been a gang, we'd have been better off. At least I could have traded some information in return for a waiver on the death penalty. Charlie could have saved his skin by fingering somebody, but there was no one to finger. I finally convinced everyone of that, and things quieted down.

Charlie had another, potentially more troublesome, dilemma facing him. Me. This was a major kidnapping trial, and I was less than a year out of law school. Worse, Sam Leibowitz wasn't around. (Believe me, I looked.) I was way out of my league, but I wasn't about to let go of the case. My resolve was quickly put to the test. I had recently been hired by a prestigious corporate law firm headed by Abe Aronovitz, who would later become mayor of Miami. Mr. Aronovitz informed me that his firm didn't handle criminal law.

"Besides, the Richters are close friends of mine," Aronovitz said. "You'll have to sit this one out, Ellis."

I had about five dollars to my name and was living in a single room at a boardinghouse. The law firm offered a bright future and financial security.

I quit. I had little choice. Criminal law was my calling.

I set up a one-room office right down the hall from Aronovitz's law firm, then rushed over to the University of Miami Law School and had a talk with Dean Russell Rasco. I asked for some advice on how to defend Charlie, then suggested that we establish a "criminal aid bureau" that would allow students to gain experience by assisting attorneys in actual trials. I volunteered to kick off the program with the Charles Johnson trial. Dean Rasco saw through the desperation that clouded my motives and realized that it was a good opportunity for the students. He gave me carte blanche to form the organization. I immediately recruited three of the brainiest students in the school, and we went right to work trying to find some way to keep Charlie alive.

Charlie had done a bad thing, no question, but I didn't think he deserved to die for it. He had too much to drink, and pulled off a stunt that in his wildest dreams he never expected would work. If he had been unable to reach one person in his chain of calls; if Ricky had been home sick that day; if the cab company or the school had questioned his authority; if Mr. Richter had been away purchasing jewelry; if he had gotten just one busy signal, the whole scheme would have blown apart. The odds against his succeeding the way he did must have been astronomical.

Charlie Johnson had winged "the crime of the century."

In his mind, it was a lark. A serious and maybe even a cruel lark, but a lark nevertheless. Charlie was surprised when he was informed that kidnapping carried the death penalty. He figured that as long as he didn't hurt anybody, it couldn't be much worse than stealing a car.

The students and I searched the law books for something, anything, to save Charlie's neck. It looked bleak. The "it was just a joke, ha, ha" defense wasn't going to fly. A couple of days before the trial, one of the students pointed out something in the state kidnapping statutes. I couldn't believe it. There it was, a loophole the size of Tallahassee! The answer had been staring us in the face all along. But could it possibly work?

It was all we had.

Judge Fritz Gordon's fourth-floor courtroom was jammed wall-to-wall for the trial. You couldn't wedge another person in with a crowbar. The reporters were everywhere. Many had come from out of town. There was no air conditioning then, and July in Miami is searing. Hand fans waved about and handkerchiefs frequently appeared to mop the sweaty brows of everyone from the judge to the jurors. The open windows merely let in more hot summer air. Everybody in the courtroom was wilting—everyone except Charlie. He was as cool as ever, and made for a great villain. He sat at the defense table in a stylish red-checked sport jacket, hair perfectly coiffured, and occasionally flashed a toothy grin so white it dazzled. Women began writing to him in jail. But even if a few ladies wanted his body, the majority of the public wanted his head.

The prosecution took three days to put on its case. It was considerable. There was the hard evidence of the money and jewelry found under his Hotel Bellamar bed, along with the bartenders and their "security" jewelry. The witnesses included Walowitz, the bartenders, their patrons, and various hotel clerks, most of whom had to be dragged in to testify. They liked Charlie, but the police pressure was intense.

"I'm sorry, Charlie," one young lady said tearfully, after identifying him as the big spender with the cash and jewels.

"It's okay, love," Charlie said, and meant it.

I was popping up and down from the defense table like a jack-in-the-box, objecting to everything, counterpunching, zealously trying to keep out the evidence by charging that the Cubans had acted unlawfully in searching, arresting, and deceiving Charlie. None of it was working. I was taking an old-fashioned, behind-the-shed whipping from veteran prosecutors Arthur Carlson and S. O. "Kit" Carson. It was so bad that when Judge Gordon finally sustained one of my objections, the whole courtroom broke into laughter, including the judge, the jury, the prosecutors, and even me. When the prosecution rested its case, there wasn't a shred of doubt in anyone's mind that Charles Johnson was guilty.

It was now the defense's turn. I stood in court and gave one of the shortest speeches of my entire career.

"Your honor, I move for a dismissal. According to State Statute 805.02, a kidnapper must have actual custody of the kidnapped person before a crime is committed. Charles Johnson never had custody of Ricky Richter. Therefore, under state law, there was no kidnapping."

There was a low buzz in the courtroom, but nothing out of the ordinary. Defense attorneys invariably open their cases with dismissal requests. Only there was a loud buzz in the judge's head, and that's what counted. He immediately called a recess for lunch, and said the court would reconvene in two hours.

When everyone returned, the judge sat down and quietly said, "Mr. Rubin's motion is granted. Case dismissed." He slammed the gavel down so hard it rang out like a shot, stunning everyone in the courtroom.

Then he stood and walked out.

For a few seconds the courtroom was silent. No one could grasp what had happened. When it sunk in, no one could believe it. The sound began to build. There was a gasp, a scream, followed by a slow rumble, building and building into a frenzy of activity. The reporters sprang from their seats, surged out the door, and fought over the nearby phones to call in the news.

"What happened?" Charlie asked me.

"You're free," I said.

"How?" he said.

"Don't ask. Let's just get the hell out of here."

I escorted Charlie up to the jail to collect his things. I was pushing him to move as quickly as possible.

"Why the hurry?" he inquired.

"I don't want the judge to change his mind," I said.

We exited the courthouse, took one step out into the sunshine, and were surrounded by police officers. They slapped handcuffs around Charlie's tanned wrists and ushered him back into the building. An officer handed me a warrant.

Charlie was charged with extortion.

I later learned that during the recess the judge had summoned Michael Zarowny, the assistant county solicitor, to his chambers.

"That son of a bitch Rubin has got us on this," the judge said. "I have to let the bastard go. But you file extortion charges immediately. I don't want Johnson to set foot outside."

Charlie was brought back to jail. His new arraignment was scheduled for the following morning in another courtroom. The change was a break, because Judge Gordon was in no mood to have mercy on Charlie or me. Actually, he didn't have a choice. Kidnapping is a capital offense, meaning it involved the death penalty. Extortion is a violation of a lesser felony law. Not only had we switched courtrooms, but we'd been transferred into a different court system.

The following day, the whole circus was moved up two floors. Same people, same faces, but a new room and a new judge—and the new judge was our old friend from the car-theft trial, Ben Willard.

Charlie and I had come full circle.

"Hello, Mr. Rubin. Hello, Charlie," Judge Willard greeted us over the rhythmic sound of the paddle fans that hung in rows from the sixth-floor courtroom ceiling. "You two have been creating quite a fuss. That was a swifty you pulled, Ellis. My compliments. Now let's get down to business. How do you plead?"

"Before I do that, Your Honor, I'd like to argue a motion to dismiss," I said.

There was audible laughter from the gallery. Even Judge Willard was taken aback, but he was not amused.

"Let's get on with the proceedings," he said.

"No, hear me out, Judge," I said. It was the first time I had ever talked back to a judge. Surprisingly, he let me.

"Okay, I'll listen, but you'd better be prepared to go to trial. There's no way you'll get a dismissal here."

"Your Honor," I said, pulling out a Florida case book, "in the precedent-setting cases, it was found that in the event of an acquittal on a kidnapping charge, the defendant is acquitted of all the lesser included offenses. Your Honor, extortion is a lesser included offense in every kidnapping."

The courtroom was silent. Judge Willard furrowed his brow, twisted his face and then exploded.

"Request denied. I don't consider a dismissal an acquittal."

He set the trial for August 12, about three weeks away.

It never happened. Judge Willard's denial had merely been a face-saving tactic. He called in the state prosecutors and they dropped the extortion charge and instantly replaced it with another one—grand larceny. That too was a "lesser included offense" and wouldn't stand, but it was a bit murkier and would keep Charlie in jail until they could find something that would stick.

The Feds came to the state's rescue. On July 30, Charlie was indicted by a federal grand jury on the charge of transporting stolen jewelry out of the country. The grand larceny charge melted away and Judge Willard publicly washed his hands of us in the newspapers. Charlie and I were shuffled off to yet another courtroom, another judge, and, this time, another building. At least we had finally escaped the buzzards at the Dade County Courthouse, both literally and figuratively.

But they had us with the federal charge. That wasn't an included offense of the kidnapping. Taking the jewels to Cuba had nothing to do with the kidnapping. I couldn't see any way of getting out of that.

As with everything, Charlie took it in stride.

"Hey, stolen jewelry, I can live with that," he said. "Remember, they were going to sit me down in that unpleasant electrical chair. The way I figure it, we've come out way ahead!"

The federal trial was put off until January 1953. The eight months in jail had faded Charlie's tan. He didn't look quite so dapper anymore. Federal Judge Charles Wyche, a colorful character in his own right, traveled from Spartanburg, South Carolina, to preside over the trial.

During the jury selection, I used my ten allotted challenges to excuse all the teetotalers. I wanted people who knew what it was like to tie one on, and, more importantly, what alcohol can make you do. I reasoned that they might relate to Charlie's state of mind when he made his calls. This logic would have worked much better had I been able to seat a jury of blind drunks, but all I could get were people who said they were "unopposed" to alcohol.

There were few fireworks at Charlie's final trial. I considered arguing that the jewelry wasn't actually stolen, but had been more of a gift, but that was really stretching it. I argued again that what the Cuban secret police had done to Charlie—an unlawful, unreasonable search based upon information supplied not by the police but by a newspaper reporter, and then arresting him without a warrant—violated the search-and-seizure laws in the United States Constitution. It was a great point—until the prosecutor reminded the jurors that the United States Constitution didn't apply to Cuba. If Charlie had only taken the jewels to Key West . . . .

I also argued that the use of the stolen jewelry in evidence infringed on Charlie's right of compulsory self-incrimination. That sounded good, but the judge didn't buy it. I scratched and clawed and objected to everything. I berated the Cuban secret police goons when they took the stand, but in the end the jury wasn't swayed an inch. They found Charlie guilty.

Judge Wyche sentenced Charlie to a stiff nine years in the Atlanta penitentiary. It seemed reasonable. Charlie wouldn't be executed. He wouldn't do life. But he would be punished for his irresponsible action, and would probably be paroled after two or three years if he behaved himself.

During the sentencing, the judge complimented Charlie on his "cultured mind, adeptness, and splendid personality." Then he and Charlie had a peculiar conversation.

"Your case has interested me a great deal," the judge said. "How many languages do you speak?"

"Two," Charlie replied.

"That's wonderful," Judge Wyche gushed. "I've always believed that's one of the finest things anyone can do. I've been trying to persuade my daughter to take up languages. How much education do you have?"

"I've been to college, sir," Charlie answered. "At Gonzaga University in Washington and a medical school in Mexico."

"I think your system is a shrewd one," the judge continued. "But I'm astounded at how reckless you were after you obtained the jewels. We probably would have had a hard time catching you, as smart as you are, if you hadn't displayed the jewels the way you did. I feel confident that you can rehabilitate yourself. I'm going to keep up with your case. I'm very much interested, and I want you to write me. I want to wish you good luck!"

Charlie's reaction to this conversation was typical.

"The judge sure talked nice, but I wish he hadn't been so free with my time."

Charlie wrote me a few times over the next couple of years. He said he had started a prison newspaper and was editor-in-chief. I suspected he had a wine press hidden in the kitchen. After those few letters, though, I never heard from him again.

I've had more than five thousand clients since Charlie. Many of the faces are a blur. But I'll never forget Charles Wesley Johnson's.

Little Ricky Richter grew up and became, of all things, an attorney. He now practices law in New Orleans.

EPILOGUE

When Charlie Johnson peered into a television camera in 1952 and said, "Get me Ellis Rubin!" it changed my life. The subsequent coverage of his trials by the new medium of television instantly elevated me into the major leagues of criminal law. Cases began pouring in. Few knew it then, but the power of television was awesome.

A quarter of a century years later, the circle would be complete. By then, television was dominating society to an increasingly disquieting degree. In 1977, the flickering images would change my life again.

But this time we were bitter adversaries.

3

PROGRAMMED TO KILL, PART I

When I said get up, she didn't want to get up. . . . And then I got scared and I said, "A gun, a bullet, oh no!" So then I pictured the little scene in my mind of her getting up, sayin' "Get out of here!" And I'd just voom, *out of the house.*
—Ronny Zamora, under the "truth serum" sodium Amytal

ON SATURDAY evening, June 4, 1977, my youngest child, Kim, was attending a confirmation party along with fifty other teenagers at Temple Emanu-El in Miami Beach. After dinner and the traditional Jewish "coming of age" ceremonies, the adults evaporated into the humid night and the kids scurried up to the reception hall for a dance. Packs of additional fourteen-, fifteen-, and sixteen-year-olds arrived to join their newly confirmed friends. Among the late arrivals was a dark-haired fifteen-year-old Costa Rican named Ronny Zamora.

Ronny was a friend of Kim's. In her teenaged eyes, he was a "very cute, very cool guy," who was "exceedingly well mannered." All of which made him a "sweetheart of a guy." His looks and charm won him acceptance in the junior high's harshly restrictive "in" clique, even though he was "socially out of his league." Most of this particular junior-high jet set consisted of upper-middle-class-to-wealthy students with fat allowances. Ronny was from a first-generation immigrant family with five children. Kim said Ronny frequently borrowed fashionable clothes from his friends to keep up.

Ronny, Kim, and most of the other partygoers were classmates at Nautilus Junior High on Miami Beach. The rest of the teenagers attended area Catholic or Hebrew schools. Kim remembers the five-foot-three-inch Ronny as being in high spirits that evening. He flashed a wad of money and said he and four of his buddies were on their way to Walt Disney World. He invited Kim and her prettiest girlfriends to go along—his treat. Kim declined, as did the other young ladies.

"He said he was leaving right then and wanted us to go," Kim, now twenty-seven, says today. "We had just gotten confirmed and were all dressed up. I said 'Ronny, you're nuts.' If he'd have given us some advance notice, we would have gone."

Or so Kim thinks. My wife, Irene, would never have allowed it. (She used to make the children leave phone numbers whenever they left the house.)

On the way to Disney World, Ronny and crew were pulled over by a Florida Highway Patrol trooper for speeding. Paul Toledo, seventeen, was driving the 1972 Buick Electra because he was the only one among the group who had a valid driver's license. Ronny had provided the car, alternately telling his friends it belonged to his father or his aunt. Considering whom the car really belonged to, and the fact that there was a pistol in the trunk that Ronny had proudly showed his friends, the encounter should have doomed their adventure right there. But the trooper took a sympathetic view of the fresh-faced youngsters going to Disney World, and didn't bother to search the car. When he asked for the car registration, Ronny took a chance and reached into the glove compartment. He found a gas-station credit card slip and handed it over. The bill was addressed to Elinor Haggart, eighty-two, Ronny's next-door neighbor. Ronny told the trooper she was Paul's aunt. The officer believed him and waved them on with a ticket and a simple warning to slow down.

The youths' spirits were buoyed higher by the narrow escape. They arrived in Orlando and spent the first night at a Ramada Inn, where they had a rousing pillow fight before falling asleep. The boys spent the next morning racing colorful motorboats and splashing down slides at River Country, Disney World's popular water resort. After drying off, they went to the main area of the theme park, took a trip on Space Mountain, then checked into a luxury suite at the ritzy Contemporary Resort Hotel on the Disney World grounds. Tanned and looking for action, they wandered around the lobby and were drawn into the video room by the beeps, booms, and rat-a-tats emanating from the multicolored machines. Flashing Ronny's money like big-timers, they shot pool, played pinball, and fed quarters into the machines being used by pretty girls. Two young ladies were impressed enough to accept an invitation to party with the good-looking boys in their rooms. Aided by an ample amount of alcohol, the impromptu festivities turned into an all-night love fest.

The Miami Beach teenagers continued their weekend of sex, booze, and Mickey Mouse on Monday morning by hanging around the hotel, going back to Disney World, having lunch, and bird-dogging every young woman who wasn't attached to her parents. They left for Miami Monday afternoon, June 6.

Back in Miami Beach, Toledo dropped off his friends and headed home. Ronny told him to keep the car for a while because his aunt was out of town.

The following day, Ronny smelled a bad odor coming from the home of his neighbor, Elinor Haggart. He sometimes helped the woman carry in groceries and assisted her with other chores, so he was concerned about her safety. He went to a back window and tried to open it, but broke the glass. He abandoned his efforts and returned home.

The next morning, Miami Beach police officers Zell Hall and Robert Gibbs responded to a call about the broken window and Mrs. Haggart's absence from her daily routines. Ronny's mother, Yolanda, met the officers when they arrived, and told them that Mrs. Haggart hadn't been seen since Saturday. Approaching the house, which was shaded by a large aqua awning, Officer Hall smelled the odor he'd come to recognize as that of a decomposing human body. Hall used a knife to pick the lock of the front door. Inside, the smell was staggering. Hall and Gibbs split up to search the home. Both immediately noticed that it had been ransacked by burglars. Hall found Haggart's body on the living room floor. She was fully dressed and had a sheer, turquoise gown covering her face. Beside her was a bottle of Old Forester bourbon and an empty, tipped-over glass. Three photographs, of her son, her mother, and her deceased husband, were scattered around her body. Mrs. Haggart had been shot once in the stomach. The .32-caliber, brown-nosed lead bullet traveled upward through her torso and lodged itself between her back and her bra strap. On the front side of her bra, the medical examiner found two diamond rings the elderly woman had hidden from her killers.

As she lay dying, Elinor Haggart's blood spilled out upon the photograph of her mother.

When Yolanda Zamora's son came home from school that afternoon, she told him what had happened next door.

"Ronny, did you have anything to do with that?" she asked.

Ronny said he hadn't.

Yolanda had reason to question her son. She knew he had gone to Disney World, and was suspicious of how he financed the trip. Ronny answered that he and his friends hit it big at the dog track. Mrs. Zamora found that hard to believe.

There was something else that disturbed Mrs. Zamora. Just a few weeks before, she had received a phone call from an administrator at Nautilus Junior High. Ronny and a friend were caught smoking marijuana in a school restroom and were suspended from regular classes for a week. In addition, Ronny was flunking because he was skipping school to stay home and watch television. When he did show up, he slept during class, was undisciplined and caused trouble. The administrator warned her that Ronny's new friend, Darrell Agrella, fourteen, had a police record and suggested that Mrs. Zamora separate the pair. Mrs. Zamora considered transferring her son to a Catholic school and sent him to a psychological counselor provided by Catholic Services. The counselor, Dr. Jack Jacobs, administered a battery of psychological tests and concluded that although Ronny was of average intelligence, he was confused, depressed, and "interprets his world in a hostile manner." Dr. Jacobs recommended that Ronny and his family go into psychotherapy.

Mrs. Zamora was shocked by the finding. Although Ronny had always been a poor student, he had never before been in serious trouble.

These thoughts raced through Mrs. Zamora's mind as an ambulance and a swarm of police cars gathered around Mrs. Haggart's house. Neighbors had crowded around the yellow tape boundaries marking off the residence. In the midst of the sirens, spinning blue and red lights, and television news cameras, Paul Toledo, Timothy Cahill, and some other friends drove by in Mrs. Haggart's blue Buick. Like everyone else, the boys slowed down to see what was happening.

No one noticed them.

They parked the car down the block and walked back to join the crowd. They asked what the commotion was about, and were told by a neighborhood youngster that Elinor Haggart had been murdered.

The name rang a bell. It was the same name on the gas slip in the glove compartment.

"We just freaked out," Cahill recalled.

Toledo then heard a news report that said the police were looking for Mrs. Haggart's blue 1972 Buick sedan. He wrote down the license number and went back to double-check the Buick. To his horror, the numbers and letters, 1WW 122, matched the radio description, as did the bumper sticker—"Warning: I Brake for Animals." Petrified, he rounded up his friends again. They confronted Darrell Agrella, outside a Burger King not far from the famous Fontainebleau Hilton Hotel. Agrella, who had not gone to Disney World, confirmed that the car had been stolen and advised them to "ditch it." The gang drove the Buick down Royal Palm Avenue and left it at 37th Street, eight blocks from Elinor Haggart's home. Darrell further advised them to wipe down the inside of the car to obliterate their fingerprints. They complied, then walked back to Ronny's house to interrogate him. Standing in the doorway and speaking in a whisper, Ronny admitted that he and Darrell had stolen the car and robbed Mrs. Haggart, but denied shooting the woman. He shooed his friends away, saying he didn't want his father to hear.

After leaving Ronny's house, Toledo had an alarming thought. The traffic ticket! The police had him nailed. Another emergency meeting was called. They decided that before the police came and carried them all away in cuffs, they had to finger Ronny and Darrell. They arrived in a pack at the Miami Beach police station shortly after 9:00 P.M.

While his friends were singing to the police, Ronny was feeling the heat at home. Mrs. Zamora continued to hound her son about the money. Ronny came unglued. He was crying, trembling, and chewing his fingernails down to the flesh. The stranger he acted, the more emotional Mrs. Zamora became. Ronny admitted that he had been in Mrs. Haggart's car that weekend, a revelation that caused his mother to become hysterical. She called her husband at the office. He came home and shook his son violently by the shoulders, demanding to know the details and threatening to give him the beating of his life. Ronny refused to say anything more. Mrs. Zamora phoned Sergeant James Harkins, an off-duty Miami Beach police officer who was a family friend. Harkins arrived within minutes and found the whole family in an emotional upheaval. The other children were crying, Mrs. Zamora was crying, Ronny was crying, and Mr. Zamora was screaming. Everyone was talking at once. The veteran police sergeant tried to calm them down, then asked to speak with Ronny privately. He escorted Ronny into the bathroom and shut the door. Ronny began to open up. His first story was that two men had driven up with Mrs. Haggart, spotted Ronny in his yard, and forced him inside with her. The men, Ronny said, ordered him to shoot her. When Harkins said he couldn't believe that, Ronny changed the story, admitting that he and Darrell were responsible.

Sergeant Harkins convinced the Zamoras that they should all go to the police station and allow Ronny to turn himself in. He advised them to request a lawyer before allowing their son to say anything. The family arrived at the police station at 9:45 P.M., less than an hour after Ronny's friends. Inside, they encountered the mothers of two of the boys pacing nervously in the police waiting room. When the women spotted Mrs. Zamora, they lashed out at her, nearly striking her in the face. The mothers blamed Ronny and his immigrant family for getting their sons involved in a murder. Mrs. Zamora was too shattered to argue, and retreated into another room.

After being read his rights, Ronny requested an attorney. The police attempted to find a public defender, but said they couldn't locate one because of the late hour. They had no trouble, however, locating a prosecutor, Assistant State Attorney Thomas Headley. Headley rushed over to advise the detectives on how to handle the sudden development. When Headley arrived, the Zamoras thought he was their public defender. Headley had to brush the emotional Zamoras off, explaining that he was on the other side.

Ronny was taken into an office by a pair of detectives. He grew impatient waiting for an attorney, and began talking. The teenager confessed two more times that evening, and numerous additional times the following day. He told the detectives that Darrell had come over the previous Saturday and said they needed money for a party. While they were discussing ways to obtain the money, he heard one of Mrs. Haggart's cats screaming next door and thought someone might be trying to break in. Ronny decided to be "Kojak" and investigate a "B&E"—pseudo-police/television parlance for "breaking and entering." At some point in their investigation, Ronny and Darrell decided to transform themselves from good-guy cops to bad-guy robbers. Elinor Haggart arrived home and caught them in the act. Since she knew Ronny, she viewed him as a naughty boy and said she would have to tell his parents. What happened next, and how Elinor Haggart ended up being shot with her own gun, took months and many doctors to determine. But as each new revelation was discovered, it all fit the same bizarre psychological pattern—a rare diagnosis that was almost impossible to believe, but seemed an inevitable result of our high-tech society.

Ronny Zamora was arrested on June 8, 1977, and charged with first-degree murder. Darrell Agrella, a handsome, blue-eyed ladies' man who already had a police record for larceny, was arrested on the same charge shortly afterward. Unlike Ronny, he invoked his right to remain silent. The police searched Agrella's home and found Mrs. Haggart's jewelry, checkbook, silverware, keys, and mantel clock. In the living room they discovered Elinor Haggart's $600 Zenith television set sitting on top of the family television. The officers also found a box in the Agrella garage inscribed with the name tag "Col. A. L. Haggart, U.S. Army": Elinor Haggart's late husband. Darrell's mother said her son explained that a friend was moving up north and needed a place to keep his stuff.

Elinor Haggart's two-carat diamond ring was located on the finger of Darrell's fourteen-year-old girlfriend. The young lady vowed to keep it, and had to be persuaded by some grim-faced detectives to change her mind.

The details of Ronny's confession appeared on the front page of the next morning's *Miami Herald.* Although it was unethical of the police, it wasn't unexpected. Edna Buchanan, the *Miami Herald*'s Pulitzer Prize–winning police reporter, had, as she'd done many times before, woven her magic spell over some cops and acquired the information. In a crime-riddled society like South Florida, the media can't play up every murder. Instead, they pick those with especially heinous or interesting elements to flesh out, thus using the one case to symbolize the overall alarm of the many. In the summer of 1977, Ronny Zamora and Darrell Agrella became that one case. Buchanan's description of the two teenagers robbing and shooting the elderly woman, then of Ronny taking her car and money and celebrating by partying at Disney World, gave the *Herald*'s readers the creeps. He was viewed as a cold-blooded murderer of the worst sort, a teenaged Charles Manson. The press coverage subjected the Zamora family to a barrage of cruel crank calls.

THE GIRL in hysterics on the other end of the telephone was my daughter, Kim. She was at a pay phone in front of Nautilus Junior High. The news of Ronny and Darrell's arrest was rocking the school like a summer thunderstorm.

"I don't see how Ronny could have done such a thing," she said, sobbing. "I was just talking to him last night. He didn't say a word about it. Not a word. You've got to do something, Daddy. You've got to get him out of jail. He'll be hurt in there."

Being my daughter, Kim had spent all her life on the fringes of murder. But this was the first time it involved someone she knew. I told her to stay put and I'd pick her up. At home, Kim continued to sob and begged me to get Ronny out of jail.

I explained to her that there was nothing I could do. I couldn't solicit a client; that was against the law. I was nearly disbarred once for coming to the aid of a fellow serviceman who had been wrongly accused of murder.* Although the laws and ethics have since changed with the advent of lawyers advertising, back then they were unbending. Before I could help Ronny, his parents would have to ask me. Kim didn't understand, as most people wouldn't, and con-

---

*The case involved an airman, Joseph Shea, from Homestead Air Force Base, who was accused in the early 1950s of raping and butchering a woman he had supposedly abducted at Miami International Airport. A cousin of mine, working temporarily in my office, called Shea's parents and offered my services. When I found out, I scolded my cousin, but made the mistake of deciding to help the airman. Some of my political enemies found out, and I was cited for solicitation. The ex-governor of Florida, Fuller Warren, volunteered to represent me before the Florida Supreme Court. I was exonerated. Shea, defended by a new attorney, was convicted of first-degree murder. *Miami Herald* reporter Gene Miller stayed on the case, wrote numerous stories about Shea's innocence, and eventually won Shea a new trial. Shea was then acquitted and Miller won a Pulitzer Prize in journalism.

tinued to cry and beg. Showing remarkable insight for a teenager, Kim said Ronny was driven to theft by peer pressure. He needed the money to keep up with his "in crowd" friends.

A few days later, Mrs. Zamora called. She wanted me to represent her son. I suspected my daughter's involvement, but didn't mention it, tightroping the ethical question. Mrs. Zamora said she had little money. I told her not to worry about paying me. I would represent Ronny as a favor to my daughter. I told Mrs. Zamora that what money she had should be used to pay doctors to evaluate and treat her son.

After visiting Ronny's mother and stepfather, I went to the Dade County Youth Hall to visit this "despicable subhuman" who had shocked crime-hardened Miami. Instead of a savage beast, I was surprised to find nothing more than a little boy. He looked more American than Latin, and appeared to have no conception of what he had done and what lay ahead of him. I'll never forget his first words.

"Mr. Rubin, when am I going to get out of here and go back to school? I'm missing all my homework."

I made arrangements to have Ronny analyzed by several top psychiatrists and psychologists. The doctors' reports were startlingly similar.

Ronny Zamora, born May 7, 1962, was Yolanda's illegitimate son. He was a "blue baby," which is a child born with respiratory problems that can cause brain damage or death. The baby survived, apparently intact. Because of his illegitimate birth, Yolanda, seventeen, was disowned by her father. She lived with various relatives for three years, then moved to New York to work as a maid. She left Ronny with friends in Costa Rica for two years before sending for him. In New York, Yolanda met and married Frank Zamora, a man she knew from Costa Rica. Life was tough on the young couple. She initially couldn't afford a baby-sitter, but had to work to survive. She also enrolled in beauty school to better herself by becoming a beautician. (She later became a nurse.) Her solution to the child-care dilemma was to purchase a television set, sit young Ronny down in front of it, and pray that it captured his attention enough to keep him safe while she was working and attending school. It did. The neighbors who looked in on him reported that Ronny was mesmerized by the images on the screen. Later, when the Zamoras were able to afford a baby-sitter, the woman they hired noted Ronny's fascination and continued to allow him to sit glued in front of the set eight hours a day, even feeding him while he watched. Television became not only his baby-sitter, but his teacher, pastor, mother, father, and school. From television he learned English. From it he learned his sense of right and wrong. He learned television's idea of morality. He learned the facts of life.

At age five, he read and memorized the listings in *TV Guide* even though he couldn't write a word.

Like Chance, the gardener in the Peter Sellers movie *Being There,* every aspect of Ronny Zamora was shaped by what he had seen on television. And if the figures given by numerous social organizations, including the PTA, are correct, what Ronny Zamora had seen on television by the time he was fifteen was twenty-thousand murders.

The doctors described Ronny as a "true television addict" whose every activity "was controlled by what he had seen on television."

Among the examiners was Michael Gilbert, a double doctor with an M.D. in psychiatry and a Ph.D. in psychology. Also present was Dr. Jorge Lievano, a child psychiatrist who had trained and worked at the world-famous Menninger Foundation in Topeka, Kansas, and had been commissioned by the President of the United States to serve in Korea as a Chief of Psychiatry and Neurology for the Second Infantry Division of the U.S. Army.

Both doctors felt that Ronny was mentally unstable, and that television had been a major factor in creating his condition. Dr. Gilbert was especially strong in making the connection, stating that Ronny's reaction to television was so overwhelming it caused him to lapse into periods of legal insanity.

"The boy had reacted more or less as an automaton at the time of the shooting," Dr. Gilbert explained.

"At that very moment he was not in contact with reality . . . he was not even aware that he was pulling the trigger," Dr. Lievano added.

During one of his meetings with Ronny, Dr. Lievano witnessed Ronny warp out right in the middle of their session. Dr. Lievano explained it in a deposition:

> Ronny looks at me . . . he had the fantasy and he projected his fantasy onto me. And then he says, apparently he was thinking of a movie that he had seen on television, and he says, "you look like Dracula." And I say, "Why do I look like Dracula, my fangs or my eyes or what?" And he looks kind of puzzled at me and says, "Well, no, you

are really Dr. Lievano," like he went back to reality for a little while right there, and he did not have a very good reality at all.

Dr. Gilbert suggested that in order to cut through Ronny's fantasy world and find out what really happened in Elinor Haggart's house that afternoon, he needed to inject him with sodium Amytal, a truth serum. The result, which has never been publicly revealed, proved that Ronny's television-related illness was embedded in his mental core.

Under the influence of the hypnotic medication, Ronny said Darrell egged him on to enter the house after they checked out the cat noise. He finally relented and Darrell followed. The way Ronny told it, he sat around dumbfounded while the more experienced Darrell did all the work, searching for money and jewelry. Shortly after they entered, Mrs. Haggart pulled up in her blue Buick. Ronny had enough time to leave, but couldn't get Darrell out of a back bedroom:

"Darrell, come on, Darrell, will you come on, you're going to get caught. . . ."
By the time we reached the door, Mrs. Haggart was walking up and she . . . noticed me first and she goes, "What are you doing here?" And I go, "I'm not doing nothin'. Please let me leave. Please. Please. Please. Let me leave. Please." And she goes, "Do you know what you are doing?" And I go, "No, I'm leavin'." And she goes, "No, you're robbing my house."
"Who, me?"
. . . She then started telling me ". . . boy, how young robbers get these days" . . . So, you know, she was smilin', so I wasn't worried too much. . . . So she said, "Well, I'm sorry, I'm going to go call the police."
. . . Darrell, he either pushed the door or he kicked it open, and from there she realized she was in trouble! He said, "All right, lady, you're on to us . . . sit down, shut up, don't make no noise and you won't get hurt." So she sat on the floor. She sat down . . . sorta mindin' her own business. And me, I was just watchin'. I mean, sometimes, you know, I feel like a bully, I say, "Oh yeah," I'm gonna tell this lady, "Old lady, get out of my way" . . . but I ain't got the heart to do it.
. . . She said, "Can you please . . . go inside that closet down there and get me a bottle of somethin', burgundy [bourbon], whiskey, rum?" . . . So I went and got the thing and brought it back. . . . She said "Will you please go and get me a glass of water?" . . . So I must have gone forth about ten times satisfying her needs. . . .

Ronny said he was calling Darrell "Tom" and Darrell was calling him "Bill," to disguise themselves. Mrs. Haggart was playing along. Sometimes she called him "Ronny," then corrected herself and said "Bill." After he got her the water and whiskey, Mrs. Haggart then asked "Bill" to go into her bedroom and find some pictures she kept in a drawer. The pictures included a photograph of her deceased husband. Ever polite, even as a robber, Ronny complied.

I showed her the pictures. The first picture was just a lake and a mountain, I think, and she just said, "This is lake such and such." And she goes, "This is my husband . . ." and she saw another, the lady was identified as her mother. So I just sat down and just lookin' at her enjoyin' herself. And then I started thinkin' . . . what was I gonna do? I'm sure the lady had identified me. I was gonna get in trouble for robbing Mrs. Haggart's house and that was that. And I was going to get the daylights beaten out of me. . . .

Then Darrell, uh, while scramblin' through some kinds of crates, or some boxes of jewelry, he found the gun. A very old, black gun . . . So I took the gun and I went, you know, to the coffee table and I started playing around. I could even have killed myself. I should've. And I was pointing the gun to my head, to my stomach, my legs, to my arms, oh, I put it in my mouth, some other stuff, stupid stuff. I pointed it at Mrs. Haggart with no intention. I pointed at the ceiling, I pointed at the piano. I pointed at the door, anything that looked big enough to hit.

. . . So Darrell was ready to start packing . . . he said, "All right, Ronny, let's get it over with." I said, "What do you mean, 'Let's get it over with'?" I said, "You, you get it over with. . . ." So he went over to another room. He brought out a pillow and it smelled kind of clean. . . . I was wonderin', "What, is this kid crazy or somethin'?" So then he took [the pillow] halfway and he folded the other half and he said, "You're going to have to muffle the sound." And I was just playing along with him, didn't want to seem stupid. I said, "Yeah, yeah, yeah." And he went around the house searchin', closing windows, shades, lamps, whatever. And I said, "Well, I'm not going to do it. I'm not going to kill nobody!" He goes, "Somebody gotta do it." I said, "Not me. You get into trouble, killing somebody."

He said, "I robbed the house. I got all the valuables. I found the $450. I found the gun, which can bring us about $50. I found just about everything. How are you going to do me like that?"

"I don't give a damn how I do you."

And he goes to me, "You gonna kill her."

"No, I ain't," I said. "If you say that again, I'm going to bust you in the mouth."

So he went over and he started playing with his jewelry like kings run through their gold. . . . I started playing with the gun some more. . . . And what really got to me was, not once, *not once* did Mrs. Haggart say, "Watch out, you might hurt somebody. . . ."

. . . She said . . . "If you leave and don't take nothin', and you leave right now, I won't call the police. . . ." Darrell heard her when he was comin' in and he said, "No way, no deal, you'd testify against us. . . ."

So I said, "Oh no, this lady's determined. What am I gonna do? Mom will—oh boy, robbin' a lady's house, that's too much . . ." and that's when the gun went off. . . . I was just holdin' it tight. I don't know why. I was scared and before I knew it, I mean, it happened so fast . . . I covered my ears. . . .

. . . I stayed sittin' on top of the coffee table. I was still thinking what I was going to tell my mother for robbing the lady's house. I had a feeling she was going to go over and tell my mother. . . . When I said, "Get up," she didn't want to get up. And then I got scared and I said, "A gun, a bullet, oh no." So then I pictured the little scene in my mind of her getting up, sayin', "Get out of here," and I'd just *voom*, out of that house.

. . . I saw a scene. I saw, not looking directly at her, I saw Mrs. Haggart rise up. I did not see no blood on her dress. She did not seem to be hit by the bullet. She came up to me, grabbed the gun, told me to leave, and I ran. . . . In that movie that I saw in my dream, the boy lived. So I said, "Oh, it happened like in the dream." And I left.

It was the most bizarre confession I had ever heard. I didn't know if Ronny was a heartless killer or a mischievous little boy. What I did know was that Ronny Zamora "re-edited" a scene out of reality as if he were acting in a television show. After the gun went off, he didn't like the result, so he yelled, "Cut," rewrote the script, and "reshot" the scene. In his new ending, he missed Mrs. Haggart and she got up, took the gun from him, and chased the foolish child away.

Dr. Gilbert was equally moved.

"This was, I felt, a very involved situation. I must confess, in the well over twenty-five years that I have been involved in forensic psychiatry, I think this is the most involved situation I have ever been in. I felt it required considerable study, considerable concern, and considerable retrospection in order to arrive at an opinion that was consistent with what had occurred."

The scene from the movie where "the boy lived" turned out to be a dream sequence from Ronny's favorite television show, "Kojak."

With his new, "Kojak"-inspired scene replacing the shock of reality, Ronny Zamora submerged himself in an even bigger fantasy land—Disney World. He never gave the shooting a second thought. He fully expected Elinor Haggart to be alive and well and out puttering in her yard when he returned.

Once the type and extent of Ronny's sickness was known, the doctors and I began to investigate the cause further.

Eighteen months before the shooting, Ronny suffered a psychologically scarring experience. While attending the eighth grade in Staten Island, New York, he and thirteen friends were playing on a frozen reservoir. One of his classmates, Scott Sefedinoski, fell through the ice. Ronny courageously dived into the frigid water to rescue his friend. He grabbed the boy's arm, but lost his grip in the struggle. Scott drowned.

That night, Ronny dreamed he had pulled Scott out. The vision was so real he woke up feeling that was what had happened. He went to school and asked everyone where Scott was. He was ridiculed by his classmates, or avoided by those who felt he had snapped.

When the truth of Scott's death finally penetrated his fantasy, Ronny was devastated. He blamed himself. Mrs. Zamora said he sat alone in his room for months, mentally replaying the scene in his mind. He began to drink, and came home drunk on a number of occasions. He told psychiatrist William Corwin that he often heard Scott's clear voice calling his name and the name of the reservoir.

In her examination, Dr. Helen Ackerman uncovered the seeds of Ronny's guilt regarding the ill-fated rescue attempt:

"As he saw this youngster go down, the youngster's hand stuck up. He saw the hand of Dracula, and it was like at one level, he wished to save him, to make the extra effort. But that hand of Dracula so frightened him that he was repulsed by it."

That forced Ronny to live with this question: Did Scott slip through his grip, or did his hand jerk back in a reflex reaction to the frightening television image his mind conjured up?

"He's a sick youngster," Dr. Ackerman concluded. "It's tragic he was not seen ten years ago. That's the unfortunate thing."

The family moved to Florida the following summer, after Mr. Zamora received a job offer to become an agent for a shipping company. Part of the reason for the move was to shake Ronny loose from the relentless nightmares. Despite the new surroundings, he remained haunted by the drowning and the voices. His only escape was to regress deeper into television.

Mrs. Zamora described how her son would pretend to go to sleep each night at 9:00 P.M., then sneak out of his room and turn the television set back on. He would watch until the small hours of the morning, frequently falling asleep on the couch or on the rug in front of the set. He did this, she said, "every night."

"Whatever he saw on the TV, it was so real to him that he believed it," Mrs. Zamora said.

What was Ronny watching and believing? He was drawn to the violent police and private-detective dramas of the late 1970s: "Kojak," "Baretta," "Police Story," "Police Woman," "S.W.A.T," and "Barnaby Jones."

Ronny's taste in music was also notable. Instead of following the current hits, his favorites were all lyrically complex songs with confounding messages. He mentioned three Beatles songs from their so-called psychedelic period in the late 1960s—"Strawberry Fields Forever," "Eleanor Rigby," and "Helter Skelter," the latter being one of the songs that was said to have inspired Charles Manson's murderous family. Ronny also liked the Led Zeppelin classic, "Stairway to Heaven," another tune with complicated lyrics.

But it was the visual stimulus of television, not music, that was Ronny's narcotic. And Ronny viewed television in his own special way.

"He can experience being in the TV," Dr. Ackerman wrote after an extensive examination of Ronny. "Everything seems so real to him. He related that he actually stands amidst all the action, hearing and seeing what is going on as if he were actually there. Ronny's sense of the boundaries of reality [is] distorted."

There was absolutely no doubt that the boy had deep psychological problems, and that those problems were either created by television or, more likely, exacerbated by the tens of thousands of hours of television violence he had witnessed. Because of television, he had a skewed sense of right and wrong. Because of the twisted inner workings of his mind, combined with the shock of a real-life drowning death, he couldn't distinguish television fantasy from reality, and therefore didn't know the consequences of his acts. Those factors fit the legal definition of an insanity defense.

Other children, tens of millions of other children, had seen the same programs as Ronny and had not been driven to murder. That was undisputed.

It was also inconsequential.

Those tens of millions of other children had watched "Superman." They didn't tie a towel around their necks and try to fly out of a fourth story window.

Ronny Zamora did.

Those other children didn't see—not imagine, but *see*—witches, ghosts, and shadow monsters in their backyards. Ronny did. According to Dr. Lievano, he threw rocks at them, chased after them, and ran from them.

These "hallucinations," as Dr. Lievano termed them, did not end with his childhood. Even as a teenager, Ronny said he heard voices calling him, people talking to one another, and saw "shadow figures staring at me." He once saw a "hairy monster" and a "bald monster" in his window. As recently as a month before his arrest, he had thrown rocks at a mysterious figure on his patio.

"When I went to the Zamora home, I asked to see the picture of Saint Martin in his bedroom," Dr. Ackerman wrote in her report, and expounded upon it in a deposition. "And there is this picture of a saint with whitish kind of eyes. . . . Ronny had related to me how the saint spoke to him with moving lips and eyes telling him what a bad boy he had been."*

Along with these psychological problems, Ronny's relationship with his stepfather was deteriorating. Frank Zamora was a decent man and good provider, but he was also a no-nonsense disciplinarian who believed in a hands-on approach to punishment. Ronny, growing more troublesome with each year, was the usual target.

"The punishment is very severe in this family," said Dr. Ackerman. "The stepfather hits the youngster around the face, head, and upper part of the body sufficient to draw blood from the mouth area."

Prior to the shooting, Ronny asked his mother if she could find him another family to live with. He also asked her if he could be treated by a psychiatrist.

"I need help," he said.

His own reasons can be seen in the results of the psychological test given by the Catholic Services doctors, a test given two weeks before the shooting. The standard test asks the patient to complete a series of forty questions. Some of Ronny's answers were normal:

---

*Saint Martin de Porres (1579–1639) was a Peruvian mulatto born of an unwed black woman and a Spanish grandee. He was a Dominican lay brother who established orphanages and a hospital for foundlings. Interestingly, St. Martin was the saint featured in rock singer Madonna's highly controversial "Like a Prayer" video in 1989.

I like: "girls."
At bedtime: "I brush my teeth."
The best: "baseball player is Pete Rose."

Other answers were quite disturbing:

I feel: "messed up."
My mind: "is all screwed up."
My greatest worry: "is me."

In 1977, Florida criminal procedures required that whenever an attorney filed a preliminary plea of "not guilty by reason of insanity," the paperwork must contain a "statement of particulars" explaining the nature of the insanity and listing the medical experts. My statement of particulars included this phrase heard around the world: "prolonged, intense, involuntary, subliminal television intoxication."

I filed the notice late in the afternoon to avoid having it picked up in the media. I knew the defense would be explosive, but unlike many of my other cases, it was the kind of defense that might be hindered by press coverage. It was too complicated to explain in a newspaper story or television broadcast, and the media were certain to react in a smirky fashion, oversimplifying the defense to "television made me do it."

Despite my attempts at concealment, our court system operates "in the sunshine." That means in public. The Zamora case was big news. Jim Buchanan of the *Miami Herald* dug the pleading out of the courthouse files almost before the ink had dried.

"Ellis, what's this 'not guilty by television' stuff?" he asked over the phone.

I explained it. The next day there was a story in the local section. I breathed a sigh of relief, figuring it would die there. Unfortunately, the Associated Press picked it up and sent out an edited version over the wires. The day after that, I was bombarded with calls from reporters around the world. Within the next few weeks there were television crews in my office from Australia, West Germany, England, France, Brazil, and Mexico, as well as ABC, CBS, and NBC. Reporters came from *The New York Times*, *Newsweek*, *Time*, *People*, *TV Guide*, and dozens of other publications, both domestic and foreign.

Once the cat was out of the bag, the best course was to accommodate the reporters in order to shape the coverage to the advantage of the client. Hide from the press, and they eat you and your client alive.

Most of the early coverage was favorable. There was widespread fear, especially among the foreign reporters, that violence on television was having a damaging effect upon children. They were particularly concerned about the proliferation of violent American programs, like "Starsky and Hutch," that were being dubbed and aired in their countries. Lost among the critical stories was the fact that Ronny's defense wasn't a wild concept an attorney dreamed up. It was the conclusion of four doctors. I didn't invent the medical diagnoses that are the crux of the television intoxication defense. I merely applied an innovative psychiatric diagnosis to the law. In that capacity, I gave a name to the legal application of a medical finding.

That being true, one may wonder why I was the first to use that defense.

Weaving a legal defense around any new and unusual psychological prognosis is a tremendous risk. Attorneys who do so subject themselves to professional ridicule, career-threatening public embarrassment, and almost certain charges from cannibalistic colleagues of "ineffective assistance of counsel." Few attorneys choose to face such intense criticism, inside the profession or out. Sadly, the majority of lawyers would have ignored the doctors' diagnoses in favor of self-preservation.

I couldn't do that. Ronny Zamora was created by television. Win or lose, society was going to have to face it.

4

PROGRAMMED TO KILL, PART II:

Trial on Television, Television on Trial

It has been demonstrated that the average child watches thousands of killings on TV. Now, a child like Ronny Zamora maybe sees five or ten times that many killings. When one has seen that many killings, the death of a human being in that type of situation is no more significant than swatting a fly.
—Michael Gilbert, M.D., Ph.D.

RONNY'S DEFENSE forced me to confront a personal dilemma. I don't like "insanity" defenses. They are overused and abused by unscrupulous attorneys. Most of the 285 accused murderers I've defended have been "insane" to some extent. I believe you have to be insane to willfully take another person's life. But every one of those 285, even the most wild-eyed, probably knew right from wrong. That's where the insanity issue gets muddy.

The federal courts and many state courts have backed away

from the long-used "M'Naghten Rule," which holds defendants legally responsible for their acts if they know right from wrong. I believe a better test is this question: Did the defendants suffer from a disease or mental defect that rendered them unable to refrain from criminal acts, or stripped them of the ability to conform to the standards of normal behavior?

I would also prefer a bifurcated trial in first-degree murder cases where insanity is an issue. That means the trial is split in half. In the first half, a jury would judge pure guilt or innocence: Did the person on trial do it? If the defendant is found guilty, then the second half would be held. In that part, the judge and the same jury would hear arguments and expert testimony pertaining to all the various insanity diagnoses. They would then determine whether the person knew the consequences of his acts and could or could not conform them to the law—or even if the person recalled the crime at all. The judge and jury would decide if a person was sane and belonged in prison, or was mentally ill and should be put in a hospital.

Unfortunately, Florida and most other states don't present this opportunity. Therefore the robbery, the murder, Ronny's "cold-hearted" trip to Disney World, and his unprecedented reaction to television had to be stirred together into one dizzying stew.

Another problem I faced was that I was unable to present proof that Ronny was insane without basing it upon the controversial television angle. And from a statutory standpoint, many of the doctors had not found Ronny "legally" insane. For the most part, they felt he knew right from wrong. In addition, all the doctors felt he was fit to stand trial, meaning he understood the consequences of the proceedings and was able to recall details to help me with his defense. These determinations again hark back to television. In its stereotypical world, television presents strong images of right and wrong when it comes to murder. Although virtually everyone kills on the action dramas, it's usually good guys killing bad guys.

But underlying this is the fact that television makes everyone a star, even the bad guys. Often, television glamorizes the bad guys. Thus the role models blur.

"Sometimes I would be the cop and the hero," Ronny told psychiatrist Charles Mutter. "Other times I'd be the bad guy and would get mad if the guy got caught."

The problem with Ronny was that instead of allowing him to

make a clear distinction between right and wrong, his television intoxication caused him to meld the two. He was like actors Michael Gross and Gerald McRaney. In their hit television series "Family Ties" and "Simon and Simon," respectively the two men play good guys. But both actors took time out from their series to give convincing performances as psychotic killers in television movies that aired in the same week as their television shows. From an acting standpoint, they put on impressive performances. But what effect did it have upon their young fans? Unable to distinguish the characters as easily as adults can, a child is suddenly faced with Steven Keaton (Michael Gross) of "Family Ties" killing FBI agents, and Rick Simon (Gerald McRaney) of "Simon and Simon" raping and murdering a string of young women.

Such identity confusion is common.

As the detective Baretta, Robert Blake was one of Ronny's heroes. In the movie *In Cold Blood,* which frequently plays on television, Robert Blake, with an accomplice, kills an entire family with a knife and a shotgun.

As Kojak, Telly Savalas was Ronny's biggest hero. In the movie *The Dirty Dozen,* he's a psychopath named "Maggot" who is so vile his evilness stood out among twelve convicts.

David Soul is Detective Hutchinson in "Starsky and Hutch." He's also the sinister killer who murdered FBI agents with Michael J. Fox's TV dad (Michael Gross) in the NBC movie *In the Line of Duty: The FBI Murders.*

But that's television and actors; everyone knows that.

Or do they?

Every actor or actress who has ever played a doctor on television can tell harrowing tales of meeting adults who believe the entertainers really are the physicians they portray. Comedian Howie Mandel, who played a doctor on the series "St. Elsewhere," incorporated these reactions into his stand-up routine. Mandel says that he "cures" these people and claims to be treating thirty regular patients.

Such mistakes aren't limited to actors portraying doctors. When comic actor John Ritter played a television evangelist in a 1982 made-for-TV movie *Pray TV,* a fake 800 telephone number was displayed on the screen to simulate how the real televangelists solicit donations. The program made headlines the following day when the phone company announced that it received thousands of calls from people, almost exclusively adults, trying to donate money to Ritter's fantasy character. This response is even more disturbing when one considers that Ritter was widely known for playing the character Jack Tripper in the long-running comedy hit "Three's Company." How many of those callers were really donating money to Jack Tripper, the bumbling buffoon with the pretty roommates?

These examples may seem comical in their absurdity, but take it a step further. A young fan killed herself after comedian Freddie Prinze shot himself in 1977. Was the girl reacting to the suicide of Prinze, an emotionally unstable cocaine addict who was often mean-spirited? Or was she reacting to the death of a character on her television set, the lovable Chico from "Chico and the Man"? This extraordinary reaction to television happened just months before Ronny Zamora shot Elinor Haggart.

The point here is certainly not to blame actors and actresses for playing diverse roles. Nor is it to blame producers and the television networks for casting against type. But society must face the fact that there are legions of people sitting in front of their television sets who think what they're seeing is real. And because of this, if an unusually suggestible child becomes so confused he does something bad, instead of putting the child into the electric chair or tossing him into the lion's den of an adult prison, we should get him help.

From a sociological standpoint, the Zamora case had immense ramifications. Dr. Gilbert put it best:

"Here's a child who commits an act of violence like this on the next-door neighbor. It's got to be explained. It's got to be understood."

For Ronny, it went beyond the conflicting images of his television heroes. He took the phrase "all the world's a stage" literally. After viewing thousands of hours of television, he became mentally unable to comprehend that when you shoot someone a half-dozen times in real life, he doesn't get up, dust himself off, and order a beer as the stuntman does in a popular beer commercial. And Ronny was mentally unable to understand that when something terrible happens, you can't close your eyes, envision a new scene, and change it.

Those with clear minds and well-adjusted children may find this melding impossible to accept. That's what I faced with a jury, and I've been able to explain it much better here than I was permitted to do in court. Even so, I never expected a jury to excuse Ronny

Zamora for what he did because he watched too much television. I wanted to get a disturbed young boy the medical help he needed to understand what he did and come to grips with living in the real world.

Without a bifurcated trial, the only way I could accomplish this was through a not-guilty verdict. Under these guidelines, the defense with which I was left was the one I dislike—"not guilty by reason of insanity." And "television intoxication" was what brought on Ronny's bizarre form of insanity.

I believed it then. I believe it today.

If the television intoxication defense wasn't unusual enough, the trial of Ronny Zamora was fated to have an additional landmark element—television itself. Radio and still photography had been banned from courtrooms in 1937 following the circus atmosphere of the Lindbergh baby kidnapping trial. Television was added to the ban in 1952. Twenty-five years later, lawyers for the *Post-Newsweek* media conglomerate argued that the technology of television and photography had improved to such an extent that the equipment was no longer as obtrusive as it had been in the past. Additionally, the journalists of the 1970s were said to be more sophisticated and less rowdy than their predecessors of the 1930s.

Twenty-seven days after Elinor Haggart's death, the Florida Supreme Court agreed to allow trials to be televised for a year on an experimental basis. At the end of the year, the televised trials would be analyzed to determine the positive and negative effects.

WPBT, which is the Public Broadcasting System's station in Miami, as well as other stations throughout Florida, began monitoring the courts to find the right case to begin the experiment. Since even public television is television, it had to be something that would capture an audience's attention. From their standpoint, they couldn't have written a better script themselves than the Zamora case. The first completely televised trial would be a murder in which television itself was on trial. It would also be a double precedent—a precedent-setting defense in a precedent-setting situation.

Unfortunately, into this unprecedented case, with unprecedented live coverage and unprecedented worldwide media attention, there was one law that outshone all the others—Murphy's. From my standpoint, everything that could go wrong did.

The first disaster struck during the depositions, the pretrial sworn statements of potential witnesses. I had decided that Dr.

Gilbert was going to be my star witness. His diagnosis of Ronny's condition was the most captivating. I had been greatly influenced by him when I decided to go with the television intoxication defense. We discussed his testimony for months. I provided him with every respected study about television violence and children that I could get my hands on. Surprisingly, there were 2,300 to choose from, and many were quite alarming. Dr. Gilbert assured me he was going to tell the jury that Ronny had a diminished sense of right and wrong from watching television, and could not separate television fantasy from reality.

The day before Dr. Gilbert's deposition with assistant state attorneys Thomas Headley and Richard Katz, I played the part of the state attorney and took him through a practice deposition. Dr. Gilbert was strong in his convictions, and gave answers that were sure to impress the most cynical juror.

The next day, Thomas Headley began questioning Dr. Gilbert. He asked him if Ronny knew right from wrong before the day of the shooting. Dr. Gilbert said yes. I sat up in my chair. Headley asked if Ronny knew right from wrong when he entered the house, when he was given the gun, and when he was holding Mrs. Haggart at bay. Dr. Gilbert said yes to them all.

I was dying. Dr. Gilbert appeared to be flip-flopping on what he had told me for the past three months.

Headley continued. He asked the doctor if at any point Ronny didn't know right from wrong. Finally, Dr. Gilbert gave the right yes answer. He said that during the two or three seconds when Ronny squeezed the trigger, he momentarily lost his sense of right and wrong.

Then came another parade of answers regarding Ronny's sense of right and wrong. According to Dr. Gilbert's new theory, Ronny was back to normal following the shooting.

I sat there in total shock. Headley looked at me and smiled. He knew the "television intoxication" defense had been mortally wounded. The "three seconds of insanity" defense might work with a husband coming home and finding his wife in bed with his best friend, but I felt it was ridiculous in this case.

I drove Dr. Gilbert to his office. Although I was ready to explode, I forced myself to stay calm.

"Mike, when did you come up with this new 'three-second' theory," I asked.

"I thought about it last night. I think it's the best way to handle it."

"Why didn't you tell me? You realize that you'll have to repeat this at the trial, and you'll be the laughing-stock of the entire medical and legal community all over the world? The prosecutors are going to turn you into an ass. How could you do this? You killed the case for this kid. And you knew the truth better than anyone."

I didn't talk to Dr. Gilbert for weeks after that. As I cooled down and studied deeper, I began to understand his thought process. With television as his teacher, Ronny did know right from wrong most of the time. Strange as the "three-second theory" was, Dr. Lievano separately came to virtually the same conclusion. He said Ronny could fade out of reality for brief periods, and had done so during the shooting. Dr. Lievano said the sensory overload of Darrell ordering Ronny to shoot Mrs. Haggart, Mrs. Haggart threatening to tell the police, and the fear that he was going to be punished for the robbery all worked to snap Ronny's fragile grip on reality.

But how could I make a jury understand that? In the narrow legal arena, such concepts would be ridiculed.

I felt, as Dr. Gilbert had originally stated to me, that Ronny's illness was an ongoing and increasing mental dysfunction that had been in the making since he was five years old. And I believed that from the moment Ronnie entered Elinor Haggart's house to the moment he confessed, four days later, he had submerged himself into a television cops-and-robbers episode, one that had Mrs. Haggart alive and well following the robbery. The post-shooting period was especially critical. While Dr. Gilbert felt that Ronny had regained his sanity, with some "impairment," following the shooting, I don't think any sane teenager could have gone to Walt Disney World with a pocketful of blood money hours after robbing and killing his neighbor.

I called Dr. Gilbert shortly before the trial and asked if he was ready to face the music. He told me he had another idea that might save the case. This was to go to the jail, inject Ronny with sodium Amytal, and get him to reenact the day of the murder. I protested, afraid of what Ronny might say. Dr. Gilbert insisted it was necessary for his evaluation, and I eventually consented. It was a stroke of brilliance on Dr. Gilbert's part. Under the serum, which relaxes the subject and inhibits deceptive thought, Ronny's description of that day, as recorded in the prior chapter, was the best evidence yet of his television intoxication. Unfortunately, when I read the transcripts, I realized I couldn't use it. There were too many things that the prosecution would jump on to hang Ronny, not the least of which was the emotional image of Mrs. Haggart showing Ronny her family photographs just before he killed her. That scene brought tears to my eyes, and those tears would have translated into juror rage.

Murphy's Law had gotten us again, and it was worse than we imagined. When the prosecutors heard what Dr. Gilbert and I had done, we were charged with smuggling drugs into the prison! We had unknowingly violated a state statute and a jail rule that an outside doctor cannot administer medications to a prisoner without either the permission of jail authorities or an order from a judge. The judge summoned us to court to "show cause" for our unlawful drug smuggling. I pleaded a variation of Steve Martin's "I forgot" defense. On one of his comedy albums, the famous comedian does a routine in which he is arrested for murder and pleads his case before a judge.

"Your honor," Martin says, "I forgot that murder was against the law."

My defense, which was the absolute truth, was, "Your Honor, I didn't know."

Nobody but jailers and a few prosecutors know that obscure law. The judge decided there was "no intent" to break a law and let it slide.

But Murphy's Law was relentless in its continuing assaults. Another disaster arrived by mail. Ronny wrote my daughter Kim a letter from jail. In it was a confession! That, combined with his having invited her to Disney World hours after the murder, and his phone calls to her after he came back, had turned Kim into a potential star prosecution witness.

One might think that, having lived my life in court, having relied upon my wife as an invaluable aide for thirty-plus years, having my oldest daughter Peri as my office manager, and having two sons become lawyers, it would be routine for a Rubin to be a star witness in a murder trial.

No way. No way in hell was I going to let my fifteen-year-old daughter go through the ordeal of being a witness against one of her friends and her father's client. And how was I going to cross-examine my youngest child? Would I be expected to do a Perry Mason number on my own kid and crack her like an egg on the stand? Kim was already so emotionally devastated by the shooting and the controversy surrounding the trial that she began having difficulty concentrating in school. Her grades plummeted.

Fortunately, prosecutors Headley and Katz were decent about it and agreed not to call her if I submitted the letter into evidence. Since I wasn't contesting the other confessions or the circumstances of the shooting, one more confession was meaningless.

That was about the only break we got. I had cringed when I learned which judge had been assigned the case. Circuit Court Judge Paul Baker and I had a long history of being at odds. It had started decades before, when he was an assistant state attorney. I took a case against the prosecutor's office for a man who claimed the state had wrongfully convicted him of grand larceny by knowingly using the false testimony of a witness. The man, Charles Horner, went from lawyer to lawyer, trying to get someone to fight the powerful state attorney's office. No defense attorney was crazy enough to risk committing professional suicide by taking his case. So of course, when Horner came to me, I accepted. I exposed the perjury in the pretrial depositions and was preparing to nail the guilty parties in court. On the morning of the trial, the attorney for the state told the judge they "admitted error" and were dropping all charges against Horner, including the grand larceny conviction. That swept everything nice and neatly under a judicial rug.

Judge Baker and I continued to cross paths under the most volatile circumstances, including one messy, front-page political battle that pitted me and Governor Claude Kirk against Baker and the state attorney.

Suffice it to say Baker's hatred of me grew with each encounter.

So naturally, of all the judges in Dade County, Murphy's Law decreed that the biggest case of my life would fall before Judge Paul Baker. Normally, when there is a history of bad blood between a lawyer and a judge, the attorney can file a motion to remove the judge from the proceeding. But Murphy's Law had that covered. The Zamora trial came at a time when I had been led to believe that Judge Baker had long since buried the hatchet. For the previous eight years he had been fair during my trials before him, had been cordial during social gatherings, and even called me periodically to ask if I would like to be appointed to this or that case. There was no reason to believe he wouldn't be fair during the Zamora trial. Filing a motion to remove him would not only have been legally questionable, but personally insulting. Because the Zamora case was so highly publicized, dredging up the past and excising Judge Baker from the trial might have held him up to public embarrassment.

ON SEPTEMBER 26, 1977, with the live eye of the television camera watching, and more than sixty reporters from around the world packing the gallery, something not to be confused with a fair trial began in Room 4-1 of the Dade County Hall of Justice. The day before, Ronny had been provided with a new suit to wear in court. He said the jailers took it from his locker and ground it into the dirty floor with their shoes, rendering it unwearable. One jailer went to his cell and taunted him by saying the electric company had offered to provide the electricity for his "death chair" for free. (The power company never made such a remark.)

I entered the courtroom under heavy scrutiny—and had both hands figuratively tied behind my back. In a series of pretrial hearings, Judge Baker proceeded to ensure that my defense went down in flames by throwing out virtually all of my medical and social science experts.

Included among these experts was Dr. Margaret Hanratty Thomas, Assistant Dean of Academic Affairs at Florida Technological University in Orlando (later renamed the University of Central Florida). Dr. Thomas is a preeminent psychologist and nationally respected expert in the field of the effects of television violence on young children and adolescents. She had published fifteen papers and was planning to enlighten the jurors, and the world, on some startling findings. The judge asked her if she had ever seen or heard of a murder directly caused by television. As Baker knew, most psychiatrists and psychologists would never answer such a question, because their science is much broader in its consideration of factors.* When Dr. Thomas tried to explain this to the judge, he unceremoniously tossed her and her expertise out of the witness box.

For a doctor or other expert, such an encounter with the legal system can be both humiliating and infuriating. These scholars dedicate their lives to a particular subject, become authorities in the

*Psychiatrists, psychologists, and medical doctors almost always speak in terms of "could have" and "may" instead of the firmer "did" and "will." Such hedging drives attorneys to drink.

field, and then are called in to testify in a big murder case. After decades of meticulous research, all in relative obscurity, the chance to share their findings in a precedent-setting trial with worldwide media coverage can be the crowning moment of their careers. They take the stand, then boom, some close-minded judge decides that they don't know squat and publicly bounces them right out of the courtroom.

That's exactly what Judge Baker was doing to my expert witnesses. I brought them in and he tossed them out, tails between their legs. He refused to consider their studies or hear their testimony concerning the damaging effects of television violence on children. Judge Baker's rationale was that the expert testimony had to be restricted to Ronny, and could not be extended to children in general. Such a decree would make most respected researchers of any topic insist that Judge Baker was legally insane. Imagine trying to prove that cigarettes cause cancer, and being restricted to one single smoker?

Similarly, the judge also refused to allow me to submit seventy-eight scientific studies and published stories on television violence and children. Many were written by prominent doctors and researchers from around the world. Judge Baker's illogic here was even more outrageous. He said I could only submit studies taken specifically on Ronny Zamora, a ridiculous and impossible restriction.

I felt like putting this reminder over the judge's bench: "The mind is a terrible thing to waste."

Incredibly, immediately after tossing out Dr. Thomas, Judge Baker came face-to-face with the power of television. The jurors had been sequestered in a local hotel and were prevented from watching the television coverage of the trial. They weren't pleased.

"Let me say that I have received the request of the jury that they be allowed to watch themselves on television with the sound turned off, just to see what you look like," Baker said amid courtroom laughter. "I can't permit that during the course of the trial, but I will arrange for it after the trial. You will all get to see yourselves on television."

Once Headley and Katz realized that the judge was sticking it to me and would sustain their objections, they went wild. Each time I tried to slip in a television-related question, the prosecutors shot out of their chairs as though a rabid rat had taken a bite out of their ankles. Headley was particularly annoying, objecting to everything and anything, even beyond the scope of television. He started his onslaught during the jury-selection process and kept it up the whole trial. The following courtroom exchange, regarding a police officer's testimony, was typical:

> HEADLEY: All right, Your Honor, may I have a continuing objection at this point, and the court can rule?
> BAKER: You may. I really can't make an intelligent ruling until I hear the response.
> RUBIN: Your Honor, I'll stipulate that he has a continuing objection since the opening day of the trial.
> HEADLEY: Very cute.
> BAKER: All right, gentlemen.

When it was his turn, Katz was in such an objection frenzy he even objected to a question asked by Judge Baker, a legal no-no. He also objected to a question, had his objection overruled, then objected again after the question was read back to the witness by the court reporter. While I was trying to question child psychology specialist Dr. Helen Ackerman, Katz objected forty-seven times over the course of about a half hour. And Judge Baker sustained most of the objections, meaning Dr. Ackerman was all but totally gagged. Some of the banished questions went right to the heart of Ronny's defense:

> RUBIN: Was there anything in the test material that showed an effect of television watching on his [Ronny's] character and his person as you see it now and as it existed on June 4, 1977?
> KATZ: Objection.
> BAKER: Sustained as to that.
> RUBIN: What kind of shows did he watch?
> KATZ: Objection.
> BAKER: Sustained as irrelevant.
> RUBIN: Did you ascertain that he watched any particular programs which he then copied in his everyday behavior?
> KATZ: Objection.
> BAKER: Again sustained.
> RUBIN: No further questions.

In essence, what little chance Ronny had left after Dr. Gilbert sprung his "three-second theory" was squashed by an unbending judge and a pair of magpie prosecutors disrupting my defense at every turn.

If they didn't believe the television-intoxication defense, if it was just one of "Ellis Rubin's crazy gimmicks," then why were they all so terrified of it?

Actually, all of this gagging of the experts wasn't that bad.

Judge Baker was smothering Ronny's defense to such an extent that I knew that if we lost, I had a solid chance of having the verdict overturned on appeal. Truthfully, I suspected that even with a supportive judge it was a hundred-to-one shot to win the jury trial. I fully expected to continue to fight the television-intoxication battle through the state appellate process.

But I had to get through the initial trial. Without the doctors, and without a defense, the only thing I had left was some razzle-dazzle. I had read that actor Telly Savalas had given a speech at Columbia University decrying television violence because it caused children to commit "copycat" crimes, a well-known phenomenon. Savalas also said he pushed to have the writers and producers tone down the violence on "Kojak." I subpoenaed him to testify. The shaven-headed actor fought the subpoena, claiming he didn't know anything about the case. His attorney filed a motion to quash his appearance. Judge Baker held a meeting in chambers to discuss it. He wanted to know the relevancy of Savalas's testimony. I explained that Ronny had conjured up a "Kojak" episode to mentally erase the shooting. Additionally, as Kojak, Savalas was Ronny's biggest hero. If Ronny's biggest hero felt that television caused children to commit crimes, that was vital. Judge Baker said he would order Savalas to appear, but that he would question him to determine the relevancy of his testimony.

"What right or authority do you have to question my witness during a deposition?" I demanded.

He replied that he was the judge and thus had the right to do anything he wanted. I countered that he could do anything except take the testimony of potential witnesses. He could lawfully attend the deposition, but all he was empowered to do was screen objections. He brushed off the legalities, insisting that he alone was going to question the television star. I felt that Judge Baker himself was becoming intoxicated by the live PBS television coverage of the trial. Bitten by the TV bug, he wanted to up the stakes and get his face on national television by questioning the ultimate "star witness." I walked out and immediately canceled the subpoena. If the judge blew Savalas out, which he was going to do, the headlines would have destroyed the case in midstream.

At this point my defense had been narrowed down to the width of a cocktail straw.

Meanwhile, Headley was encountering a few problems of his own. Linda Agrella, Darrell's mother, refused to respond to his subpoena to testify. The judge had to order a writ of attachment and have her brought in. When she arrived, her lawyer said she was psychologically unable to take the stand. He produced psychiatrist Bryan Weiss, who took the stand in her place. Dr. Weiss testified that Linda Agrella was "in a psychotic condition and cannot differentiate reality from her fantasies . . . at the present time, she is not capable of differentiating right from wrong."

Headley and Judge Baker promptly accepted the single diagnosis of Mrs. Agrella's mental state, excused her, and waived the charge of disobeying a court order. The prosecutor and judge then went back to their virulent attacks on my doctors' diagnoses of Ronny's insanity.

Despite the suffocating restrictions placed upon me, I fought on and managed to win a few rounds. I begged the judge to allow me to use the tape of the truth-serum test. That was my Br'er Rabbit, "please don't throw me into the briar patch" strategy. Headley correctly argued that the Florida Supreme Court had ruled that truth-serum tests weren't admissible without both attorneys agreeing. Since Judge Baker thought I wanted it in so badly, he naturally refused to allow it. That kept Elinor Haggart's emotional family photo album scene out of the hands of the prosecutors and the minds of the jurors.

There were other minor victories. Mrs. Zamora held up under the strain considerably better than Mrs. Agrella had. She took the stand and emotionally and effectively detailed television's effect upon her son and his mental disintegration after his friend drowned:

> The way he learned English [at age five] was watching TV from the time he got up in the morning until he went to sleep. . . . I had to go out and work. My husband had to go out and work. . . . Ronny was very active and I was afraid he would run away or something, you know, open the door and let anybody in the apartment. So I thought of watching TV, and for him watching TV was the greatest thing in the world.

Even as a teenager, Ronny's devotion to television remained unwavering:

> He would stay home and watch TV. . . . He didn't want to do his homework. He didn't want to read. He . . . would just watch TV.
> . . . A lot of times when my husband was not home Ronny asked me many, many times, he actually begged me to convince my husband to have his [Mr. Zamora's] head shaved like Kojak. . . . My

husband was going to do it, but then one day he was mad and he said forget about it. . . . Ronny was very upset because we almost had him convinced that he was going to shave his head like Kojak.

Then Ronny's friend Scott drowned, the boy's life literally slipping through Ronny's fingers. About this incident, Mrs. Zamora said, "I was worried because Ronny had changed completely. He was not the same person I knew. . . . He was losing his mind or something."

When it came time for Dr. Gilbert to testify, it took me fifteen minutes just to list his credentials, including his double doctorate and his stint at St. Elizabeth's Hospital in Washington, D.C., a seven-thousand-bed mental hospital. A brilliant man, Dr. Gilbert had been admitted in court as an expert hundreds of times—for both defense attorneys and prosecutors.

Headley objected to his admission as an expert.

In fact, Headley put up a fierce objection, arguing that the doctor had formed his opinions based upon the illegal sodium Amytal test. Dr. Gilbert insisted that he hadn't, explaining that the truth serum merely confirmed his earlier diagnosis. Legally, Headley was splitting hairs on a microscopic level.

Miraculously, Judge Baker didn't pounce upon this to bounce Dr. Gilbert. Apparently he realized that he had to leave me with at least a skeleton of my defense, or the appellate courts would have his head.

"I'm not about to sit here and rob a fifteen-year-old boy of a defense. I'm just not going to do it," Baker said.

Because Dr. Gilbert had personally analyzed Ronny and was the defense "psychiatrist of record," Judge Baker had no right to gag his testimony or limit his diagnosis as severely as he had with the other doctors. That crack in the door was all I needed. Despite having painted himself into a corner with his "three-second theory," Dr. Gilbert gave a sweeping display of mental prowess. At one point he testified in French, German, and Spanish to make a point. The following exchange was especially captivating regarding Ronny's television intoxication:

DR. GILBERT: It has been demonstrated that the average child watches thousands of killings on TV. Now, a child like Ronny Zamora maybe sees five or ten times that many killings. When one has seen that many killings, the death of a human being in that type of situation is no more significant than swatting a fly. This develops a concept, an attitude, a distortion of reality, if you will, that the shooting of a person is of no greater consequence, let us say, than the swatting of a fly.

Now, the reason is, you see, if a shooting in television were accompanied by the physical agony of the person who's shot, the bleeding and suffering, and we're also shown the funeral, and also shown the suffering of this person's family, his children or his parents or what have you, all as a consequence of this shooting, as contrasted with "bang, bang," and the scene goes on. They don't look [on television] to see if the person is alive or dead or still bleeding or he can be saved or whatever. And then [the child] gets a distorted concept of what television death is, what death by shooting is, whereas if he saw all these other things which are reality, then he has a realistic concept of what death is. But [television], then, gives him an unrealistic concept of what death by shooting is. It's not real. It's distorted. And this is what happens in the case of an adolescent in Ronny Zamora's situation.

RUBIN: Did it have anything to do with the shooting of Elinor Haggart?

DR. GILBERT: It certainly did.

RUBIN: Can you explain that, please?

DR. GILBERT: . . . At the time he first gets the gun, this to him is not a weapon. It's a play toy, because he describes he opened the barrel, he spun it around, he waved it here, he pointed it there . . . put the barrel in his mouth . . . aimed it at the ceiling, aimed it at various things. He was playing a game with a toy.

Now then, Mrs. Haggart makes a statement to the boys. She says she knows he's the next-door neighbor and she is going to tell the police. It is at that point that Ronny told me the gun went off accidentally. . . . Now then, if this child has been exposed to thousands and thousands of situations where he has seen, when you are threatened, bang, you shoot. You take this emotionally disturbed child in a situation which is foreign to him—he's never been a robber before, he's never held a gun in his hand before, but he has been conditioned that the proper thing or the thing to do is to shoot. He has no conscious awareness, intention, volition, if you will, of what he is doing. But the trigger finger reflexively contracts over the trigger and the gun goes off.

. . . Up to that time he knew the difference between right and wrong. At the time of the shooting, he did not know what he was doing. Therefore, he could not know the nature and consequence of his act, since he did not know what he was doing. And therefore he can't, couldn't judge that what he was doing was wrong.

If I could have gotten Dr. Gilbert off the stand at that point, we'd have had a slim chance. Unfortunately, he had to be cross-examined. Dr. Gilbert, for all his double doctorates, had a tendency to appear smug and pompous. Knowing this, I could suppress the characteristic by playing to his intellectual ego. However, when challenged by an enemy, these negative traits tended to surface. During the depositions, Dr. Gilbert had been condescending to Headley and Katz and had shown an obvious disdain for their inability to quickly grasp and accept his innovative concepts. He even went so far as to correct Katz's grammar, and followed up by correcting Headley's grammar in open court on live television! Obviously, this didn't sit well with the two prosecutors. I could see Headley practically salivating as he left the prosecutors' table. He took Dr. Gilbert through Ronny's sanity as before, and was told that Ronny was sane up to and after the shooting:

> HEADLEY: Now, when it comes right to the moment that the gun is shot, it is your opinion that the defendant went from sane to insane and back to sane in a matter of two or three seconds?
> DR. GILBERT: That is correct.
> HEADLEY: Now, the exact time—which we can't reconstruct—but would the time period be from when the trigger was pulled until he heard the noise and this brought him back to his senses?
> DR. GILBERT: More or less.
> HEADLEY: This, then, could be no more than a second.
> DR. GILBERT: Second or seconds. I think by the time the noise subsides and one gets his faculties back where he can look around and see what happens. Probably, let us say a few seconds, but I think we're really pulling at hairs here. A second, a few seconds, or ten seconds. I don't think it's of any great consequence.

But the jury did. Adios, Ronny. See you in twenty-five years.

In defense of Dr. Gilbert, when psychiatrists talk about the inner workings of the human mind, time can be meaningless. Scientists have long had a different view of time. They see it as relative. Ten seconds in a courtroom is a blink of an eye. Ten seconds with one's foot in a fire is an eternity.

But three seconds of insanity from watching television? A jury couldn't comprehend that. And just in case some of the jury members were swayed by Dr. Gilbert's oration, the prosecutors had their own experts to dismantle his diagnosis:

> DR. WILLIAM CORWIN: It is completely unlikely that in the space of a brief period, like one to two or three or four or five seconds, the time in which it would take to pull a trigger, which in itself required some effort and conscious volition, it is completely unlikely that he would be, at that moment, legally insane.

While the television-intoxication defense was being skewered in court, the other precedent-setting aspect of the Zamora trial was meeting with far greater success. The cameras-in-the-courtroom experiment, at least from the viewers' standpoint, was a rousing success. Miami's PBS station edited each day's trial footage into two- or three-hour segments that were aired the same evening at eleven-thirty. During the course of the nine-day trial, it was the highest-rated program in its time period, a rarity for PBS. In fact, the Zamora trial was crushing the time period's previously indomitable leader, Johnny Carson.

But the high Nielsens weren't helping me one iota in court. By the closing arguments, I was ready to be carried out on my shield. The prosecutors naturally invoked their right to make opening and closing summations, sandwiching me in between. Headley gave Katz the opening half and saved the critical last word for himself. He was brutally effective:

> My God, where have we gotten when someone can come into a court of law and, with a straight face, ask you to excuse the death of a human being because the killer watched television? The defense in this case could have just as easily have been too much violence from reading the Bible, too much violence from reading history books, too much violence from reading the papers. Unfortunately, we do have violence in this world and we're exposed to it. But exposure to that violence does not make you legally insane, or we're going to have free license to do whatever. And what did the defense do to establish their defense?

What indeed? It was Headley who pleaded with Judge Baker to gag my experts and thus sabotage my defense. But those are the breaks, and in the summations—especially the final, uncontradicted summation the prosecutors are gifted with—no prisoners are taken.

Dr. Gilbert, the grammarian, also felt the sting of Headley's tongue: "The whole case depends on Dr. Gilbert. You heard his testimony. I didn't understand too much of it, to be honest with you. . . . I suggest that the testimony offered by Dr. Gilbert is something that if you were at a friend's house, you would listen to politely for a few minutes and then throw up your hands and say, 'Nonsense. Nonsense.' "

Which basically sums up the reaction of the jury. They were out two hours, an unusually short time for deliberations in a murder trial. It wasn't surprising, though. Judge Baker spared them the effort of having to glance at any of the seventy-eight articles on television violence I was prevented from submitting. But, hey, it was only a boy's life.

On October 6, 1977, Ronny Zamora was found guilty of murder, burglary, armed robbery, and possession of a weapon. On November 7, Judge Baker sentenced Ronny to life in prison with no chance of parole for twenty-five years. (During his opening argument, Headley had announced he wasn't asking for the death penalty.) Ronny was also given two other twenty-five-year sentences on the burglary and armed-robbery charges, and three years for possession of a weapon.

Prior to the sentencing, Judge Baker commented on all the advice he had been getting:

"In the weeks since this trial, I have received phone calls, letters, and petitions even from Dr. Karl Menninger himself, telling me what to do. And it is not their business. It's unfortunately mine."

Dr. Menninger is the renowned Nobel Prize–winning psychiatrist who created the respected Menninger Foundation. He had recommended that Zamora receive medical treatment. Regarding Judge Baker's comments, Dr. Menninger recently responded: "The judge is right: it is his business; but he is not right that it is none of ours. It is some of our business to be sure that the judge is acting in a way that a modern and intelligent judge should."

A member of the jury explained the verdict in this quizzical way to PBS:

"I endorse any and all television. It's police shows, it's—what it is doing is bringing the everyday violence that occurs out on the street into your home and you're getting more educated."

The television-happy juror was equally elated about televised trials.

"I think it's really one of the greatest achievements in a long time, the television. The public gets a chance to view and also be the jurors."

Judge Baker himself termed televised trials a success. He explained his reasons to PBS narrator Richard Reeves, the syndicated newspaper columnist and national editor of *Esquire* magazine:

"I define 'success' as not having an impact on the witnesses to the extent that they were given to overstatement or that they were intimidated. I define it as having little or no impact on the jurors' ability to consider the testimony. . . . I think as an educational tool and as news, it was successful, since it gave the public an opportunity to see what goes on in a courtroom. And most of them have not had that experience."

However, Dr. George Gerbner, professor of communications and dean of the Annenberg School of Communications at the University of Pennsylvania, offered PBS some words of caution. Dr. Gerbner, a noted television researcher and authority, expressed concern that television has a tendency to change and overwhelm whatever it touches, and reminded everyone that many judges are elected officials. He felt that the constitutional separation of powers that is at the heart of the legal system might be compromised by "centralized" and "organically programmed" television.

"There are hundreds of trials going on every day," Dr. Gerbner said. "Who is going to . . . decide what will be selected out for either regional or national television? The medium itself? On what basis will it select? On the same basis on which it selects everything else—the basis of sales, the basis of ratings, the basis of entertainment."

FOLLOWING THE verdict, my plan was to exhaust all state and federal appeals. Besides the judge's actions, Headley had made a serious mistake. After the verdict, I was told by the father of one of the witnesses that during the trial, Headley and his investigators had told a prosecution witness to call a defense witness to try to find out where the jewelry and gun were. The parties involved were Ronny's junior-high classmates. Apparently, rumors about the missing gun and the remaining pieces of unrecovered jewelry were running rampant at the school. One of the Disney World boys was summoned to the state attorney's office and instructed to call a girl who supposedly knew who had the evidence. (The girl was one of my daughter Kim's friends. I still give thanks to God it wasn't Kim.) The boy called her twice. Sure enough, the girl made a series of incriminating statements that could have sent the little valley-talking fourteen-year-old away for a long stretch. During the call, she repeatedly refused to come forward and vowed to lie in court if asked. Both calls were taped, and the tape was played in front of two additional state witnesses. Since all the witnesses had been ordered not to talk about the case to each other, such a call, and the playing of the tape, was in gross violation of the judge's strict witness-sequestration order.

When I called the teenage girl to the stand to testify, I was totally in the dark about the clandestine kiddie wiretapping operation. Headley jumped up and informed the judge there had been a violation of the separation order because of a telephone call. Sure, he knew. He caused it! Headley, of course, didn't mention that. He skirted serious judicial punishment by graciously saying that although he should object to her testimony on the grounds of the call, and because she had admitted to watching some of the trial on television, he wasn't going to. Even so, four prosecution witnesses had been compromised, and a fifth was later told about the taped calls and was subsequently tainted. All five should have been eliminated from the trial, not only for violating the sequestration rule, but because of the fear-provoking tactics used by the state. The wiretap operation no doubt scared the life out of the impressionable teenagers who heard the tape, and may have caused them to alter their testimony. Also, it could be viewed as an underhanded tactic to get rid of a defense witness and deprive Zamora of a fair trial.*

Besides the teenage girl, the "tainted five" included all four of the boys who had gone to Walt Disney World with Ronny. Without their critical testimony, which Ronny said was full of lies, it might have been a whole different case.

I informed Judge Baker. He was upset about what had transpired, but ruled that it had no bearing on the outcome of the trial.

In the initial appeals, I protested both my inability to present my case and the problem of the tainted witnesses. While the appellate judges also condemned the prosecutors' actions regarding the witnesses, they refused to order a new trial. The next step of the appeals process was federal court. That's where I felt we had our best chance. I was confident that a federal court would never tolerate the judicial abuses that occurred during the Zamora case. But before I could appeal, Frank and Yolanda Zamora decided on a different tack. They switched attorneys and attacked me for "ineffective assistance of counsel."

---

*The attorney for the state argued during the appeal that the wiretap information was being gathered for the upcoming trial of Darrell Agrella. However, there was no mention of Agrella on the tape, and four of the five witnesses were scheduled to testify in the Zamora trial within a few days of the call. The two teenagers discussed the trip to Walt Disney World, which had no bearing on Agrella's case because he didn't go. Further, the missing gun was critical in the Zamora trial, because Ronny was the one who had pulled the trigger.

Ronny's new attorneys went from court to court, trying to get somebody to rule that I had been ineffective. They were shot down at every turn, including Florida's Third District Court of Appeals, the U.S. District Court, and, as recently as 1988, the U.S. Eleventh Circuit Court of Appeals in Atlanta.

The Third District Court of Appeals stated that "defense counsel cannot be faulted for selecting a tack which, by allowing for the presentation of evidence as to the defendant's unfortunate background, may have at least evoked the sympathy of the jury and a consequent jury pardon. . . . Whether viewed in its individual segments, in different series, or as one entire picture, [the defense] does not project an image of ineffectiveness."

In 1986, U.S. District Court Judge Eugene Spellman wrote: "This court sees this situation as a rather bleak but not uncommon one—a lawyer faced with the task of representing a 'client with no defense.' "

The Atlanta court concluded: "The evidence suggests that counsel was prepared and that he attempted to develop a defense in a weak case."

I was happy to be vindicated, but I disagree that Ronny Zamora was a client with "no defense" or a "weak case."

Although the accusations of incompetency hung over my head like a sword for more than a decade, I can't blame the attorneys for attacking me. I knew the risk when I offered the defense. The media make a big deal about "ineffective assistance of counsel" charges, but actually they're a routine appeal tactic. Defense attorneys get slapped with thousands of such charges every year. However, I felt that the logic behind the motion was disturbing. Instead of pursuing the errors made by the judge and prosecutors, Ronny's new lawyers kept hammering away at the ineffective counsel charge. Even if the courts had found that I was ineffective and had ordered a new trial—a rare occurrence—Ronny simply would have been convicted again. What was the point? At least my way, we had a remote chance of winning the case, and a solid chance of winning an appeal and getting Ronny the medical help he needed.

But I wasn't the victim. While I was being professionally attacked, Ronny Zamora was growing up in prison. If he was so impressionable that television had distorted his mind, I'm almost afraid to consider the effect of twenty-five years in prison.

EPILOGUE

Shortly after the Zamora trial, on June 6, 1978, a year and two days after Elinor Haggart's death, Judge Baker sentenced Agrella to three life terms in prison. He served eight years and was paroled on November 5, 1985.

The televising of the Zamora trial, a true acid test, was judged by the higher courts to have had no negative effect upon the fair dispensation of justice. Cameras have been allowed in Florida courtrooms ever since. As of 1989, more than forty states have followed suit. Federal courts, however, have remained in the dark.

AS FOR the latest developments in the ongoing debate as to whether or not viewing excessive television violence by teenagers leads to criminal acts, 1989 saw the release of new studies confirming that "television viewing is linked to about half of the 20,000 homicides that occur each year in the United States" (the results of a seven year study by a professor at the University of Washington School of Medicine). The study also said: "While television clearly is not the sole cause of violence in our society, and there are many other contributing factors, hypothetically if television did not exist, there would be 10,000 fewer homicides a year."

And for the first time in the thirty years since Congress first debated the effects of television violence, both the Senate and the House have agreed on legislation seeking to tone it down. A bill passed in 1989 "would grant the networks, local stations, producers and cable operators a formal exemption to antitrust laws in case they voluntarily decide to get together and talk about ways to lessen the daily murder and mayhem depicted in non-news shows."

OF THE multitude of bizarre cases I've tried in my years as a defense attorney, none have haunted me like the Ronny Zamora case. Regardless of what I do the rest of my life, the headline of my obituary will probably read, ELLIS RUBIN, INVENTOR OF THE TELEVISION INTOXICATION DEFENSE. It's shadowed me in everything I do. To this day, I still can't determine whether the overall effect has been positive or negative. It made me famous and it brought me ridicule. I was deemed innovative and was accused of making a mockery of the law. In the past twelve years, hardly a week has gone by without someone calling about the case—be it a journalist, a university professor, a college student, a doctor, or a high school student.

I owe a major part of this legal immortality to the Public Broadcasting System. PBS edited the trial down into an award-winning, two-hour special that has been aired around the world. The reviews, like the ratings, were overwhelming. WPBT collected some of them:

> "It's the most important WPBT production to be fed over the PBS network, an instant historical document that illustrates perfectly the capabilities—and limitations—of opening trials to the electronic media."
>
> *—Variety*

> "Perhaps the most significant program this year. . . . If I could fly a Goodyear blimp over this column to call attention to it, I would."
> —Kay Gardella, the New York *Daily News*

> "It made 'Perry Mason' look like 'The Katzenjammer Kids.' "
> *—Daily Variety*

> "One of the most . . . fascinating programs in recent years."
> —Jim O'Brien, *Philadelphia Daily News*

> "A fascinating documentary."
>
> *—TV Guide*

> "Just when you're considering donating your set to Goodwill, a program lights up your brain as well as your screen."
> —Mike Drew, *Milwaukee Journal*

One newspaper wrote that more people have seen Ellis Rubin try a case than all the other defense attorneys in the history of the world put together—times 100 million. That put my head in the clouds for about a second, until I realized that more people have seen Ellis Rubin *lose* a case than all the other attorneys in history.

Looking back, my only regret is that I was never able to present the case I wanted. Thus, I was unable to adequately explore the question of television violence and the danger it may present to young minds. And by losing the case, I probably set back the cause of those who diligently warn of the possible dangers.

As for the future, the next watershed case involving television may have nothing to do with the unanswered questions about violence. Broadcast television used to have strong moral images of right and wrong. That eroded with the advent of bed-hopping soap operas like "Dallas" and "Dynasty." Although they may be entertaining, these sex-soaked programs and others like them glorify adultery and a cornucopia of other forms of what used to be known as "sexual immorality." That may be okay for adults, but do our children really need to see J.R. Ewing's wife, Sue Ellen, jump from bed to bed in one drunken stupor after another?

Probably not. But since televised immorality and its effect upon rampant teenage sex is a social problem instead of a criminal violation, the effects of televised bed-hopping—including X-rated movies on cable television—may never have a landmark court case.

Or maybe it will. Ironically, the same day this epilogue was written, there was a story in the *Miami Herald* about a trio of Miami Beach elementary school students who seduced, and sometimes forced, their classmates into committing a series of homosexual acts in a school restroom. The sexual bullies were aged twelve, eleven, and ten, and they had preyed upon at least six willing or unwilling victims. The abuse had gone on for three months.

Among the things the police said the three boys had forced their victims to do was perform oral sodomy.

One of the arrested youths told the police he had been influenced by watching oral sex on late-night cable television.

5

THE SHEIK, PART I

Lifestyles of the Incredibly Rich and Obnoxious

Money makes people rot.
—Sheika Dena al-Fassi

IN LATE 1980, all of South Florida was atwitter with the news that Prince Turki bin Abdul-Aziz and his vast entourage had alighted in Miami. Prince Turki, trillionaire brother of zillionaire King Fahd of Saudi Arabia, had taken up residence on the top floors of the Cricket Club, an exclusive Miami condominium and hotel complex on the shores of Biscayne Bay.

The Cricket Club was then owned by one of Miami's more colorful residents, attorney-turned-real-estate-baron Alvin Malnik. On April 25, 1982, the *Miami Herald* published a rather voluminous splash of journalism recounting "twenty years of accusations" that Malnik was a close associate of the late mob boss Meyer Lansky, and had business dealings with some other mobster types. Malnik once again denied the charges, as he had for the previous two decades. The *Herald* quoted a state gambling regulator who claimed otherwise. As is frequently the case with such stories, absolutely nothing came of it. Malnik has never been convicted of any crime.

Among Malnik's possessions is the nationally famous Forge Restaurant, an exclusive dining spot on Miami Beach's Arthur Godfrey Road. The Forge is the place where Lansky's stepson, Richard Schwartz, got into a squabble with another man with Mafia bloodlines, Craig Teriaca, the twenty-nine-year-old son of alleged underworld honcho Vincent Teriaca. In October 1977, Teriaca and Schwartz, forty-eight, were arguing over which Mafia prince owned a ten-dollar bill lying on the bar. Schwartz pulled a gun in the crowded lounge and shot Teriaca dead. Revenge was swift. Four months later, while out on bond awaiting trial, Schwartz was gunned down coming out of his restaurant on Bay Harbor Island. He died on the pavement beside his blue Cadillac.

For once, though, it was a guest, and not the owner of the Cricket Club, who was making all the news. And for once it was positive. Except for a few isolated pockets of resistance from Jews on Miami Beach, the Arab prince and his trillions were welcomed to Miami's melting pot.

The wealthy residents of the Cricket Club and the adjacent Jockey Club, where bayfront condominiums can cost as much as $1 million, were made to feel like paupers compared to the Arab. The prince rented an entire traveling circus to perform at a birthday party for his three-year-old daughter and two-year-old son. The mini-prince showed up wearing shoes sprinkled with two-carat diamonds. The tennis courts were covered with a tent, which proved to be no match for the strong bay winds and blew off, much to the delight of many of the condo owners.

Something occurred during this awesome display of wealth that is more revealing. The private circus performance was staged on Halloween, a coincidence based upon the prince's daughter's birthday. The Cricket Club's vivacious social director, Bobbe Star, joined the costume parade as a mermaid princess. On her head was a sparkling tiara. Her Highness, Princess Hend Turki, caught sight of the beautiful Star and boiled with jealousy. She demanded that Star hand over the tiara on the spot to the true princess. Star complied. Princess Turki placed it upon her own head and wore it proudly.

"I don't know what all the fuss was about," Star said. "I bought the damn thing at Woolworth's for $1.98."

While one might snicker at the princess's foolish pride, the incident was a foreshadowing. Had Starr's tiara been a valuable family heirloom, the princess still might have taken possession. Her menacing security force would have seen to it. On the other hand, had Starr held out and offered to sell her cheap party crown, she may have received upwards of $100,000 or more. The "Beverly Hillbilly" Arabs were a paradox of arrogant demands and immense gullibility. They could take or be taken, and the sums either way were often vast.

The prince's honeymoon in South Florida didn't last long. Soon a dark and troubling story emerged. One of the prince's servants escaped and went directly to the Metro-Dade police department. The servant told detectives a tale of slavery, beatings, and abuse. The chief abuser, the servant said, was Princess Hend. The servant begged the detectives to free her companions from their life of misery.

The Metro detectives didn't take the servant's story lightly. They began investigating and uncovered enough supporting information to get a warrant to check out what was going on. When a team of eight detectives and officers arrived, they found that His Highness was surrounded by an elite force of international bodyguards who felt no obligation to obey American law. Even if they had, Princess Turki wasn't about to let the officers inside her suite. She screamed orders for her men to impede the actions of the police any way they could. The bodyguards, a grizzled band of mercenaries and karate experts, stomped the cops. The princess was said to have joined in, spitting, biting, scratching and yanking on the hair of a female officer named Connie Kubik. Many of the officers were badly injured, including Kubik. She was lifted off the ground like a hapless professional wrestler and body slammed into a wall.

Suffice it to say, the officers were unable to locate any servants held against their will.

Following the incident, one of the battered officers, Sgt. John Collins, came to my office. He wanted to sue the Turkis for causing his injuries. All the officers were in rough shape, especially Kubik, and it ticked me off.

We sued.

The state attorney was also upset about the incident, and was planning to prosecute the royals.

Down from the north came a representative from the U.S. State Department. According to the *Miami Herald,* the representative turned out to be former U.S. Ambassador to Saudi Arabia John West. West, a former governor of South Carolina, was a member of the board of directors of the Whittaker Corporation, a California-based company that made millions doing business with the al-Fassi family. Some strings had been pulled, and Prince and Princess Turki were retroactively awarded a sweeping blanket of diplomatic immunity. The immunity included the prince's staff, bodyguards, and, I presume, any slaves.

That meant no prosecution, no arrests, no trial, no human-rights investigation. And no civil lawsuits on behalf of the injured officers. There wasn't a damn thing we could do about it. When Uncle Sam throws his red, white, and blue blanket over a foreigner like that, the foreigner can do anything short of raping the President's wife and get away with it.

"That's the government for you," said Officer Michael Fisten. "We're only a bunch of peon cops. It's all right for us to get our asses kicked."

I really felt sorry for the police. They were asked to do their job, did it, risked their lives, and were injured, only to have some guy and his crass wife laugh at them from their perch high above the city.

Fortunately, public sentiment turned against the prince, and he soon bade Miami farewell. But that wasn't the last the city heard of the obstinate Arabs. Princess Turki left behind her wayward little brother, one Sheik Mohammed al-Fassi.

And that's when things really went haywire.

MOHAMMED AL-FASSI is a five-foot-four-inch, 125-pound, wiry little dude with thinning black hair, a thick black mustache, a perpetual five-o'clock shadow, crooked teeth, and a fortune estimated at $6 billion. He first touched down in Los Angeles in 1975, where he attended college and tried to buy his way into the Hollywood scene by throwing lavish parties. In 1978 he paid $2.4 million in cash to purchase one of Beverly Hills' most famous mansions, a thirty-eight-room palace known as the "White House." That nickname was the first thing to go. The sheik painted the house pea green, then made international headlines when he had an artist highlight the genitalia and add pubic hair to statues surrounding the home. The neighbors were aghast. (The home can be seen in the movie *The Jerk.* It was used in the comedy to demonstrate Steve Martin's exaggerated concept of the good life.)

The Hollywood and Beverly Hills set quickly tired of the sheik and his vulgar ways. Miffed, he packed up his sixty-five servants, four kids, two wives, and five hundred suitcases, hooked up with Prince Turki and Princess Hend, and wandered around the world for a few years. While they were gone, one of Mohammed's ex-chauffeurs torched the Beverly Hills mansion to cover up the theft of valuable paintings. Neighbors were reported to have gathered around the flaming structure, chanting, "Burn, baby, burn."

In 1981 the sheik and his contingent landed in South Florida—reportedly by mistake. They thought they were going to Walt Disney World, but overshot Orlando by about 250 miles. No matter. They decided to stay anyway.

The sheik was twenty-six when he arrived. In family tradition, he set up shop on the forty-fifth and forty-first floors of Irving Cowan's beautiful beachfront Diplomat Resort Hotel, located in Hollywood, Florida. The sheik booked about seventy luxury rooms, along with two convention halls and two meeting rooms to store his goods. Among the seventy $175-a-night hotel rooms, four were used solely to accommodate the sheik's wardrobe. That included one room for his shoes, which were laid out in colorful rows upon the two king-size beds and on the floor. Not to be outdone, his two wives also had a room each for their shoes, similarly lined up on the beds and floor. They had enough shoes to make Imelda Marcos fly into a jealous fit! The sheikas also had separate rooms for their purses.

The tab for the hotel, figuring in the restaurant bill and other incidentals, totaled about $25,000 a day. That came to $750,000 a month—not including tips. And that doesn't reflect the massive security force Mohammed hired. At one point, more than one hundred off-duty Hollywood police officers were on the sheik's payroll at eleven dollars an hour. This home-team protection was further bolstered by dozens of off-duty officers from surrounding communities.

Instantly forgetting the bad experience with his brother-in-law, Miami was soon atwitter again. The sheik wooed local politicians and scattered money to the winds. He and his clan bought $17 million worth of local property. He made generous donations totaling $240,000 to city governments, local charities, children in hospitals, and adults with sob stories. He made many an area merchant richer.

He tantalized the society set with his fabulous parties. When his son turned four, the sheik decided to throw a birthday party. He had the police round up twenty children, dubbed "rent-a-kids" by the local newspapers. Mohammed leased an eighty-five-foot boat and filled it with puppeteers, magicians, clowns, and musicians. For the adults, there were five hundred shrimp, 250 lamb chops, two hundred servings of filet mignon, and twenty-four pounds of succulent roast beef. The party cost $150,000. Reporters and photographers who came to cover the event were offered hundred-dollar tips for their troubles.

A similar party was staged for selected residents of Golden Beach, a ritzy community of waterfront homes where al-Fassi's younger brother, Tarek, had chosen to live. This bash included a thirty-yard-long buffet table decked with lobster and filet mignon and set against the Intercoastal Waterway, in the backyard of Tarek's $750,000 house. Describing the festivities reminds one of the carol "The Twelve Days of Christmas." The young sheik gave his Golden Beach "true loves" thirty-one waiters, an eighteen-piece orchestra, six strolling violinists, three ice sculptures, and a $60,000 rose display. If he would have thought of it, I'm sure he would have included a partridge in a pear tree.

Tarek, by the way, had once given a local drugstore manager $10,000 in cash for a giant display bottle of Paco Rabanne cologne. The plastic bottle was filled with colored water.

All of which paled in comparison to the palace Mohammed was building on Star Island, a secluded neighborhood of million-dollar homes just off the picturesque, tropical causeway that links Miami and Miami Beach. The sheik spent $1.5 million to buy two adjacent mansions, which he promptly demolished, and made arrangements to purchase a third. The rebuilding costs were budgeted at $15 to $25 million. The complex was designed to include two new houses, a $125,000 domed mosque, two bowling alleys, a theater in the round, a beauty salon, five waterfalls, three fountains, a glass-bottomed swimming pool perched over the living room, a 145-foot water slide, motorized closets the size of a two-car garage, a clock that spoke three languages, front doors that would open when the sheik clapped, a racquetball court, an ice-skating rink, a shooting gallery, Jacuzzi rooms equipped with a light show controlled by a tub-side switch panel, a sauna, and a monorail encircling the compound. Inside, there were fifteen-by-fifteen-inch Italian marble tiles, silk-upholstered walls, and a black ceiling dotted with tiny disco lights. The bathrooms were purple onyx and turquoise, with the requisite gold fixtures.

Mohammed shared his wealth with seemingly everyone—except the Diplomat's president, Irving Cowan. After paying his massive hotel bill diligently for eight months, enriching the Diplomat by about $6 million, the sheik began to lapse.

As spring burned into summer, the hotel tab soared past $500,000, past $750,000, past $1 million, and was closing in on $1.5 million. Rumors circulated that the sheik had a spat with the departed Prince Turki, and his allowance had been cut off. Cowan and his employees were getting nervous. There were reports that the sheik was planning to sneak away, beating the hotel for the bill. Every time they asked the sheik or his advisers to pay up, the Diplomat officials were told not to worry, they'd be paid, but the sheik couldn't be bothered with such trifling sums right then.

A trifle to Mohammed was a million-five to Irving. When the Diplomat finally got a check, it bounced. In fact, thirty-six of the sheik's previous checks were being "held" by his Swiss bankers until the account could be replenished. In short, they all bounced.

On a hot July afternoon, a group of grim-faced Diplomat officials, backed by a squad of on-duty Hollywood cops, forcibly evicted the sheik and his seventy-five-person entourage. They impounded $40 million worth of jewels, antique furniture, cars, prayer rugs, linens, clothing, and shoes. They charged the sheik with "defrauding an innkeeper," a third-degree felony in Florida. He was forced to cool his heels at the Hollywood police station for six hours while he waited for a bondsman to post a $1,000 bond. For some reason, the sheik could never wangle the diplomatic immunity his brother-in-law had acquired.

Royally peeved, Mohammed and his band retreated to his father's $3.2-million Miami Beach mansion. Those of his retinue who couldn't fit into the limited space of the mansion were ensconced at the Everglades Hotel in downtown Miami, or at the Moulin Rouge Hotel on Miami Beach. The new innkeepers gladly welcomed the business.

It was then that I received a call from one Ali Jamel, the sheik's right-hand man. As he talked, I noticed that Jamel had a Brooklyn accent. I would later learn that Ali Jamel, chief adviser and business manager to Sheik Mohammed al-Fassi, was actually Eli Gamel, a nice Jewish boy from Brooklyn. Gamel met al-Fassi in London, where Gamel owned several businesses. The two hit it off, went into some successful business ventures together, and Gamel was invited aboard full-time. He accepted, switching a consonant and a vowel transforming himself into Ali Jamel.

Ali/Eli explained that the sheik was having some problems with a local hotel. He wanted to retain me to take care of that and some other legal problems the young man was encountering. I agreed to meet him at his home the next day. At that point, what little I knew about the sheik was positive. He had been praised in the media for his generosity and benevolence, and appeared from a distance to be a decent fellow. Like everyone else in Miami, I was curious to see what went on inside his inner circle and get a taste of what it would be like to have limitless wealth. As for the Arab/Jewish aspect of the matter, it was never a consideration. That's a battle fought in another world. I prefer to view people the same way the law views them, as individuals. Besides, it's virtually impossible to live in Miami very long and still harbor ill feelings toward any racial or religious group. There's not enough hate in the worst bigot to cover the variety of people one encounters in a single Miami day—or in my office lobby.

Visiting the sheik proved to be a tedious process that consisted of being stopped at the guardhouse at the gate, getting permission to enter the compound, stopping again at the door, getting permission to enter the home, and finally being escorted into a waiting room. The only interesting part of the ordeal was the compound. That's where the sheik had his cars. The sheik had every kind and color of sports and luxury car one could imagine. There were six Cadillac stretch limousines—dark blue, light blue, burgundy, black, and a pair of white ones. Each was equipped with a television set and a full bar, even though the sheik didn't drink. Surrounding the limousines were a Maserati, a white Excalibur convertible, a Ferrari Mondial 9, a cherry-red Mercedes 500SL convertible, a Rolls-Royce, a Jaguar, a gold-plated Stutz Blackhawk, a Lamborghini Countach, and a few other makes I've forgotten. Every car was clean and waxed to a high gloss.

In the waiting room, one would wait, and wait, and wait, anywhere from an hour to forever. During the times I visited, I encountered doctors, dentists, jewelers, politicians, journalists, fellow attorneys, and businessmen of every stripe waiting in the "lobby" of the house. Once I found boxer Muhammad Ali sitting in a daze, waiting patiently to see the sheik. Another time, actor Omar Sharif was waiting.

Everybody waited. Everybody but Ellis Rubin. It didn't take long to figure out the sheik's game. He loved to keep people waiting. The more important they were, the longer they waited. After about forty-five minutes, I got up to leave. Jamel quickly rushed over and escorted me into a huge living room bathed in white—white rugs, white furniture, white drapes, white everything. The sheik came downstairs and greeted me. He seemed nice enough at first, but was shorter, skinnier, and balder than I expected. His eyes gave him away. The sheik had treacherous eyes. We agreed on my retainer, and I told him not to worry about the Diplomat problem.

After a week of legal scuffling, I managed to move the conflict from the criminal courts to the civil courts. That was a critical victory. No one would be coming to arrest the sheik again, at least not on these charges. I then scheduled an emergency hearing to deal with the impounded property.

I felt that the Diplomat had grossly overreacted. Sure, if someone runs up a $1.5-million bill, that might make you sweat. But if you're holding $40 million worth of that person's property, including $15 million in furniture and jewelry, what's the big deal over $1.5 million? What's $1.5 million between friends? All they had to do was grab a handful of diamonds, as the sheik suggested, and erase the bill. Of course, the Diplomat didn't see it that way. Being tossed a diamond the size of a golf ball isn't the kind of payment your basic hotel treasurer knows how to handle.

As weak as the Diplomat's case was, it blew totally apart when the hotel's attorneys made a huge blunder during the hearing. I had brought the sheik's top aides into the courtroom to testify. After my first witness told his story, the Diplomat's attorneys invoked a rule that all upcoming witnesses must wait outside. This prevents them from hearing each other's testimony and synchronizing their stories.

While the Diplomat's treasurer was testifying, in walked the hotel's general manager. He was their star witness. He sat through virtually all of the treasurer's testimony. I couldn't believe it. He was then called to take the stand.

I objected.

After a half hour or so of arguments, the judge ruled, repeatedly, that since the Diplomat's attorneys had invoked the "witnesses-out" sanction, they would have to live by it. Adios to the Diplomat's star witness. Not only that, but they had no one else ready to take his place and had to rest their stillborn case.

Unfortunately, they had another, better witness they didn't even know about. It was a dead poet who resided in Judge Joe Price's head. When he reached the critical point in a long speech rendering his judgment, the judge quoted Wordsworth:

And the night shall be filled with music,
And the cares that infest the day,
Shall fold their tents like the Arabs,
And as silently steal away.

Wonderful. Although I had thumped the Diplomat's attorneys like a dishrag, I was beaten by a literary allusion to thievery from a poet who died 130 years ago. The judge refused to grant my motion to dissolve the writ locking out the sheik from his property.

Actually, it was only a minor defeat. After six hours of bickering in court, we came up with the brilliant solution that if the sheik paid his bill, the Diplomat would release his property.

Shrewd.

I handed the Diplomat's attorney three cashier's checks totaling $1.56 million, and a few days later the sheik carted out his belongings.

At the same time as I was handing over that check, a parade of twenty-five other creditors, everyone from a painter to a shoe repairman, began showing up at the door of one of the sheik's financial law firms, Thomas and Thomas. The merchants demanded and received payment for a score of other rubber checks.

The sheik, still seething, demanded action against the Diplomat. Six weeks later we struck back. I filed a suit in Broward County Circuit Court against the hotel and its owners. The suit stated that al-Fassi had "suffered humiliation and embarrassment, nervous shock to his mind and body, defamation, libel, slander of his good name and reputation throughout the world, false arrest and false imprisonment, and damage to his credit." The Diplomat was additionally accused of "wrongfully terminating services and overcharging, inflating, and inventing said costs and charges."

We asked for $1 billion in damages—$300 million in compensatory damages and $700 million in punitive damages. And that didn't include interests, costs, and attorneys' fees.

Mohammed's problems with the Diplomat, reported around the world, spurred an interesting phenomenon. Hotels began vying for his business. The Holiday Inn in Miramar, a city close to Hollywood, goaded its rich, big brother Diplomat by awarding the sheik a key to the motel and making him an honorary innkeeper. A group of businessmen threw him a picnic and begged him not to leave town. Two children, moved by his financial problems, broke open their piggy banks and mailed the sheik $1.09 and fifty cents. That moved him the most.

"For a child, $1.09 is a lot of money," he said. "Americans have good hearts."

Nowhere were the "good hearts" more evident than in St. Louis. A disc jockey named Bob Wilke started a campaign to entice the sheik to move his operation there. Although it began as a joke, the sheik responded and St. Louis got serious. The sheik was given a personal invitation by the mayor to come for a grand visit. Al-Fassi sent Jamel and me instead. We were treated so royally that after the first couple of hours I phoned my two sons, Mark and Guy, and, quoting a favorite movie of mine, said, "Meet Me in St. Louis!" We had a great time and met some good people, including baseball great Stan Musial and the Busch family. They even flashed WELCOME TO ST. LOUIS, ELLIS RUBIN AND PARTY! on the scoreboard at Busch Memorial Stadium during a St. Louis Cardinals baseball game. I reported back to the sheik, and that was the last I heard of St. Louis.

Back in Miami, the sheik's peace was about to be shattered in a manner that would make the Diplomat Hotel battle look like nickels and dimes. The prior January, wife number one, Sheika Dena, had flown the coop. The Italian beauty had been unhappy for years, starting with the addition of wife number two, American actress Victoria Sosa. Sosa lasted only a year, but the damage was done. In Miami, the sheik added wife number three, a raven-haired Saudi Arabian named Aptisam. Sheika Dena was exiled to the east wing of the Diplomat while her husband cuddled with Aptisam in the forty-fifth floor master suite. Dena told me during a deposition that the sheik's staffers supplied her with cocaine and tricked her into taking Quaaludes by saying they were aspirin. Once, while she was zonked out on the non-aspirin Quaaludes, she said she was sexually assaulted by the husband of one of her maidservants.

Escaping this nightmare, she returned to the West Coast, where she fell into the waiting arms of a member of rock singer Rod Stewart's band, identified in the deposition as lead guitarist Jim Cregan. They had met earlier in Miami, had a brief affair, met again in New York, then became reacquainted in San Francisco and Los Angeles.

But Dena would be back—with a vengeance.

Sheika Dena al-Fassi returned to Miami in August 1982 with celebrity divorce lawyer Marvin Mitchelson in tow. They were coming to get what they felt was theirs. And what they felt was theirs were four children and $3 billion.

Three billion dollars.

It would be Marvin Mitchelson versus Ellis Rubin, one on one, for the highest stakes in a child custody suit in the history of the planet Earth.

6

THE SHEIK, PART II:

The Billion-Dollar Babies

I'VE PROBABLY held more than five hundred press conferences in my life. I've spoken into five thousand microphones, looked into a couple of thousand news cameras, and fielded more than ten thousand questions from reporters.

Yet, for sheer variety, I've never experienced a media circus the likes of the one that surrounded the al-Fassi custody battle. Never before had I seen a *National Enquirer* reporter bumping shoulders with a *New York Times* reporter. Never had I seen a *Wall Street Journal* correspondent shouting down a *People* magazine scribe. Never had my secretary handed me a message that *U.S. News & World Report* called, and, under it, a message to call the *Midnight Globe*. And trying to determine who the mob of foreign reporters was, or even what countries they represented, was futile.

Love, money, sex, drugs, and fame. The world never tires of it.

THE ROMANCE of Mohammed al-Fassi and Diane (Dena) Bilanelli had been the stuff of a television miniseries. They met in a London clothing shop in 1975. He was nineteen. She was fifteen. He was soon to be a billionaire. She was a shopgirl with a billion-dollar face. The young Dena was Sophia Loren and Gina Lollobrigida rolled into one, a dark-haired, creamy-skinned Italian beauty with the biggest, most alluring eyes God ever set in one of his creations. The teenaged Arab was smitten the instant he saw her. They married less than a year later.

At the time, al-Fassi was a well-off foreign student, but nothing out of the ordinary. His sister, Hend, was the companion of Prince Turki, and that gave al-Fassi what leverage he had. Actually, the al-Fassi clan was nothing more than a band of Morrocan nomads who settled in Saudi Arabia, looking for a better life. Mohammed's father, Shamsuddin Abdullah al-Fassi, operated a small trading company and a tobacco shop and was once jailed for speaking out against the Saudi government.

Mohammed and Dena moved to Los Angeles, where they settled into a $200-a-month apartment. He bought a Buick. She cooked for him and washed the clothes. They both remember this as their happiest time together.

Then things changed dramatically. Hend al-Fassi, a secretary for a foreign company, was promoted from Prince Turki's consort to his wife. That made her a princess of considerable clout. Prince Turki is one of the numerous sons of former Saudi King Abdul Aziz. The prolific King Aziz is known as the founder of modern Saudi Arabia. Thanks to Hend, the entire al-Fassi family was swept into the oil-soaked Saudi royal family. Many people, both inside and outside the prince's entourage, swear that Hend al-Fassi had some sort of "black magic" hold over Prince Turki that enabled her to lure him into the marriage and control him afterward. In any case, their family's fortunes rocketed. Papa al-Fassi, the one-time antigovernment rebel, was not only dubbed a sheik, but picked up an honorary doctorate from a Korean university as well. His stature leaped from convict to the double titled Dr. Sheik. His trading company was awarded lucrative government contracts, including the medical supplies concession in Saudi Arabia. That gave "Dr. Sheik" the wealth to back up his titles. Hend's four little brothers also became sheiks and instant millionaires.

Mohammed al-Fassi ushered his Italian bride into a life of unimaginable wealth. Paris, Rome, New York, Los Angeles, Miami, London—the world was their playground. In Saudi Arabia they had five hundred servants. When they traveled, at least fifty servants went with them. Wherever she wanted to live, they lived. Whatever she wanted was hers. Jewels. Furs. Cars. Clothes.

They had two children and adopted two more.

But Mohammed's money and Dena's beauty couldn't shield them from the same problems that affect so many couples, especially those who marry as teenagers. They simply grew apart. Coming to America didn't help. Dena matured and wanted more out of life than to be one of the sheik's four allotted wives. She found that the stringent rules and cultural limitations expected of her as a Saudi sheika conflicted tremendously with the free and equal status of the English and American women she had come to know in London and Los Angeles. In Saudi Arabia, few women are allowed to work or even drive, and it's preferred that they cover their faces with veils.

Dena liked America. She started changing, growing, becoming Americanized. She liked to visit discos and dance the night away. She liked wearing flashy clothes, the latest hairstyles, and shopping on Rodeo Drive and in Bal Harbour.

Al-Fassi, for all his worldliness, wanted his domestic life to be guided by Arab tradition and the Moslem religion. The woman's place was in the home. She was to be the veiled mother, the nurturer, the keeper of the household. He preferred his wives in traditional Arabian robes. He didn't want them at Regine's at 5:00 A.M.

A teenage marriage combined with the changing role of women in American society. Those conflicts have torn apart a million American couples. Imagine the schism it created between an Arab sheik and his Italian bride.

Dena blamed the money.

"L'argent pourrit les gens," she says in lovely French. "Money makes people rot."

Dena had also grown weary of globe-trotting and being imprisoned in hotel rooms. She wanted to settle down in one place, where her children could lead a normal life. Mohammed wanted to keep wandering the world, invading hotels like Howard Hughes, shaking things up, then moving on.

They argued. Al-Fassi couldn't understand the new Dena. Their problems escalated.

"We had fights, fistfights, arguments," Dena told me in a deposition. "I tried to defend myself. He pulled my hair in front of everyone."

Of all the bright new American traditions Dena enjoyed, she particularly liked California's fifty-fifty community property law. Mitchelson had filed the divorce suit there to take advantage of the generous statutes. California Superior Court Judge Harry T. Shafer ruled that his court had jurisdiction to decide the $3-billion divorce case, but decreed that a Florida judge had to decide the custody battle and the visitation guidelines. Mitchelson had to come to Miami to get the kids—Hessha and Turkei, both five, and Rahad and Abdula-ziz, both three. He also needed cash for Dena's upkeep pending the court decision. In truth, regardless of which judge claimed jurisdiction, and how hard they shook their legal fists in California, Mitchelson would have to come to Florida to collect anything he won.

Thus, the bloodiest battles were destined to be fought in Miami.

One of the smartest things Mitchelson did before he arrived was to hire Miami matrimonial attorney Melvyn Frumkes to assist him. Frumkes is sharp. He's also one dogged and determined SOB—attributes that make him one of the best divorce lawyers in the country. If you want a peaceful settlement, hire a good divorce lawyer. If you want to purée your spouse into a puddle of proto-plasm, hire Frumkes.

From a legal standpoint, Frumkes is admired for being able to ferret out all the money and goods a wealthy spouse has hidden from his or her partner, whether it's in a Swiss or Cayman Islands bank account, a dummy corporation, a mistress's apartment, or buried in a hole in the backyard.

Frumkes is also known for papering his adversaries to death with motions, pleadings, and requests—a trait that makes oppos-ing lawyers and the targeted spouses want to stick his head in a shredder.

Together, Mitchelson and Frumkes were a force. They went right for al-Fassi's jugular with their opening maneuver. The two attorneys did an end-run around the judge handling the case, and obtained an emergency writ of *ne exeat* from a weekend duty judge. *Ne exeat* is a holdover law from the Dark Ages. It is one of the most unfair laws in the entire legal system. What it means is if someone can convince a judge that their husband or wife is about to skip town with disputed property or children, the judge can have that person arrested and tossed into jail. No trial, no hearing, no due process, right to the slammer. It's the "Monopoly rule," as in "go directly to Jail, do not pass Go, do not collect $200."

The Florida Supreme Court, aware of the severe consequences of the *ne exeat,* handed down this caution in 1932: "In view of the fact that this writ tends to abridge the liberty of someone, it should be granted with caution. . . . Excessive and unreasonable bail should never be required; as the writ is purely a civil writ, it should not be allowed to be used oppressively."

Many attorneys aren't even aware of the *ne exeat.* I was, because I'd used it once. The son of the Prime Minister of Iceland had grabbed his children from his wife, and was on a jet ready to fly them home. I obtained a *ne exeat* and had some deputy sheriffs yank the man and the kids off the plane. But even then, I waived jailing the guy.

A jet taxiing down the runway is one thing. A sheik tanning himself by his pool is quite another.

I was rocked out of a nap that Saturday afternoon in August 1982 by a call from a frantic member of the sheik's entourage. He said there were cops trying to arrest the sheik. I quickly dressed and drove to Dr. Sheik's mansion. Outside the gate were five carloads of sheriff's deputies and Miami Beach police officers. They were being held at bay by the sheik's regiment of bodyguards. It was about ninety degrees, and the sun was frying everyone's nerves. Remembering the Prince Turki incident, I feared a bloodbath was in the making.

"What's going on here?" I shouted to the officers. Before they could answer, I spotted Melvyn Frumkes standing among them. He had a grin on his face the size of a crescent moon. I demanded to see "the papers." They obliged. The *ne exeat* order not only sentenced the sheik to jail, it stated that he had to post a $1-million cash bond to regain his freedom. One million! So much for the Florida Supreme Court's decree against "excessive and unreasonable bail." It's virtually impossible to get a million in cash on a Saturday, which Frumkes knew. Even the sheik didn't have that much lying around the house.

"This is just like you Melvyn, to pull this on a Saturday," I said. "How the hell did you get a judge to sign this without telling me? You know I'm the sheik's lawyer."

"We got word he was going to leave," Frumkes said, still grinning. He was having a great time. He knew he had my ass in a wringer.

"The sheik isn't going anywhere until I talk to the judge," I told the police lieutenant in charge. It was a bluff. I didn't have the power to stop the police. But I've learned that if you speak with authority, it works. The police agreed to hold off until I could reach the judge.

I was ushered inside and taken straight to the sheik. There was no waiting this time. I'd never seen him so scared.

"Please, Mr. Rubin, I don't care what it takes or how much it costs. If I go to jail, I'll be beheaded," he wailed.

The sheik had told me before that under the laws of his country, if he ever set foot in jail, in Saudi Arabia or anywhere else, he would have his head chopped off. I don't know if this is true, but he appeared frightened enough to believe it. I told him to calm down and stop worrying, that he wasn't going to be jailed.

Actually, the sheik was in grave danger of doing some time— and getting his noggin' lopped off. But I wasn't about to let it happen without a fight. What I needed was to locate Judge George Orr and find out how he could have signed such an order without a hearing or even notifying me. I called for nearly an hour before I got him.

"Judge, how's it going to look that you signed this order without being shown any proof he was leaving?" I reasoned. "You've ordered a member of the Saudi royal family to be jailed without a hearing or due process. How's that going to look around the world? Do you understand the consequences of what you are doing? He'll have his head cut off in his home country! How did this case get before you anyway?"

"I'm the duty judge," Orr explained.

"Isn't it obvious the original judge should rule on this?" I continued. "Mitchelson and Frumkes specifically waited for the weekend to get you to give a blind order!"

Judge Orr asked to speak to Frumkes. We sent someone for him, and courageously he waltzed into the enemy camp. I was afraid the sheik was going to impale him on a gatepost the moment he got inside. Frumkes argued with the judge to keep the original order, and continued to claim that the sheik was planning to flee. I argued that he wasn't going anywhere. The judge decided to hold off until Monday morning, and throw the issue back into Judge Jack Turner's court. Turner was handling the custody case and should have ruled on it in the first place. Frumkes was not pleased.

"Nice try, Melvyn," I said as he left. "I'll see you Monday morning, you son of a bitch."

As Frumkes and the police departed, cheers rang out all over the mansion. The sheik was so elated he took me outside and presented me with a brand new, fire-engine-red Mercedes 500SL convertible—a $60,000 chunk of German machinery. I drove it home. That night, the sheik threw my wife and me a grand feast, the likes of which I'd never experienced. There were a dozen or so courses, with dates, figs, grapes, nuts, chicken, lamb, vegetables, soup, rice, and tabouleh (buckwheat soaked in water, mixed with chopped parsley, chopped tomatoes, cucumbers, and sesame seeds, spread over a bed of lettuce).

As we ate, the sheik's resident holy man wandered around the table, showering me with elaborate blessings. He was dressed in a blue robe with a matching turban, and had a long beard. He looked like the Ayatollah Khomeini.

On Monday morning at eight-thirty, we appeared before Judge Turner. As I expected, the judge wasn't happy with "The Marvin and Melvyn Show," and wanted to know why they hadn't made the *ne exeat* request on Thursday or Friday when he could have handled it. M&M said they got word of the sheik's supposed departure too late. Judge Turner canceled the *ne exeat* writ. On top of that, I argued and won the right for the sheik to take the children with him on trips outside Florida, a major victory.

The sheika, meanwhile, was hardly waiting tables. The sheik had put her up in a suite of rooms at the Everglades Hotel in downtown Miami. He gave her $200 a day in cash, as well as unlimited charging privileges, provided her with thirteen servants, and allowed her to keep the children for days on end. And each child had its own personal nanny.

Frumkes complained that the sheik had also provided twenty bodyguards, which he claimed were spies. Frumkes said the bodyguards presented "no opportunity for a free flow of love" between the mother and her brood.

"This woman can't take the children to the restaurant downstairs without permission," Frumkes argued. "All the children see are bodyguards watching their mother."

I countered that the sheika was being treated like a queen and had no cause for complaint.

After those fireworks, it was time to deal with the big battle, the custody case. I scheduled the sheika for a deposition, and Mitchelson and Frumkes howled. They scheduled the sheik for a deposition, and I howled. Mitchelson tried to ban the media from the depositions, and they howled. The media called their attorneys, and they howled.

Things were getting out of hand.

After a week or so of haggling, we finally gathered for the formal deposition of the sheika. Mitchelson opened by again asking the reporters to leave. I said that under Florida law, they could stay. Al Messerschmidt, a reporter for the *Miami Herald,* piped up and began speaking better legalese than Mitchelson, Frumkes, and I combined. He cited cases and quoted judges, the whole works. We were all stunned and sat quietly as Messerschmidt lectured us on media law. It was the only calm moment of the deposition.

We ended up calling Judge Turner, and he said the reporters could stay. We moved on, but before I could get anywhere, things bogged down. Aside from Mitchelson and Frumkes, Frumkes had brought in a third lawyer, Cynthia Greene. They were all objecting and interjecting, and it was getting ridiculous. I demanded that one person represent the sheika, and the other two shut up.

> RUBIN: If we can't agree, then it's no holds barred and dog eat dog and bury your dead. Is that what you want to do?
> MITCHELSON: No, nobody wants to bury any dogs. We want to conduct this in an orderly fashion.

My point exactly. Surprisingly, Mitchelson agreed, and said Frumkes would do the objecting.

That worked for about thirty seconds. We continued to argue over what I could ask. I wanted to talk sex, drugs, and rock and roll. Mitchelson and Frumkes obviously didn't, especially with Messerschmidt there. Frumkes kept objecting to everything, even simple questions concerning the sheika's background and how the sheik supported himself and the source of his money. I couldn't get a word in, so I called a recess and walked out. That meant they wouldn't be able to speak to the sheik at all, since his deposition was not to be taken until the conclusion of the sheika's. As I left, I heard Frumkes fuming after me about holding "Sheik Mohammed al-Fassi in contempt for his flagrant violation of the court order in not appearing!"

We tried again a week later. This time we had a referee, Special Master Mallory Horton. The former district court of appeals judge would rule on all our squabbles much as he would if we were in court. For example:

MR. FRUMKES: Now he is trying to intimidate her.
DENA: He doesn't.
MR. FRUMKES: He intimidates me.
MR. RUBIN: I intimidated you the day I was born.
HORTON: Let's go ahead.

That helped. Things went a little better.

As I questioned Dena about cocaine, Quaaludes, and adultery, Mitchelson objected and asked to make a statement for the record. He then proceeded to give a tear-jerker of a speech on male chauvinism and women's rights. He concluded by heartfully proposing a brave new era of jurisprudence in which these kinds of prying questions won't be asked of people. What a wonderful world that would be, especially for Mitchelson's legion of adulterous clients who are trying to squeeze the life out of their rich, old Hollywood husbands. As I reached for a tissue to dab my eyes, I remembered all the lurid celebrity cases that earned Mitchelson his national reputation. Fortunately, the special master ignored him. Finally, thanks to Horton, we got through the depositions. The hearing was set for the following week.

Before we could get to court, the sheik managed to embroil himself in another headline-grabbing controversy. Three weeks earlier, the sheik had given the Yellow Thunder Indian tribe in Rapid City, South Dakota, a $10,000 donation for the care and education of Indian children. Then, without warning, American Indian Movement leader Russell Means surfaced in Davie, Florida, held a news conference, blasted Mohammed, and announced he was returning the sheik's check—or at least $8,592.34 of it. Means's complaint was that the sheik had made the donation as a bribe to meet actor Marlon Brando, a longtime supporter of Indian causes.

"He wanted me here, really, to bring Brando to him for his own infantile ego," Means told the reporters, adding that Brando was "insulted and infuriated" by the donation. Means explained that the refund was short $1,407.66 to cover expenses involved in the sheik's visit to the tribe. The reporters gleefully splashed Means's insults in their newspapers. The sheik was incensed and threatened a libel suit, screaming once again that he was being humiliated around the world. He countered that Means had tried to squeeze him for $2 million to build a housing project, and was upset by the "paltry" $10,000 donation.

The next day I called a press conference and merrily jumped into the fray.

"Heap big Indian speaks with forked tongue," I told the reporters, giving the incident the dignity it deserved. I also demanded that Brando surface from his island, or wherever the hell he resides, and "confirm or deny the accusation of the Indian."

Brando stayed secluded, and the flap quickly died.

THE BILLION-DOLLAR Babies hearing finally got under way on Friday, September 10, 1982. The sheika looked ravishing. The sheik looked short and skinny. The media looked eager. They weren't disappointed. There were enough stories of cocaine, Quaaludes, and Rod Stewart and the boys to keep them all happy. The sheika had an almost childlike attitude about her sins. I asked her what the cocaine did for her.

"Nothing special," she said. "They just tell me the name, cocaine. I never knew what it was. It was a bottle they had with them."

Mitchelson, whom the reporters came to see, had to take a backseat to Frumkes in the hearing. Florida and California laws differ, and Mitchelson didn't appear to be a man who enjoyed the boring intricacies of the law anyway. Frumkes, the paperman, loves it.

The sheik, with his claims of strict Moslem abstention from alcohol, cigarettes, or drugs, looked like a monk compared to the sheika's world of cocaine and rock stars. Not surprisingly, after I gave my word that Mohammed wouldn't take the children out of Dade County without permission, Judge Turner awarded custody to the sheik. The judge gave Dena generous visitation privileges.

At that point, I had thumped Mitchelson and Frumkes in virtually every battle. Mitchelson decided to go back to California and push his divorce case back on his home turf.

Despite my victories, I was growing weary of the sheik. I had only represented him for six weeks, but it seemed like forever. At his house, he abused and humiliated his servants so badly it was embarrassing. He would throw garbage or food right on the floor just to watch them run over and clean it up. He chomped on Indian nuts all the time, and did so by breaking the shells with his crooked front teeth and then blowing them out on the floor. This was combined with his incessant habits of spitting and cursing. My wife thought he suffered from Tourette's syndrome, a neural disorder that causes inappropriate reactions, including cursing, spitting, and barking like a dog. (She heard about it on "Donahue.")

I just figured the sheik was an uncouth little worm.

To accommodate his filthy habits, he had the entire mansion dotted with Kleenex boxes. My wife counted eighteen in one room. He had tissues in every color of the rainbow. He'd spit into a Kleenex, wad it up, and throw it on the floor. Sometimes he wouldn't let the servants clean them up until he left the room. During some of our meetings, the revolting pile would reach mountainous proportions.

Sheika Aptisam was normally reserved, but she too had her idiosyncrasies. She'd be chatting quietly in the living room, then, without warning, let out an ear-shattering banshee wail for her servant. The maid would humbly bring the sheika her Evian water. Aptisam would continue her conversation for a while, then let out another piercing yelp that would all but knock us off the sofa. The maid would come and take the bottled water away. The sheika would talk some more, then wham, another blood-curdling shriek. The maid would bring the bottle back. It would go on like that, back and forth, for hours. One afternoon I was afraid my wife, Irene, was going to leap off the sofa and strangle the life out of Aptisam if she screeched one more time.

Residents and employees complained bitterly that during their stay at the Cricket Club, the Turki and al-Fassi clan routinely urinated in the elevators, hallways, or anywhere else they felt the urge. By the time they vacated the place, the stench was said to be unbearable.

The sheik was also setting a poor example for his children. One of his sons was a spoiled brat of *Guinness Book of World Records* dimensions. He would spit on the floor just to see the servants wipe it up. He'd throw his food on the rug and carry on like a little demon. Once, while they were staying at the Diplomat, the children were given a litter of kittens as a present. They took them down to the swimming pool, where at least one child began tossing them into the water, clapping and laughing while the animals struggled to stay alive. A number of the tough, burly bodyguards, who were never allowed to interfere with anything the children did, broke precedent and rescued the terrified kittens. They confided to me that the kitten incident was the most heartbreaking thing they had ever witnessed.

During the custody hearing, a child psychiatrist was ordered to evaluate the sheik's bratty son. The report said he was "unmanageable" and had a "foul mouth."

Then there was the sheik's trip to Midland, Pennsylvania. Al-Fassi dangled a $3-million offer in front of the noses of depressed steelworkers in the financially strapped town of 4,300. The catch? They would all have to sign a waiver promising not to vote for Ronald Reagan in the 1984 elections. Most of the people were eager to accept, especially when it was discovered they were almost all Democrats anyway. The State Department said the offer violated federal vote-buying statutes and threatened the sheik with a two-year prison sentence. The sheik publicly thumbed his nose at the State Department, but privately backed off.

The whole scene was beginning to repulse me. I had taken the case out of curiosity, to see what it was like to be a billionaire. In this case, it was disgusting. The sheik was the biggest horse's ass I had ever known, and I've represented hundreds of accused murderers. And he was starting to play his money games again. Once, when I asked him for a payment, he spat on the rug next to my foot and walked out of the room. I was going to quit right then, but every time I tried, Ali Jamel or one of the other aides would beg me to stay. The sheik's father even called from London or Saudi Arabia twice, asking me to stay. Apparently, I was faring better than his other lawyers had in winning legal battles and keeping him out of trouble.

I agreed to remain because I had a feeling it wouldn't be much longer. The sheik was itching to leave Miami, and I could sense it. I had given my word that he would stay and not take the children, but it was apparent that he cared nothing for my word, and less for American law. Fortunately, there were so many people in his own camp who hated him that every time he coughed, Dena would be notified. A week or so later, he tried to slip away to Orlando, and someone in his camp contacted Dena and the police. The state attorney ordered a "sheik watch" at Miami International Airport, and a judge called an emergency hearing. In fitting fashion, it was scheduled for midnight at the judge's home.

The judge was Richard Feder. He's probably the only judge in America who requires the attorneys who practice in his court to don black robes, a practice I support wholeheartedly. It lends dignity to the proceedings.

I rendezvoused with the sheik at 79th Street and Biscayne Boulevard. Although that junction sits between two major arteries connecting Miami Beach with the mainland, our meeting point was a section of town overflowing with drug dealers and hookers. The sheik arrived with Aptisam, the four children, and their four nannies. I brought my wife along. We went caravan-style to Judge Feder's house. On the way, the sheik and I argued about his attempt to violate the court order.

"Fuck the court order," he said.

"Well, then, you're going to jail," I countered. "Say good-bye to your head."

That shut him up. I also took the opportunity to make him pay the $20,000 he promised for my services. He gave me a check.

When we arrived at the judge's house, the street was lined with police and federal agents. Waiting inside were Judge Feder, an assistant state attorney, Dena's attorneys, a court reporter, and nationally famous attorney Henry Rothblatt. Without my knowledge, Rothblatt had been added to the sheik's team and had come to silently observe. We sat in a circle in the living room, with the babies crying, and had a bizarre hearing that my wife refers to as "the séance." All we needed was a medium and a crystal ball. After the arguments, the judge ruled that the sheik could take his children on the grand tour of America that he had planned. There was one catch. Mohammed had to bring me along to keep him in line. The sheik, surprisingly meek, agreed, and told the judge he was going to dole out $2 million in donations to various city governments, hospitals, and local charities.

The next day, the sheik spat at my feet and said he was going without me. That afternoon his $20,000 check bounced. That was it. I went to court, obtained an emergency hearing, and "fired" the sheik as my client. Rothblatt, famous for handling the My Lai massacre, Watergate, "Happy Hooker" Xaviera Hollander, and unhappy political wife Martha Mitchell, was now the sheik's new mouthpiece. Feder issued a temporary order freezing the sheik's bank accounts until Judge Turner, who was out of town, could return. Rothblatt was beside himself and raised such a ruckus that Judge Feder had to order him twice to cool it.

The following morning there was a big story in the newspaper about my "firing" the sheik. The Associated Press picked it up and sent it worldwide. Apparently that caused Mohammed even more "shame and humiliation all over the world." A few nights later, he called my home after 1:00 A.M. Irene answered. The sheik forced an embarrassed aide to read a list of twelve threats and demands. The demands said that I was to continue as his attorney, and continue to handle the custody case for a specific fee and a new wardrobe. If I refused, he would hold a press conference and say I had asked him for money to bribe Judge Turner and Turner's secretary. He also threatened to charge me with stealing the red Mercedes. I wasn't about to knuckle under to that, but Irene was nervous and said she would take the car back. She drove over the following evening, and had our daughter Kim follow in a separate car to bring her back.

When she arrived, Ali Jamel met them at the door and tried to smooth things over. He invited them in for coffee. What happened next is best told by Irene. She had to give a sworn statement about it to a Dade County assistant state attorney.

> Ali was shmoozing up to us the way he always did, trying to be nice but actually being a jerk. He looked at Kim, then twenty-one, and asked, "Could I have permission to make love to her?" I told him I'd kill him if he tried.
> About five minutes after we sat down in the living room, we saw the sheik come in and sit on a sofa across the room. He was facing away. He was wearing his white pantaloons, white T-shirt, and was barefoot. Then this good-looking blond man came into the house wearing jeans and a colored T-shirt. He greeted the sheik with hugs and kisses, and was presented some folded linens by a servant. He left the room. Ali Jamel excused himself. A few minutes later the young man came back wearing the same white outfit as the sheik. He sat beside the sheik on the couch. The two began kissing on the mouth, teasing each other, and grabbing each other's genitals.
> "Mom, I know that man," Kim said. "That's . . ."
> [Kim identified the visitor as the son of a prominent Miamian.]
> Well, he and the sheik began to really get it on, and Kim and I were getting disgusted. Jamel returned and I said, "Do you see that?"
> And he said, "Yeah, so what? They do that every Sunday."
> "Where's Aptisam?" I demanded.
> "She's upstairs praying," he said.
> I told him I wasn't sitting still for that, and Kim and I left!

That was an interesting development. The "Arabs Invade Miami" story had come full circle. It started with a bitchy princess battling the cops in Alvin Malnik's Cricket Club, and was ending with a romp between the princess's weaselly brother and a young heir.

Ending, but not quite ended.

The sheik's final act in America presented me with a major legal dilemma. A short time after the midnight hearing, I received a call from someone inside the sheik's camp that he was leaving for good. The bags were packed, reservations were set, everything was in order. And unlike the previous times where he was just traveling out of state to tour other cities, this time he was picking up and going back to Saudi Arabia. Leaving the country would violate numerous Florida and California laws and court orders. He would become a wanted man.

That meant he would probably never come back to America.

When he had tried to flee before, someone always alerted the police directly, or called Dena. This time, no one knew but me.

My dilemma: violate the attorney-client privilege and rat out my own former client, or maintain the privilege and let him escape? The fact that he was a *former* client didn't overrule the attorney-client privilege, and was clouded even further by the sheik's insistence that I was still his attorney.

I considered the law. The attorney-client privilege is a shield against past crimes; it is not a sword to use to commit new crimes.

In the end, it was not only a clear-cut legal and moral question, but a human one as well. If the sheik left the country, chances were that Dena would never see her children again. I couldn't do that to anybody, attorney-client privilege or not.

I called Judge Turner and alerted him to what was in progress. He ordered a "sheik freeze" at the airport. Unfortunately, the sheik anticipated it and slipped out of Miami. He chartered a private 707 in Norfolk, Virginia, flew to the Bahamas, then caught a jet to Saudi Arabia, taking the children with him.

And that was the last anyone heard of Sheik Mohammed al-Fassi in America.

EPILOGUE

After the sheik's sudden departure, it was discovered that he had ripped people off for staggering sums. He left his multimillion-dollar Star Island mansion in mid-completion, and hadn't paid the contrac-

tors in months. He owed them millions. They ended up cannibaliz-
ing the opulent palace, turning it into a mildew-infested eyesore.

Area merchants called my office wondering if, or how, they
would be paid. We received more than 150 calls. A startling pattern
emerged. People had given the sheik tens of thousands of dollars in
goods "on approval." Jewelers would bring him suitcases full of
valuable gems and leave them behind without getting a cent in
return. Many of the gleaming cars in front of the sheik's house had
been leased, or bought with little concern as to when he would
actually pay for them.

Many people had fallen all over themselves to give the sheik
their valuables. Everyone figured he was so rich he'd pay for it all
eventually. Not to worry.

And most were too ashamed to complain. The typical Miami
Beach shopkeeper wasn't about to let everyone know that in his
greed, he went whoring after an Arab, and, in his stupidity, got
ripped off to boot. What would they say at temple?

Gone with the sheik was the billion-dollar lawsuit against the
Diplomat Hotel. Gone was the trillion-dollar lawsuit another lawyer
filed against the Hollywood, Florida, police department. And gone
were hundreds of thousands of dollars' worth of goods from local
merchants.

Gone also was Dena's $3-billion California divorce action,
which she won in the sheik's absence. The judgment was eventually
knocked down to a paltry $84 million when Mitchelson could docu-
ment only $168 million worth of the sheik's holdings. Mitchelson
has been combing the world the last seven years trying to collect
Dena's $84 million, and appears to have had some luck. As of 1989,
the California attorney said he'd rounded up about $20 million
worth of cash and property.

"And I'm still looking," he vowed.

Mitchelson added that Dena has seen her children a few times,
but would not elaborate on how this was accomplished or where the
meetings took place.

Alvin Malnik moved to Saudi Arabia to become an adviser to
Prince Turki. The newspapers said he grew a long beard and con-
verted to Islam. He later returned to Miami. His son Mark also
moved to Saudi Arabia, ditched his wife, and married Hoda, one of
the al-Fassi sisters.

As for everyone else, hopefully, we all learned a lesson.

* * *

OVER THE years, there have been occasional reports of the sheik popping up here and there in other countries. In 1984 he swarmed into the Hyatt Regency in Casablanca as a guest of King Hassan of Morocco. There were also reports that he had spent time in Tunisia. Aides say he desperately longs to come back to America, but remains unable to get the diplomatic immunity that would wipe out all the crimes he committed while here. As it stands, he could get up to twenty-five years for his various acts of "uncivil disobedience."

A year or so after he left, Irene was on a commercial airliner over London, and ended up sitting next to a dignified Saudi gentleman. They began talking about al-Fassi. After going on about what a terrible embarrassment he was to his people, the Arab gentleman related that al-Fassi had continued his obstinacy at home and was publicly flogged. A number of other people would relate the same news, and the story was published in some newspapers.

We tried to confirm it, but no one inside Saudi Arabia would acknowledge the punishment. Those traditions, we were told, are not to be shared with the world.

During August of 1988, I received a telephone call from a strange voice indicating that he was a business acquaintance of Sheik Mohammed al-Fassi . . . that he was interested in clearing up the $20,000.00 bad check I had been given. After some negotiations, my claim was settled and I agreed to cancel the grand larceny warrant that had been issued for the arrest of the sheik.

7

THE DEATH OF A DEBUTANTE, PART I

It's the ethical nightmare dreaded most by criminal defense attorneys.
—*Time* July 21, 1986

IT WAS Passover, 1984. Only the blood was on the bed inside the Abramsons' large, luxurious home, not on the door. And the Abramsons' firstborn, Erinn, was gone. Her body was discovered the next day, lying in an empty field across from a garbage dump. She had been slaughtered beyond anything ever done to a sacrificial lamb.

Erinn Abramson, eighteen, was found wrapped in a light yellow blanket and a light orange bedspread—even Miami's murders come in pastel hues. Over the next three years her death would be shrouded in a darker blanket of mystery. When it was over, not only would the convicted killer be in jail, so would I. And although my jailing received more attention than the murder itself, the critical elements that compelled me to take my controversial stand have never been revealed.

Until now.

THE BROWN cardboard box sitting on my office doorstep startled me. With my clientele, and those I've gone up against, it could have contained anything from a Sandinista bomb to a mutilated chicken from a Haitian voodoo curse. I stepped around it, but couldn't fight the urge to peek inside. The box contained oranges, cucumbers, and tomatoes. They were dusty, and some had the stems still attached. They looked as if they had just been picked from one of the steamy farm fields that still surround Miami. I was relieved, but curious.

Entering the building, I asked the office manager, my daughter Peri, about the box. She said some ragged-looking lady had brought it for me.

"Her name was Holly. Holly something," Peri said.

"Sanborn," I said. "Holly Sanborn."

That explained it. Mrs. Sanborn's son Russell had been arrested a month after Erinn Abramson's death and charged with the murder. A year had passed, and his trial was coming up. Mrs. Sanborn had written me a few times, and then called for the first time the day before. She begged me to take her son's case. She had somehow become convinced that I was the only person who could save him.

She called again. I thanked her for the gift and told her the same thing I had said before: changing attorneys at this late stage was not in her son's best interest. Russell's court-appointed attorney, Bill Surowiec, was an excellent trial lawyer from a well-known Miami law firm. He and his associates had prepared for months to represent her son. As for me, I was swamped with cases of my own, and I hadn't even read the Abramson story in the newspaper. I assured her again that her son was in good hands.

The next morning there were *two* boxes on my doorstep. It startled me again. I didn't connect them with Mrs. Sanborn until I saw the red tomatoes. She called and said she had gotten up at dawn and picked them herself. I invited her to come to my office. She said she didn't have a car, so I sent someone to pick her up. I was somewhat surprised when I saw her. She sounded intelligent and educated on the phone, but in person she was ragged and soiled, as my daughter had described. She was heavy, had a round face, light hair, and was wearing a ratty sweater and a gray skirt. She looked like Shelley Winters dragged through a potato field.

She pleaded with me anew to take her son's case, repeating that I was the only person who could save him. She cried. I was weakening, but it still wasn't the best move for her son. I explained that I wasn't the magician she had come to believe. The stories she had read about me in the newspapers, and the talk around the jail, were probably exaggerations. I had won some big cases, but I'd lost my share, too.

The following morning, there they were, the boxes of cucumbers, tomatoes, and oranges. Only now Holly Sanborn was sitting next to them. The tears were streaming down her face.

"Please, Mr. Rubin, please. He's my baby boy."

She touched me on the arm and looked up into my eyes. I could see the dirt under her fingernails and the dust in the crinkles lining her face.

We went inside. She sat down and handed me a letter she had written. It was more of the same, pleas to take her son's case and charges that he had been framed, but there was something else, something that caught my attention. She promised to sign over her $600 monthly disability check for the rest of her life if I'd defend Russell. It was her sole income, aside from the few dollars she made picking vegetables and selling them at a stand near her home. The check was the only thing that kept her alive.

Whatever button I have, her tremendous sacrifice pushed it. I would take the case, and she could keep her checks.

I visited Russell at the Dade County Jail. He greeted me with a great sense of relief. He shared his mother's conviction that I was his emancipator. He told me passionately that he was innocent.

I had decided, against all logic, to represent him. It was a decision that came from my heart, not from my head.

THE HAD been a number of versions of what happened to Erinn Abramson that night, and, more important, who was responsible. From the police reports and trial testimony, a strange story finally emerged.

Erinn and Russell were an unusual pair. She was a beautiful, auburn-haired college freshman pampered by her wealthy parents.

Life was a whirl of shopping for the latest fashions, going to the beach, and cruising the malls. At night she'd dress up in expensive outfits, drive around in her parents' $40,000 Mercedes sports car, date nice Jewish boys from equally wealthy families, and hit the exclusive private clubs like Turnberry Isle, where Gary Hart and Donna Rice hooked up. Her father, Herbert Abramson, was not only a prominent criminal defense attorney; he was a charitable man who gave both his time and money to help establish a local branch of Here's Help, a drug-rehabilitation center. Erinn had jetted in for the holidays from Santa Monica Junior College in California. Her father had set her up out there in an $850-a-month apartment in exclusive Marina del Rey. She had talked of becoming a doctor, but had dropped two of her four classes that semester. A bit homesick, she called her mother nearly every night.

Russell "Rusty" Sanborn, twenty-six, was a crude, prison-hardened veteran of four stays in Florida penal institutions. He was a muscular man about five feet ten, with long red hair combed straight back, and a smattering of freckles dotting his pale complexion. A high school dropout, he was the son of a long-gone father and Holly, a farm worker. An itinerant plumber by trade, his résumé included convictions for robbery, forgery, petty larceny, and possession of marijuana. He remained on probation for grand theft and for marijuana and barbiturate possession.

Rusty and Erinn had made love the last night of Erinn's life, but love had nothing to do with it. The pair were linked by something more powerful than love or sex.

Cocaine.

He had it. She wanted it. The drug is the great equalizer. It knows no class distinction. It's blind to social status, race, color, or creed. Erinn had met Rusty years before at the beach. He gave her a Quaalude. Although they were from different worlds, they became friends after a fashion. Erinn knew Rusty was always "holding," meaning he could be counted on to have drugs.

Erinn gave him her money, then her body, to get those drugs. But even that wasn't enough to satisfy her craving. When her credit ran out, and Rusty lost interest in her body, she became desperate. Erinn devised a plan. She recruited a friend to disguise himself, come over to her house, and rob her rich parents of their money and jewelry. In return, she would score another day or two's supply of cocaine.

The friend agreed.

On April 16, 1984, a car containing two people pulled to the side of the road outside the spacious North Miami home of Herbert Abramson. It was about 4:30 A.M.

"I'll be out in a few minutes," the passenger said. "Wait here."

The man fished in his pocket for two keys. One disarmed the Abramsons' elaborate burglar alarm. The other opened the front door. Inside, the intruder walked through the familiar surroundings and entered Erinn's room. She smiled and said hello. Erinn had given him the keys earlier that evening. It had all been arranged.

After chatting with Erinn in her bedroom for a few minutes, the intruder slipped a nylon stocking over his head and entered the master bedroom. Herbert and Barbara Abramson were awakened around 4:45 A.M. and were forced to live out the harrowing nightmare feared by virtually everyone. A masked man, waving a knife and barking commands, had invaded their home. The terror of such an event, in which you are shaken from a dead sleep to confront a scene out of a horror movie, is something a person never forgets.

In a rough, gravelly voice, and using language Barbara Abramson would later describe as "tough prison talk," the intruder threatened to kill them if they didn't keep quiet.

"I have already killed four people," he said. "It doesn't make much difference."

He demanded their money and jewelry, then grabbed Barbara. When Herbert tried to protect his wife, the intruder slashed the attorney's ear with the knife. A stream of warm blood dripped down Herbert's neck and shoulder. Though terrified, the Abramsons began to notice that the intruder was acting strangely. He appeared to be confused about what to do. He didn't have a flashlight and asked Barbara Abramson if she had a small light. She suggested that he turn on the closet light, and he did. He had nothing to tie them up with, and had to improvise by using the cut cords from a clock radio and their cable television. After ordering them to lie facedown on the bed, he bound their hands and legs and put a pillow over their heads. As the intruder searched the room, he carried on a running conversation with the Abramsons. He said he knew that they had a "big son" sleeping in a nearby bedroom, and told them that if the son woke up he would have to kill him. Scott Abramson, sixteen, slept through the entire incident.

The intruder seemed in no great hurry. He began to pick

through Barbara Abramson's jewelry box like a child looking for the best marbles. Angered that the contents appeared to be mostly inexpensive costume jewelry, he started grousing and making threats. Barbara Abramson began describing from memory, as she lay on the bed, which pieces were the most valuable. Herbert Abramson, trying to add a measure of sanity to the burglary, suggested that the intruder take the whole box. The masked man told him to shut up or he'd kill him, then went back to searching through the contents.

The intruder kept leaving the room and coming back. The Abramsons could detect his movements from the squeaking sound of the bedroom door. Each time, he would return with what appeared to be new instructions on what to look for. He was also growing angrier and more frustrated, as if he had expected much more. It wasn't until his third visit that he thought, or was told, to take the chain from around Herbert's neck.

After filling a sock with a meager $2,000 worth of jewelry and $140 in cash, the angry intruder left the master bedroom for the last time.

Erinn's friend had been inside the house nearly an hour, keeping the driver waiting nervously outside. When he finally emerged, he was carrying a large object over his shoulder. The driver would later describe it as looking like a rolled rug. The intruder opened the door of the Abramsons' brown Mercedes 450SL convertible, heaved the object into the passenger seat, got behind the wheel, and drove away. The driver, curious about the change in plans, followed him for a while, lost him, then drove to Russell Sanborn's apartment to see if he ended up there. Sure enough, the brown Mercedes was gleaming in the parking lot, already covered with a coat of water from South Florida's staggering humidity. The driver drove away.

More than an hour later, the Abramsons struggled free from their bonds and called the police. In Erinn's room they discovered a large, circular bloodstain on her mussed bed. Scott, who had returned that evening from an exhausting weekend fishing trip, was still sleeping soundly in his room. The Abramsons told police officer Richard Conover that their daughter had mentioned that she was expecting someone named "Rusty" to visit her late that night.

"Don't worry, he'll only stay ten minutes. I'll push him right out," she had promised her mother.

Sometime around 10:00 A.M., Erinn's body was discovered in

the lot about six blocks from Russell Sanborn's apartment. When the yellow bedspread and orange blanket were removed, the officers found the stiff figure of a young woman lying faceup. She was wearing jeans and a dark T-shirt, was barefoot, and her left arm was crossed over her eyes as if to shade them from the bright Florida sun. A closer inspection revealed that she had been stabbed more than fourteen times, including four times in her chest, six in triangle patterns on her back, a number of huge gashes in her arms, and one in each of her wrists. The medical examiner said the locations and time sequence of the wounds—the nonfatal ones occurring first— indicated that Erinn had been savagely tortured before she was killed.

The next day, the brown Mercedes was spotted in a parking lot a few blocks from the dump. Among the items found in the car was a single white Jox gym sock, stained with blood. It was the kind of sock a teenager would wear with her Reebok sport shoes.

Late that afternoon, the police received a call from Alvin Lindner, the owner of the J&L Coin Shop in the Diplomat shopping mall in Hallandale, a retirement community halfway between Miami and Fort Lauderdale. The morning of the murder, Lindner had purchased a gold Rolex watch and a pear-shaped diamond ring for $1,300 from a muscular, red-haired man. The man had identified himself as Peter Martin Bean, and offered Lindner a crumpled birth certificate as the identification required by Florida law to pawn jewelry. After the transaction, the red-haired man spoke of having more jewelry to sell. Lindner, growing a bit suspicious, told the man he would need a driver's license or some other form of picture identification. The man returned about ten minutes later with a ragged woman in tow, identifying her as his mother. The pair had an assortment of jewelry, including a gold initial ring with the letters "ESA," a man's gold bracelet with the name "Herb," and a gold charm formed in the letter "B." As they spoke, Lindner noticed that the woman called her son "Rusty." Lindner offered them $600 for the batch, and the man presented his mother's driver's license to secure the deal. The next day, Lindner was showing some of the jewelry to a customer. The customer looked at the name on the bracelet and initials on the other pieces and said, "This looks like the stuff from the Abramson murder!" Startled, Lindner called the police. Metro Dade County homicide detective Roosevelt Turner responded. Lindner showed him the two sales registrations. The second one was signed "Holly Sanborn."

All the jewelry was later identified by Herbert Abramson as his, his wife's, or his daughter's.

Turner, a veteran detective who had investigated more than four hundred murders, visited Mrs. Sanborn at her home. She explained that her son had asked her to drive him to the mall to sell the jewelry. She said he told her a friend had given it to him as payment for a debt. She added that her son had moved to Miami Beach, she didn't know exactly where, and had used some of the jewelry money to buy a 1978 silver AMC Concord. The purchase order showed that Rusty had made a down payment of $560 and listed the telephone number of a woman named Mary Jo Mercado. Mercado, a former girlfriend, told the police where Rusty had previously lived in North Miami, and added that she had sold him a sofa bed with a yellow blanket and orange bedspread. She later identified them as the blanket and bedspread wrapped around Erinn Abramson's body.

Turner put out a BOLO on Russell Sanborn. That's police terminology for "be on the lookout." He was wanted for questioning in the murder of Erinn Abramson. A few days later, the detectives had a warrant to search Rusty's North Miami apartment. Despite the lapse in time, the search proved fruitful. In fact, there was no indication that Rusty had moved out. They found large bloodstains on the living room rug, smaller stains on the sofa and windowsill, and a copy of *Cheri* magazine with Erinn's name and telephone number written in the margin of the table-of-contents page. In the bathroom they found, wrapped in toilet paper and tucked inside a toilet brush holder, a piece of gold-and-diamond jewelry in the shape of a lightning bolt. The charm was identified by Barbara Abramson as Erinn's favorite piece of jewelry.

Although blood was found on Erinn's bed, the amount found in Rusty's apartment indicated to the detectives and laboratory experts that most of the wounds, and probably the fatal ones, occurred there.

Outside, in a vacant lot next to the apartment, the police investigators found the keys to the Mercedes, a bloody T-shirt, a pair of expensive ladies' high-top tennis shoes, and a white Jox gym sock stained with blood. The sock matched the one found in the Mercedes.

Meanwhile, Rusty had gotten wind that the cops were on his trail. He dyed his hair brown and booked himself into a cheap

Miami Beach motel. He alleviated some of the boredom of hiding out by befriending a young Latin girl named Ana Ortiz, whom he met on the beach. They hit it off so well that two days later he moved into her small room at the Paradise Motel. He told Ana, a beauty school student, that he was lying low because some Cubans were looking for him to "collect their share." He let her use his newly purchased car to attend class.

During this time, Rusty decided to write an impassioned letter to Detective Turner, plucking Turner's name from a newspaper story about the murder. Rusty pleaded his innocence and fingered a friend and fellow convict named Ron Chica. Rusty said he left Chica and Erinn together in his apartment from midnight to 4:00 A.M. When he came home, Erinn was gone and his buddy had some jewelry to sell. Rusty bought the jewelry for an ounce of cocaine and quickly converted it to cash at the pawn shop.

That last action completed the typical Miami "food chain"— cash to drugs to gems, and back to cash—the drug-culture cycle of life.

Rusty wrote that when he saw the news of Erinn's death on television, he panicked and went into hiding. He was on the run, he explained, because he didn't want to go back to jail for buying and receiving stolen property. He added that his mother knew nothing about the jewelry being stolen, and that he would be long gone by the time the letter made it to the detective.

Detective Turner wasn't impressed, nor did he believe Rusty had skipped town. He intensified efforts to find him. Teams of officers combed the parking lots from one end of Miami Beach to another, looking for the silver AMC Concord. They found it on May 9 in a parking lot across the street from the Paradise Motel. They swarmed into the room where they were told the car's owner lived, but instead of Rusty, they found the terrified Ana Ortiz. She told the detectives that she and Rusty had a spat—she caught him naked on the beach in the arms of another woman—and she kicked him out. He moved somewhere nearby in the surrounding maze of small art deco motels. While the detectives were in her room, Rusty called. She told him the police were looking for him, and asked what he had done. He told her he had sold some hot jewelry involved in a "bad" crime. He didn't say where he was. The police notified the phone company to trace all calls coming in to Ana's line. They waited for Rusty to call again. He did. By the next day, they knew exactly where Rusty was hiding. They picked him up without resistance that evening.

Meanwhile, Detective Turner had put out a search for Ron Chica, a small-time criminal known to him. Chica was proving to be more elusive. Still, it was Sanborn they wanted, and they had him.

After downing a Burger King Whopper and a large order of fries in the interrogation room, Rusty repeated his story to the homicide detectives, again fingering Chica. Turner was skeptical. When the laboratory report came in, his skepticism intensified and his efforts to locate Chica diminished. Russell's red pubic hair chemically matched the hair found on Erinn's body. His blood type matched the semen they discovered in her vagina. The blood found on his living room carpet matched Erinn's. Russell's fingerprint was found on the seat-adjuster knob of the Mercedes. Combined with the socks, keys, blanket, bedspread, and jewelry, Rusty had provided the police with enough hard evidence to convict ten murderers. He was charged with first-degree murder and hauled off to jail. The police felt the case was airtight. They had every reason to.

Rusty stood by his story. He didn't do it, he insisted. It was his friend, Ron Chica. Feeling railroaded, he again put pen to paper. A cellmate was being represented by Herbert Abramson. The prisoner suggested that Rusty take his case directly to Erinn's father. Rusty thought it was a swell idea. The letter, written in a combination of prison and drug-dealer language, began to unravel the mystery of why things went bad that evening.

Rusty wrote that Erinn came by early that Monday morning, sometime just before or after midnight. They did some coke, "then we got a little intamet [*sic*], what a man and woman do when their [*sic*] alone and like each other." According to Rusty, Chica arrived around 2:00 A.M. By then, Rusty said he and Erinn had snorted four grams of cocaine, a considerable amount. Chica was holding four "D's," slang for Dilaudid, a powerful narcotic. Chica swallowed the D's and became "totally wasted." Rusty borrowed Erinn's car and drove to a nearby store. That's why, he said, his fingerprint was on the seat adjuster. When he returned, Ron and Erinn had concocted a plan to rob Erinn's parents and score more cocaine. Rusty agreed to supply the cocaine if they came back with anything worthwhile. He even fronted Chica an eighth of an ounce.

Rusty told Erinn's father that he went to a nightclub and hung out from 3:00 to 6:00 A.M. while Ron did his thing. When Rusty returned to the apartment, only Ron was there. They bickered over the economics of the jewelry-for-cocaine transaction, with Rusty finally agreeing to trade two ounces for everything Ron had.

Rusty didn't stop there. In his letter he speculated as to how the deal had gone sour. According to Rusty, Chica left Erinn at Rusty's apartment and went to rob her parents. While he was gone, Erinn's high began to wear off. The terrible scheme against her own parents didn't seem so cool anymore. When Ron returned, still flying on the four D's, he was in no mood, or position, to alter the plan. The deed had been done. He "freaked out," thinking Erinn would rat on him, and killed her.

Rusty ended the strange letter by saying that Erinn was a beautiful girl. "I loved her and still do, we are all sure she is in heaven, their is no other place for her."

Incredibly, Rusty thought such a letter would gain him sympathy. In reality, it painted a picture of Erinn's lifestyle that did nothing to endear him to her parents.

The letter did contain one subtle clue that supported his mother's belief in his innocence. Rusty's "theory" of what happened that night failed to consider a critical point: if Erinn waited at Rusty's apartment while the robbery took place, then whose blood was on her bed? If Rusty was unaware that she had been home that night during the robbery, and that she had apparently been stabbed there, then he didn't do it.

Unfortunately for Rusty, his proclivity for letter-writing would backfire. Before he was arrested, he wrote an unmailed letter to a buddy back in prison. Detective Turner found it on top of Rusty's television set when they searched his apartment. In it he said he was dodging the police because he had committed a burglary, then added, "I got this bitch, fine to death." The jumbled wording of the line was a mystery.

In a medium-sized city, or even some of the bigger cities with a less frightening crime rate, the story of Rusty and Erinn would have been big news. The media would have leaped upon every revelation. In Miami, it was just another drug-related murder. Erinn was rich enough, and came from a good enough family, to merit the initial burst of stories. But Miami is awash in violence, so the case was quickly forgotten. It would have stayed that way if it weren't for two things: Russell Sanborn's inability to get along with his lawyers, and Holly Sanborn's relentless determination to have me represent her son.

Rusty began going through attorneys the way George Steinbrenner goes through managers. He rejected the first public defender assigned to his case, Richard Houlihan, claiming the man wasn't paying enough attention to his case. It's a common charge made by criminals against the overburdened public defenders, and is no reflection upon Houlihan's abilities. Privately, Houlihan was no doubt happy to be dismissed. No one, even a harried public defender, likes to be saddled with what looks like a guaranteed loser.

Circuit Court Judge Sidney Shapiro then appointed René Sotorrio, a private attorney, to be Russell's new champion. After perusing the files, Sotorrio quickly argued that he didn't have the time to handle the massive workload of a first-degree-murder case. Shapiro accepted Sotorrio's explanation and this time appointed a law firm headed by Paul Pollock, a well-known Miami defense attorney. Pollock assigned the case to William Surowiec. Surowiec, a bright defender, did the best he could, gathering evidence and preparing to go to court.

That's when Holly Sanborn began her fruit-and-vegetable campaign for me. After I agreed, I told her to have Russell ask the judge to let me be his court-appointed attorney. Judge Shapiro refused, and expressed anger over the last-minute switch. What that meant was he would not authorize the court to pay a minimal fee for my services, as he had for Russell's previous attorneys. Holly offered her disability check again, but I said it was unnecessary.

A few days after my first conversation with Rusty at the Dade County Jail, he appeared before Judge Shapiro. As Shapiro would later relate, Rusty practically got down on his hands and knees and begged him to allow me to represent him. Shapiro relented, but again refused to have the court pay for my services.

Surowiec was overly friendly as he handed me his materials. I sensed that he was trying hard to suppress his delight. That was disturbing. When an attorney breaks his back working on a case, and some new guy comes in at the last minute to steal all the glory, the reaction is often rage. But when an attorney breaks his back, then gleefully hands you the materials, he is transmitting an unmistakable message: "Thank you for removing this defeat from my record."

When I looked over the prosecution's case, I could see why. Rusty looked as guilty as sin. The physical evidence was brutal. There was also a little surprise in the packet. Public Defender Houlihan had arranged to have Rusty take a polygraph examination, or, as it's commonly known, a lie-detector test. The finding was "inconclusive," which is often a nice way of telling an attorney that his client failed.

Despite all this, I began to work intensively on his case. Holly Sanborn continued to insist that her son was innocent, and I continued to give her the benefit of the doubt. A closer inspection of the evidence revealed that almost all of it could be explained by Rusty's relationship with Erinn. He had made love to her that night, so the hair, blood, and semen samples were immaterial. Lie-detector tests are far from infallible. And I had once handled a similar case in which all the physical evidence had been fabricated by the police.

The strange wording in the letter to his cellmate, "I got this bitch, fine to death," was too ambiguous to be allowed in court. That could simply be prison slang for "I've got a fine-looking woman." And the letter itself said the police were after him for a burglary, not a murder. That might have referred to any burglary. If he was confessing to his old prison buddy about the Abramson case, why not confess to the murder as well?

There remained a doubt in my mind as to whether Rusty had killed her. It didn't make sense. Why? They were friends. It actually was more logical that a mutual friend, in a drug-induced frenzy, had murdered Erinn in Rusty's apartment while Rusty was out.

Judge Sidney Shapiro grudgingly granted a trial delay, giving me forty-five days to prepare a defense. I put my staff attorneys and secretaries on it, and gave it my full attention for the month and a half we'd been given. That was $75,000 worth of fees down the drain, plus another $75,000 we could have made working for a paying client. But Holly Sanborn's sacrifice kept me going. I couldn't give her anything less than my best. The fees are just money. The cases are people's lives.

We went down the list of prosecution witnesses and took depositions from them. Things grew bleak. Then I noticed that the man who lived near the junkyard, the one who had reported seeing the brown Mercedes that morning, had never been interviewed, either by the police or by the prosecution. That can sometimes be a good sign. Maybe he knew something they didn't want anyone to know.

Maybe he saw Ron Chica, the man Rusty kept saying was the real murderer.

I had my son and law partner, Mark, take his deposition. The man said he not only saw the car, he saw it roll in. He watched a medium-sized, muscular, red-haired man get out of the car, pull something from the seat covered in a orange bedspread, dump it on the ground, then drive away.

He was a sensational witness—for the prosecution!

Still, it supported my theory of what could have happened. Rusty returned to his apartment and found Erinn dead on his living room rug. His natural inclination would be to dump the body. He was too involved to call the police. The problem was that it definitely made Rusty an accessory to murder, and getting a jury to believe that he hadn't actually killed Erinn would be tough.

I drove to the Dade County Jail and had a serious discussion with my client. He was intent upon testifying, and I felt that was sure suicide. Unless he admitted the accessory charge, his story would have more holes than Bonnie and Clyde.

"Mr. Rubin, if I don't testify, I'm a dead duck."

"If you do, and try to tell them you had absolutely nothing to do with it, you're going straight to the electric chair. I can't allow you to testify." (Rusty knew I had to let him go on the stand if he wanted to.)

He frowned, then brightened.

"You come back tomorrow and I'll tell you what I'm gonna do."

The next day I brought another attorney from my office, Matt Fuqua. I wanted a witness.

"Mr. Rubin, I'm going to testify. And here's what I'm going to say."

Rusty then proceeded to change some crucial elements of his story. He still maintained his innocence, but the new version deviated from what he had previously said and written. He now claimed to have spent the night weeping at the hospital bedside of a sick ex-girlfriend. On top of that, he said he had two witnesses who would back him up, including the woman. Smiling brightly, he gave me the phone numbers of the pair, insisting they would corroborate his new story and give him an ironclad alibi.

"It's all set," he said. "In the bag."

"Rusty, your story doesn't sound true to me, but I'll call your witnesses," I promised.

I had Matt call them later that afternoon. The girl backed Rusty's story—for about an hour. Then she called Matt back, frightened and crying, and said she had been paid to testify for Rusty. She asked Matt what she should do. Matt didn't hesitate.

"You don't go anywhere near that courtroom," he said. "That's a felony. You want to go to jail with him?"

The other witness, a fellow drug dealer, refused to back Rusty from the outset.

"You think I'm crazy?" he said. "Rusty's history."

Not only was Rusty lying, but he couldn't even deliver his phony alibi witnesses.

Worst of all, my belief in his innocence had been shattered. As Rusty explained his plan, I had seen something frightening in his eyes, something that made a chill run up my spine.

The mysterious Mr. Chica eluded police for over a year. He was finally located in a jail in Ohio. He heatedly denied robbing the Abramsons or killing Erinn, and took a lie-detector test to prove it. He gave detectives blood and hair samples, and neither matched any of the evidence found at the crime scene or on Erinn's body. He was never arrested.

Rusty remained intent on going with his new, highly original "sick friend" defense. He was convinced that when push came to shove, the witnesses would back him once they were forced up on the stand.

I was in a bind, and the biggest bomb was yet to drop.

8

THE DEATH OF A DEBUTANTE, PART II:

The Driver

ATTORNEYS ARE not allowed to deceive a jury by presenting testimony they know to be false. There are a dozen state statutes, rules of conduct, ethical codes, and even legal precedents that make this clear. Attorneys have been disbarred for doing what Russell Sanborn wanted me to do.

Still, it's done all the time—so often, in fact, that the statutes and codes of professional conduct decrying such tactics are widely ignored in favor of a defendant's right to defend himself.

Yet, incredibly, in my thirty-eight years as a lawyer, I've never known a client to work out a fabricated story beforehand and ask me to help him present it. I've had clients who I suspected might be lying, but I couldn't be sure and therefore was able to do my job and defend them. If Rusty had kept to his original story, one that I believed might possibly be true, I could have gone on. If there was any doubt whether it was Rusty or Ron Chica who had killed Erinn, then the law says Rusty deserved to be free. But to go into court with a blatant, preconceived plan to deceive a jury—that was something else. Even before the possibility fully hit my brain, it began churning in my stomach. My body was telling me that to do this would be a terrible betrayal of my profession and, even more, of myself.

While I contemplated how to handle this, I decided I owed it to Holly Sanborn to tell her what was happening. Maybe she could help persuade Rusty to stay off the witness stand. I sent someone to bring her to my office the following day. It was Saturday, and the trial would begin Monday.

Time, as the cliché goes, was running out.

Mrs. Sanborn arrived in my office looking as unkempt as ever. I told her, as gently as I could, that all the evidence, including the eyewitness, pointed to her son as the murderer. I explained what Rusty wanted me to do, and that I wasn't going to be able to do it. Instead of breaking down in tears, she sighed and said she wasn't surprised.

What she told me next nearly knocked me out of my chair. I've heard a lot of surprise confessions in my life, and I've learned never to be shocked by anything, but this one hit me like a Mike Tyson uppercut.

Holly Sanborn proceeded to tell me that she was the person who drove "the intruder" to Erinn's house that night. She waited diligently while her son was inside, and watched him carry the "rolled carpet" to the Mercedes. She followed him, lost him, then saw the Mercedes at his apartment. Then she went home. A few hours later, Rusty showed up at her house with the jewelry. She helped pawn it for him, signing the papers. Holly Sanborn claimed to be unaware of what had actually happened, but I found that difficult to believe, especially since the robbery was reported to have happened between 4:00 and 5:00 A.M.

On top of this, when Matt called Russell's ex-girlfriend, the supposed "sick friend" alibi witness, guess who paid her the bribe to back Russell's new story in court? Yep, Holly Sanborn. And what was the bribe? Cocaine. At the time, I wrote it off as a desperate mother's love.

Some mother! My sweet fruit-and-vegetable lady, the one who seduced me with her crying eyes and so protectively offered me her disability checks, was building quite a rap sheet. At the very least, she was an unknowing accessory to her son's burglary. At most, she may have been an accomplice in a burglary that resulted in a murder. Under recently tightened laws, that made her susceptible to a murder charge. She had additionally lied to the police, bribed a possible witness, and trafficked in cocaine, and she was planning to commit criminal perjury in court.

After she left, I sat stunned in my empty office. I'd been snookered big time. When the shock wore off, I began to reconsider my harsh indictment of Mrs. Sanborn. Rusty had not broken into Erinn's house that night. He had walked through the front door. Erinn was his friend. The whole thing had been planned. Mrs. Sanborn probably didn't have a clue as to what was going on. And what mother could honestly believe her son could be so savage a murderer?

I couldn't even be upset about her deceptions. Clients' lies are something you learn to live with. Over the years, I've been lied to by clients so often it rarely fazes me. In fact, there hasn't been a single case I've tried—and I've tried three thousand—in which some surprise revelation didn't come out during the trial. Usually, it's some damning fact that my client "overlooked." Even the innocent clients lie, believing some skeleton in their past will make them appear guilty. One of the secrets of winning court cases is to survive these booby traps, recover, and go on.

You can't get angry with the client (or his family). It's his neck on the line, not yours. He comes to you in a state of panic, sometimes even shock, and is as desperate as a human being can be. He, or a loved one, is facing death or, what may be just as bad to some, incarceration in a violent prison. It's hard for clients to place their trust in anyone under those circumstances. They invariably feel that if they tell you the truth, you won't take the case, or won't defend them with the same vigor. You can explain the need for them to tell you the truth until you're blue in the face, and in virtually every instance, the client will do everything but.

And any lawyer, policeman, or psychiatrist who claims to be able to determine whether a person is lying is either naïve or is deluding themself. Some people are such great liars they could convince you they were orbiting Venus at the time of the crime. Others are pathological liars, and are thus so convinced of their version of events that they truly believe it themselves. These people can even pass lie-detector tests. I try not to delve into psychology, nor do I judge people. I leave those tasks to others. I just defend them to the best of my ability. It's better if they tell me the truth, but I've learned to accept that it's a rare client who does.

However, that doesn't mean I have to go into court and participate in what I know is a planned deception of the jury. I can't, and I won't. A lawyer is sworn to uphold the law. There is no loophole, no exception. Presenting known perjured testimony to a judge or jury is breaking the law. Plain and simple. It must never be done under any circumstance.

In a case like Russell Sanborn's, the best you can do is to try to keep him off the witness stand so he can't lie or hang himself with his own thin fabrication. Then you do your damnedest to make sure the prosecution legally and lawfully presents its case against him. If they mess up, which they usually do in some area, then you can attack there. You make them do their job in proving your client's guilt beyond a reasonable doubt. If they don't, you explain it to the jury.

In the face of overwhelming evidence against a client, this is just one of the many acceptable tactics a defense lawyer can use. Additional techniques include pleading insanity, intoxication from drug or alcohol use, self-defense, other mitigating circumstances, or uncovering doubt as to who the murderer really was. But you don't lie. You don't create a fabricated story, nor do you allow the client to use his friends, relatives, girlfriends, or debtors to back his phony story by perjuring themselves on the witness stand.

Unfortunately, the law itself has some glaring imperfections. It was one of these imperfections that tied my bonds tighter—this time around my own neck. Despite all the rah-rah codes of pristine judicial ethics, Florida law, like the law in nearly every state, is murky on the issue of what exactly should be done in a case of premeditated perjury. The law states that an attorney, faced with a client intending to commit perjury, is first supposed to attempt to talk the client out of it. If the client remains insistent, the attorney is to file a motion to withdraw from the case. However, to protect the client, the details behind the request are not disclosed. The attorney can only note that the problem relates to the professional code of ethics. (Mentioning the code of ethics, along with additional legal wording in the motion, is usually enough to give the judge a hint that the conflict involves perjury.)

At this point, the guidelines become even more tangled. The individual judge is allowed to rule on the matter as he sees fit.

In the case of Judge Sidney Shapiro, he saw fit to deny my motion to withdraw. He ordered me to go back into the courtroom and allow Russell Sanborn to get up on the stand, swear to God to tell the whole truth and nothing but the truth, then tell one whopper after another. And I, as Sanborn's attorney, was supposed to help him deceive the jury by calling him as a witness and allowing him to lie. Admittedly, Judge Shapiro was also in a bind. I was Sanborn's fourth attorney. The case had been delayed a number of times because of the switches. The judge and the prosecutor felt that Sanborn might have been purposely sabotaging his trial with eleventh-hour attorney switches. That enabled him to avoid a conviction and remain in the less horrid Dade County Jail instead of going to the chair or doing hard time in the hell of Raiford Prison.

In addition, the attorney-client privilege prevented me from telling the judge exactly what Sanborn was planning to say, and how much of it I knew to be false. On top of that, I couldn't mention Mrs. Sanborn's involvement. That was privileged information that would convict my client.

Still, knowing what I knew, there was no way I could go on with the trial. The depth of the deception was staggering, and I knew far too much. Besides, it would have turned the trial into a farce. The parade of fools I'd have had to march up to the stand to back Rusty's story, including two shaky alibi witnesses who had already copped out, would have been a travesty.

I protested anew. Judge Shapiro consulted some precedents and worked out a plan. He said I was to put Russell Sanborn on the stand and let him tell his story without any questions from me. Then I was not to use any of his false testimony in my opening argument or summation. Shapiro knew that while the law states that a defendant decides how to plead and whether or not to testify, it's the defense attorney who controls all the other witnesses. It was understood that I just wouldn't call any supporting witnesses who also planned to lie. That meant Rusty would have to fly solo with his "sick friend" defense. I asked Judge Shapiro if his decision could be appealed. He agreed. The trial was delayed a few months to enable the appellate judges to rule. They backed Judge Shapiro's compromise.

Even with the judicial blessing, it remained a terrible solution. Sitting back silently while your client commits criminal perjury is no less an offense than participating. In addition, my sudden muteness was sure to alert the jury that something was wrong. I might as well walk up to the jury and say, "Hey, my guy's lying his head off because he's guilty. Let's save some time here and convict him." If the jury didn't catch on, then allowing Rusty to twist in the wind on the witness stand, without the aid of a trained attorney to guide him through his critical testimony, was certain to assure him a cell on death row. That also would turn the courtroom proceedings into a circus. If, by some miracle, Rusty managed to get his story out in a coherent fashion, my leaving the seemingly vital testimony out of my summation would further confuse the jury.

And once on the stand, Rusty was sure to blurt out, "And I have witnesses to prove it, but my attorney won't call them!"

That could have caused a mistrial.

On the other hand, disobeying a judge's order is a serious offense. By standing up for my principles, I would be facing a jail term and the possibility of a disbarment proceeding. The latter could result in a professional "death sentence," stripping me of my license to practice law.

I called a meeting with the other attorneys in my law firm, including my son Mark. All but Mark advised me to protect myself, my career, and the firm by doing as the judge ordered. In their view, the ethical problem had been lifted from my shoulders and placed upon those of Judge Shapiro and the appellate judges. I disagreed. The ultimate responsibility was mine.

As I maintained my defiant stance, I could see the anxiety in my associates' eyes and feel the tension in the room. They kept reminding me of the ramifications of my decision. Was it worth it to risk everything to accomplish so little? Would my refusal of Judge Shapiro's order do anything to stop the increasing problem of perjury in the courts?

I had to admit that it probably wouldn't.

My son Mark was particularly apprehensive. He knew I wasn't going to back down. I had preached ethics and integrity to my children since they were babies. Mark could already visualize me being thrown in jail. The thought terrified him.

That evening, something occurred to me that further solidified my position. One of the questions I ask potential jurors to determine their character is, "What's the most important thing that you teach your children?"

I've asked that question of hundreds of people. Invariably, the answer is the same.

"I teach them to be honest and truthful."

Honesty and truthfulness. That's what it was all about. The average American citizen walks into a court of law and sees a judge in a black robe sitting upon an elevated bench. The judge is surrounded by the flag and federal, state, or county seals. The citizen usually knows little about the intricacies of the law, but believes that justice can be found in the simple ideals of truth and honesty that are taught to a child.

Could I betray this public trust by presenting a defense that was constructed around bribes and lies?

Despite my colleagues' views on the futility of my stand, I was also concerned with the legal precedent that was being set. If I obeyed the judge, then criminals across the country would be free to blackmail their lawyers into presenting, or allowing their clients to present, elaborate fabrications before a jury. All they would have to say was, "The Rubin case says you have to let me lie." Further, does the acceptance of false testimony open the door for the submission of false documents to support that testimony? It would appear so. Say a criminal plans to commit a crime on a certain date. All he has to do is mail one of his bank cards to a friend in another state, give them the secret code number, and have them make a withdrawal from a twenty-four-hour banking machine in Wyoming or somewhere. The receipt is dated to the exact minute of the transaction. *Voilà*—an instant, ironclad, documented alibi placing the accused far away from the crime scene. And I, as that man's lawyer, am charged with submitting this or other false documents to the court to back his planned deception, even though I know it's a sham.

Let's take the "silent treatment" solution further. Say I follow Judge Shapiro's order and sit reading a "Spiderman" comic book while Rusty flounders through his testimony. Then I put on some headphones and listen to Michael Jackson's greatest hits while Assistant State Attorney David Waksman rips out Rusty's jugular in the cross-examination. Then I follow that by not redirecting testimony of my client to seal up some of his spurting arteries. Then I follow this demonstration of legal brilliance by not mentioning the heart of Rusty's defense in my summation.

Rusty is convicted, and his new attorneys slap me, or any attorney in a similar bind, with an incompetence charge of unprecedented proportions. Even if I had notified the court in advance, they could argue that I had no right to judge my client guilty and not help him with his testimony, call his witnesses, and highlight it in my summation.

Rusty could get a new trial.

And I'd be up the creek.

Worse, whether the defense attorney mentions the phony alibi or not, after the client loses, what stops the convicted person from saying it was the defense attorney who dreamed up the perjured testimony, and the scam cost him a guilty verdict? The client could get a new trial, and the defense attorney would face disbarment amid glaring newspaper headlines sullying his or her reputation, regardless of the final ruling.

Considering all this, it's no wonder the American Bar Association rejects the "silent treatment" as the solution to client perjury. But their recommendation isn't legally binding, and the ruling of Judge Shapiro and the appellate court was. I was ordered to proceed. I told Judge Shapiro I couldn't do it. Judge Shapiro was just as adamant about getting this long-delayed trial over with as I was about sticking to my principles. By killing an attorney's daughter, Sanborn had stuck a dagger into the heart of the judicial fraternity. In the same way police departments hunt cop-killers more intensely than they pursue other murderers, courts are equally driven to seek justice when someone murders one of their own. While I can sympathize with Judge Shapiro, what he did next was excessive. Sentencing me to thirty days in jail was overkill. Forty-eight hours, maybe. But thirty days?

When the producers of the television series "L.A. Law" jumped on my predicament and jailing, the television judge jailed conscience-stricken attorney Michael Kuzak (played by Harry Hamlin) for a weekend only. That made sense. As I watched Kuzak stand before his client's mother, attempt to solicit perjured testimony, then completely freeze up as his conscience screamed at him, I was happy that they had humanized the feelings that were running through me. But the bizarre web of deceit involved in my case far exceeded anything the "L.A. Law" writers could dream up.

I appealed both the decision and my subsequent contempt conviction, over and over, all the way to the Supreme Courts of Florida and the United States. Both courts ducked the sticky problem by deciding not to hear the case. To the lower court judges who did render decisions, and to many attorneys and prosecutors, it remained a simple matter of legal discipline. Attorneys are to do as the court orders. You obey, you don't make your own rules. The judges were also mindful of the dilemma of criminals telling their attorneys they were planning to lie, bouncing out one lawyer after the other, never going to trial.

That was a possibility, but one that could be remedied by

allowing the accused four changes of attorney. Fire the fourth, and you defend yourself. That actually happened in a case once, and it appears to be a good solution.

In the meantime, while I was fighting to stay out of jail,* Russell Sanborn was given his fifth attorney, had his trial, and was allowed to testify. Prosecutors David Waksman and Kevin DiGregory ate him alive, and the jury promptly convicted Rusty of murder and a whole host of other crimes. Judge Shapiro gave him one of those sentences comedians always joke about—life in prison plus six concurrent 134-year terms for burglary, armed robbery, three counts of kidnapping, and armed aggravated battery.

What isn't so funny is that the case was appealed at an additional cost to taxpayers of thousands of dollars. I'm all for appeals; I've filed a few hundred myself. But in the Sanborn case, his sixth attorney appealed the three kidnapping charges. He won. Now Sanborn has life and only three 134-year sentences. That makes a world of difference.

It's interesting to note what Judge Shapiro said to Rusty during the sentencing:

"It is this court's desire that you never see the light of day again as a free man. You have shown by your animalistic actions that you cannot function in our society. It is my hope you're never given the opportunity again."

Shapiro added that he would have given Rusty the chair, but the jury had recommended life by a nine-to-three vote.

This was the guy Judge Shapiro wanted me to waltz up on the stand, knowing he was going to deceive the jury? Just because that final jury saw through him doesn't mean mine wouldn't have swallowed his story. Holly Sanborn fooled the hell out of me. I'm sure she'd have had the jury crying big, wet tears. And what if I'd have given an effective summation? Combined with Rusty's and Holly's stirring testimony, they might have let him walk.

I have two daughters about the same age as Erinn.

Defense attorney Herbert Abramson once had one.

---

*Because of the contempt charges leveled against me, lawyer-client confidentiality was legally superseded by my need to defend myself. I never mentioned the specifics of Russell and Holly Sanborn's deception during my early appeals, but was legally allowed to do so in subsequent hearings.

9

THE JAILING, PART I

OWING TO the intricacies of the law, the unsanitary conditions of the jail, and the fits and starts of the appeal process, I was jailed three times on the contempt charge. The first time was on July 11, 1986. The worst part of this nine-hour jailing was having to stand silently before Judge Shapiro and listen without recourse as he distorted the facts and ripped me apart in public:

> Mr. Rubin, you are free to disagree and maintain your personal view of what the law is or ought to be, but as the appellate court stated, the decision of mere mortal judges . . . must be obeyed. . . .
> In every case, one side proves to be right, the other wrong. The "wrong" side is certainly entitled to representation, and his counsel is not unethical for championing his causes. You would like this community to believe that you would never represent a client if you believed him guilty or suspected his version of the facts was tainted.

That wasn't the case at all, and he knew it. Lawyers frequently represent clients they perceive to be guilty. The issue was this: Can an ethical attorney be ordered by a judge to willfully present perjured testimony in a court of law?

But when an almighty judge looks down upon the mute condemned, His Honor can say anything he wants.

Fortunately, the newspapers came to my rescue. An editorial in the *Fort Lauderdale News/Sun-Sentinel,* under the headline "Highest Obligation Is to Truth," said in part:

> The Rubin case raises serious issues about legal ethics, the role of a defense attorney, the right of a guilty person to lie to protect himself and the nature of the attorney-client relationship. . . .
>
> Does every defendant deserve representation by an attorney? Of course.
>
> Should an attorney be forced by a judge to represent a client against his will? Of course not.
>
> Is it ethical for an attorney to represent a client he suspects is guilty? Of course.
>
> But must that attorney knowingly allow his client to lie on the witness stand? No way.
>
> . . . Rubin had a duty to his client, but he had a higher duty, as an officer of the court, not to suborn perjury. Rubin's point is well taken. He shouldn't have to go to jail to prove it.*

Lawyers around the nation began taking their own stand, either at the request of local reporters, by writing law review articles and letters to the editor, or by arguing among themselves at the corner bar. Anne Spitzer, a University of Florida law professor, responding in the *Orlando Sentinel,* voiced the most popular view among my peers:

"Florida rules [of professional conduct] tell you if your client is going to commit a crime—and perjury is a crime—you're obligated not to assist him in doing it and to inform the authorities to keep it from being done. But he (the attorney) must, under our rules, obey the court's order even though he believed it to be wrong."

That is the easy way out. Pass the buck. The world learned at the Nuremberg trials, and continues to learn in subsequent trials of other Nazi Germany war criminals, that the defense of "I was only following orders of superiors" has no legal foundation and is morally reprehensible.

Although the majority of attorneys condemned my stand in going against the court order, there were a few who did support me.

*Reprinted with permission of the *Fort Lauderdale News/Sun-Sentinel.*

Robert Dempsey, at the time the Commissioner of the Florida Department of Law Enforcement, was the most notable. He wrote me these encouraging words:

> As a law enforcement officer for thirty-five years and a member of the Bar both in New York and Florida over the past twenty-five years, I have strongly objected to the concept that an attorney must do anything in the interest of his client, including subornation of perjury. I have consistently been sickened by the actions of attorneys in civil as well as criminal cases who turn a deaf ear to confessions, admissions against interests, etc., and not only conceal such information but actively concoct lies, half-truths, and misstatements on behalf of their clients, all under the guise of their duty to their client, which is the paramount interest. . . . I for one certainly appreciated your going public and exposing this terrible hypocrisy that exists among members of the Bar, including those on the bench. . . . Your cause is right and ultimately you will prevail.

What was especially encouraging was the reaction of the public. I received letters from people around this country and Canada. One in particular bolstered my spirits. It was written by a man named Kenny Shaver, Minister to Youth at the Duncanville Church of Christ, Duncanville, Texas:

> A couple of evenings ago, I saw a report on "CBS Evening News" about your plight with the court system in Miami. My heart went out to you and I was also proud of your stand for the truth. In our day and age, we need more people who will stand up for their convictions—especially when they have to do with truth and integrity. I applaud your stand. I wish I could do more for you.
> I am currently teaching a class that around eight hundred teenagers will attend. The theme of my class is integrity. When I saw the report about you, I knew that I had to use it as an illustration of standing for the truth, no matter what the consequences. Teens today do not get that kind of role model very often. I am glad they have one in you.

The letter was signed by Shaver and dozens of teenagers in his classes. I took that letter and others like it into jail with me and reread them whenever I became depressed. And I did become depressed. Standing up for a principle is one thing; actually seeing those bars slam in front of you is quite another.

"ELLIS, I'M sorry I have to handcuff you," one of the corrections officers said that first day.

"You don't have to do that," I said. "I'm not going to escape."

The officer told me to put my hands behind my back and

pretend I was handcuffed. I complied. The police and corrections officers treated me well. I've represented the individual policeman many times, and I had represented separate groups of black and Hispanic corrections officers in various labor disputes. Most of them acted embarrassed when they saw me.

"What are you doing here? You don't belong here," one said, expressing the prevailing view.

They supported the stand I'd taken in court. Surprisingly, even the other prisoners didn't feel I should represent a liar. That was unexpected, but as I would learn during my later incarcerations, there exists considerable honor among the men and women behind bars.

I didn't encounter many fellow inmates on this visit. What I did experience was four hours in the prisoner booking area. As I sat waiting to be processed, I was given a view of humanity one rarely experiences. The doors kept opening, each time bringing in new denizens of the underbelly of society. One woman was dragged in by the hair. That's about all the officer had to hold on to, because she was naked. The others were in various states of disarray. There were drug addicts crashing, drug addicts soaring, drug addicts passed out, silk-suited drug dealers, white-collar criminals in three-piece suits, derelicts, robbers, murderers, and rapists. Some came passively, others fought as if they were possessed. Corrections officers have to be the most underpaid and unappreciated people in the world.

The holding cell was a junction where all these fine citizens gathered together. It was a room of unmentionable filth punctuated by a staggering stench. There were things on the floor that do not warrant mention.

For me, it was just a brief introduction. A Florida Supreme Court justice, acting on my son Mark's request for a writ of habeas corpus, called and ordered me set free pending their decision to hear the appeal. I walked out a few minutes after 11:00 P.M. and did several live interviews on the late news. Many people, noting my image as the "Electronic Lawyer," accused me of planning it that way, but it was merely a coincidence.

I shed my prison uniform and climbed back into my pinstriped suit—just in time to take one of the strangest cases of my career.

But they saved a cell for me. And I would be back.

10

PRENTICE RASHEED AND THE TUTTI-FRUTTI DEFENSE, PART I

I didn't kill Odell Hicks. The system killed Odell Hicks.
There's many more Odell Hickses out there that are
already dead. They just haven't fell over yet.
—Prentice Rasheed on the CBS TV program "60 Minutes"

"MY NAME is Dr. Earl Wells," said the man on the phone. "I'm president of the Liberty City Merchants Association. Have you heard about what happened to Prentice Rasheed?"

I certainly had. The news about Rasheed was everywhere. The Vietnam veteran's clothing and sundries store had been burglarized seven times in the previous months. The thieves were driving him out of business. To stop them, he rigged an electric grate under the hole the robbers had chopped in his ceiling. On September 30, 1986, burglar number eight broke into the store through the attic, somehow climbed down the grate unharmed, and began carting out goods, pushing them through the steel bars protecting the back entrance. When the burglar climbed back up the grate to escape, he was electrocuted. Now the state was trying to convict Prentice Rasheed of manslaughter.

I also knew Liberty City, a Miami neighborhood that isn't featured in the tourist guides. It's the area of town that was set aflame during one of America's worst race riots of the 1980s.

"We would like you to meet with Mr. Rasheed," Wells continued. "He needs help."

The Greater Miami Yellow Pages devotes eighty-five pages to attorneys. According to the Dade County Bar, there are more than nine thousand. Yet, despite a probability of sizable proportions, I wasn't surprised by the call.

WHEN I was a youngster in Binghamton, New York, my father owned and operated Larry's Army/Navy Store. He sold work clothes and a few scattered military items, and barely kept the family afloat.

In 1942, a few months after Pearl Harbor was bombed, the army stationed a battalion of about one thousand black military police outside Binghamton. There was some whispered concern among the mostly white Binghamton residents, but it was wartime, so even the most fervent racists couldn't protest too loudly.

My father decided to make the most of this influx of soldiers by going to New York City and ordering "tailor-made" uniforms, buttons, belt buckles, boots, and dozens of other army items. The U.S. Army issues a uniform and other essentials, but the quality is mediocre and the fit can be terrible. Soldiers are allowed, at their own expense, to purchase tailored uniforms made from better fabrics.

My father's store was soon overflowing with black soldiers buying uniforms, brass buttons, leather boots, and anything else that caught their fancy. The atmosphere at the store changed from sleepy to bustling. My mother used to handle the money and make change. I remember how happy she was with all the excitement. My father's income increased considerably. He went from struggling to solvent.

I was in high school, and worked at the store after class. The soldiers I waited on were only a few years older than I, so we got along. I joked with them, picked up their colloquialisms and culture, and got to know many of them personally. While other teenagers were growing up in a world of racial separation, my Pavlovian response to blacks is something entirely different. I have memories of my mother's laughter as she shared stories with the men, of the prosperity they brought to my father, and of good times and good friends.

You can imagine my shock when I encountered the other, more prevalent view, in a Southern court. My very first case was the defense of Henry Larkin, a black man accused of murder. In addition to the fact that it was my first case, I still had a stammering problem. I'd gotten through my opening statement without stumbling over a word, and was just beginning to feel confident. I started to cross-examine the first witness of my career, a black man named Clarence Williams.

"Now, Mr. Williams . . ." I started.

"Bailiff, take the jury out!" bellowed Judge Ben Willard, drowning out the rest of my sentence. I was petrified. What had I done? How did he know I stammered? Was he going to banish me from court, killing my dream of being a trial attorney?

"Lawyer," Willard said, "where are you from?"

"Upstate New York, Your Honor," I gulped.

"Well, I don't care what you do in upstate New York, but we don't call nigras 'mister' in Miamaaa. If you want to practice in this court, you'll address colored people by their first names."

Judge Willard turned to the witness.

"What's your name, boy?" he said.

"Clarence," the man replied.

"See?" Judge Willard said. "It's Clarence. That's what you call this boy, ya hear?"

I remember feeling sick inside. My mother's smiling face flashed before me, as did the faces of many of the soldiers who came into the store. They were proud men who had told me stories about their homes, parents, and girlfriends, and had shared with me their dreams and aspirations. I turned around and walked to the bench, fighting tears. It was the first dilemma I would face in a long career of facing, and spitting into the face of, legal wrongs. But this was my first case. I was a stammerer. Could I disobey a judge and ground my career before it even took off?

To hell with Judge Willard, I thought. I would start my question the same way and take my chances. Then I saw one more face, Henry Larkin's. He knew what I was going through. He knew my feelings. The look in his eyes said, "Don't do it. Not here. Not now." And he was right. My first obligation was to keep Henry Larkin out of the electric chair. I could fight racism later.

So I called Clarence by his first name. I was too angry to think about stammering, and I didn't. I also won the case. A few years later, I set up a law office in the Sir John Hotel, in the heart of the black section of Miami. That first year, I represented more than two hundred blacks free of charge. I was fueled by pure indignation. If I couldn't call a black man "sir" or "mister," I sure as hell could fight to keep some innocent black men and women out of jail. And every chance I got, I'd "slip" and call a "nigra" by a respectful title. (The famous "Fight Doctor," Ferdie Pacheco, was similarly motivated and started a medical practice in an adjacent black neighborhood. Dr. Pacheco later became Muhammad Ali's physician and is now an NBC fight analyst.)

I went broke, but I was chosen one of Florida's five Outstanding Young Men of the Year in 1954, and was nominated for the national award in 1955.

It took me more than twenty years to strike back on a higher level. As I became more experienced, I waited for the right case to come walking into my succession of offices. In 1973 it came. Johnny Brown, a city busdriver, was ordered to send his children across town to integrate a white school. Brown didn't want his two young daughters bused so far away, so he tried to register them in the nearby Dade Christian School. When he brought the girls to the office, he was handed a card that stated, "We do not practice integration in this school."

The irony gets a bit confusing here. School busing was designed to help minorities by equalizing educational opportunity. Yet Johnny Brown was against busing. When he tried to get around it the same way whites did, by turning to private and religious schools, he had the door slammed in his face—again! It was a strange beginning to what would be a landmark racial discrimination case, but most of my big cases seem to be anchored in paradox.

On behalf of Johnny Brown, I fought the case for the next five years, all the way to the U.S. Supreme Court. It was a tough battle. On the plus side, there was a national court order to integrate public schools, and a Supreme Court decision outlawing discrimination in private schools. But there existed no precedent for religious schools. They were the last stronghold because, in order to defeat their policies, a lawyer had to confront the ironclad separation of church and state laws. The Dade Christian School's attorneys argued that separation of the races was an integral part of that school's religious foundation, and the almighty First Amendment guaranteed them freedom of religion.

As a Jew who was sent to Holy Cross College by the navy, I've had a well-rounded religious education. I couldn't recall anything in the Bible, Old Testament or New, that ordered the separation of the races. I was curious as to how a Christian school could embrace that policy. Sure enough, during the deposition of the school's principal, I discovered that, far from being a long-standing religious tenet, the Dade Christian School's administration, faculty, and parent groups had merely voted on integrating, and had decided against it.

I also determined that they had altered regular textbooks by removing all photographs that portrayed blacks and whites together, and replaced them with photographs of whites only.

Because of these discoveries, I won in federal court. The school appealed its case to the U.S. Fifth Circuit Court of Appeals in New Orleans. At that level, a lawyer presents his case before thirteen sitting judges—an experience that's the ultimate test of advocacy. Their Honors sit in two tiers and rain questions down upon the lone attorney. Not only must the attorney battle the collective wit of thirteen esteemed judges, but he or she must also fight the feeling of being overwhelmed by the splendor of the arena.

I presented my case and fought off the probes. It boiled down to a question of superiority, not of blacks and whites, but of law. Which law was superior, the free exercise of religion or the civil-rights laws?*

The judges favored the civil-rights laws—just barely. They voted seven to six in June 1977 to allow Johnny Brown's children to attend the Dade Christian School. The school appealed to the U.S. Supreme Court. The Supreme Court upheld the decision in

---

*The law I used here was the same one used in *Runyon v. McCrary*, the Virginia showdown over discrimination in private schools. It is 42 U.S. Code 1981, an obscure, post–Civil War act, passed in the 1800s that gave black men equal standing in contracts. It is based upon the Thirteenth Amendment, which, along with outlawing slavery, gave Congress the power to pass laws that would bolster the antislavery act.

Feburary 1978, effectively ending discrimination in private religious schools in the United States of America.

As is often the case with precedent-setting rulings, Johnny Brown's daughters would not benefit from the long battle. They had grown into teenagers, assimilated into their current schools, and had no interest in being unwanted pioneers at an all-white Christian school that had fought so hard to keep them out. (They've since graduated from college and graduate school.)

But that was okay. I had fought the battle for Mr. Clarence Williams.

I VISITED Prentice Rasheed at his Liberty City store.

"Mr. Rubin, you're the right man for this," he said. "I'm in a lot of trouble."

I told him not to worry. That's one of the main functions a lawyer can perform. Calm the client, show him you're in charge, and assure him that he's in good hands. Rasheed explained what he had done and why, and then pleaded poverty. I found him to be a gentle man, a devout Muslim who was intelligent and articulate in his own colorful way. I liked him from the start. He was forty-three and had a lovely wife and two daughters. Rasheed's father had been a share-cropper on a peanut farm near Dublin, Georgia, and Rasheed, form-erly Prentice Edwards, grew up picking cotton in the hot Georgia fields. After combat duty in Vietnam, he returned to America and worked hard to better himself. He became a watch repairman, con-verted to Islam, and opened a series of small businesses.

Every Friday, Rasheed and his employees would close the store, kneel, and pray. They faced east, toward a nearby Winn-Dixie gro-cery store on Dr. Martin Luther King Boulevard.

I offered to represent him without charge. He couldn't believe it. In return for my services, I made him promise to follow my advice. I make all my clients promise this, but I presented my standard edict to Rasheed as if it were a trade-off. That enabled him to keep his dignity, which is vital when someone is facing a trying ordeal. The agreement was that no matter what anybody else told him, and what he felt we should do, he had to do it my way. Unfortunately, he would forget this promise later.

From my standpoint, Rasheed's story was perfect. He had tried every way humanly possible to get protection for his store. He had called the police and begged them to increase their patrols in the

Liberty City neighborhood surrounding his business. The police weren't keen on responding. The riots in 1980 were touched off by the acquittal of five white police officers charged with beating a black insurance agent to death following a traffic violation. After that, the bad blood between the police and the Liberty City residents intensified. Frustrated blacks would gather at the slightest police provocation and toss cement blocks through the windshields of cars and throw bottles at the heads of the officers. Even if the police arrived to arrest a neighborhood felon, a mini-riot would develop. For everyone involved, it was best to keep the two parties as separate as possible. This led to something of an *Escape from New York* situation in Liberty City, where the thieves and drug dealers ran wild. As time passed, the emotions subsided, but the memories and crime lingered.

Into this uneasy history entered Prentice Rasheed with his demands for a higher police profile in his neighborhood. He even appeared before the Dade County Commission and pleaded with the commissioners to give him and his fellow Liberty City merchants the same police protection that was afforded the richer, white merchants who owned stores in Coconut Grove, a trendy area on the southeast side of Miami. Without such protection, Rasheed warned, he would be forced to act on his own.

"You might turn me into a criminal," he told the commissioners. "I'm not a criminal. But eventually, if a man's got to survive, he's gonna do what a man's got to do."

Rasheed's pleas fell upon deaf ears. He couldn't afford a burglar alarm, and insurance was too expensive in his neighborhood. Realizing he was on his own, he traced the burglars' path through the roof and into his store, and dotted the trail with nails. It didn't work. The thieves learned to negotiate the nails and continued to plunder the store. The hole in Rasheed's roof widened. He was losing his ability to provide the simple necessities of life, including food for his children. Rasheed's solution was to take a couple of steel-mesh grates, the kind that cover store windows in rough neighborhoods, and set them in an inverted pyramid under the hole. He was told by a friend that the upside-down-teepee configuration was necessary to allow an electric current to flow through. He then took a simple electrical cord, cut one end to expose the wire, hooked the exposed wire to the grid, and plugged it in.

Rasheed thought, as most people probably would, that the

110-115–volt electric current coming from a wall socket was not enough to kill. People take full hits of this kind of current around their homes all the time. The injuries range from nothing to slight burns. Rarely does someone die from the standard household current. Rasheed figured the burglars would touch the grid, get shocked, and go away.

It only took two weeks before the device was tested. Actually, it's not known how many times it worked as Rasheed thought it would, or how many burglars it chased away. What is known is that on the morning of September 30, Rasheed's assistant manager, John El-Amin, opened the store and immediately saw a man's body in the grid. The man had been carrying a large portable radio that was still blaring disco music. El-Amin thought it was a careless burglar who had fallen asleep, and poked him a few times to rouse him. When the man didn't budge, El-Amin called his boss and told him the trap had killed someone. Rasheed told his employee to call the police.

Detectives John Spear and Steve Vinson arrived and demanded that Rasheed come to the store. He refused, knowing full well that they intended to arrest him for something. They eventually located the frightened shopkeeper and charged him with manslaughter. Wells and the Liberty City Merchants Association came to Rasheed's aid, taking up a collection to post his $6,500 bond. He was free, but he was in serious trouble. Florida law prohibits the use of deadly force to protect one's property unless a life is in danger. You can't place the value of material goods over the life of a human being—even a lowlife human being. The American Civil Liberties Union and the local criminal law experts at the area colleges and universities quickly condemned the "vigilante" mentality and were calling for Rasheed's hide.

In a court of law, I was sunk.

I decided to try the Prentice Rasheed case in a higher court. The court of public opinion.

The first love of my life, my junior high school teacher
Helen Foley. She gave special attention to a shy kid
with a severe speech impediment. I wasn't the only one
smitten. Rod Serling based a ''Twilight Zone'' episode
on her.

Even as a child, Rod Serling's mind soared beyond the problems of a young boy with a handicap.
He taught me to stretch my mind and never give up. That's us, second row from the bottom, the
third and fourth scouts from the left. *(The Rod Serling Foundation)*

Ellis Rubin

Rod Serling *(The Rod Serling Foundation)*

My mom, dad, and sister Jeanne, seeing me off after I joined the navy during World War II.

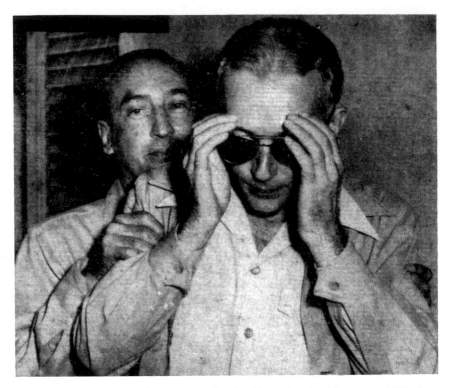

The infamous Charles Wesley Johnson, adjusting his shades after his arrest in 1952. Don Johnson of "Miami Vice" never looked so hip. *(The Miami Herald/Steve Wever)*

The Agony of Defeat. The television intoxication defense goes down in flames. Ronny reacts to the guilty verdict. *(Wide World Photos/pool)*

Billionaire Arab Sheik Mohammed al-Fassi and wife number three, Aptisam, get the key to Miami as former heavyweight boxing champ Muhammad Ali looks on. The sheik and the Greatest were planning to go into the fast-food business together. *(The Miami Herald/Bob East)*

The chic sheik and Aptisam head to a deposition prior to the "Billion-Dollar Babies" trial. *(Wide World Photos/Kathy Willens)*

Wife number one, Sheika Dena al-Fassi, with her top-gun divorce lawyer, Marvin Mitchelson. Dena infused the proceeding with elements of sex, drugs, and rock and roll. *(Wide World Photos)*

Beauty . . . the lovely Erinn Abramson. She had it all—looks, wealth, loving parents, fun, sun, the beach, the malls—and cocaine. She ended up paying a ghastly price.

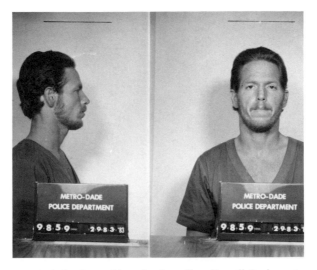

. . . and the Beast. My refusal to allow Russell Sanborn to commit perjury sent the case spiraling into a legal twilight zone.

Rapist/burglar Odell Hicks steals his last radio. His life of crime and repeated sexual assaults was put to an end by merchant Prentice Rasheed's electrified trap. It was estimated that Hicks had raped as many as seventy-five women.

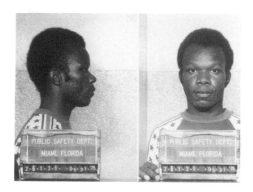

Odell Hicks.

Rasheed and I awaiting the grand jury's verdict. Little did we know that a glorified rat named Tutti-Frutti had become the key element. *(Bett-mann News Photos/Jim Sherry)*

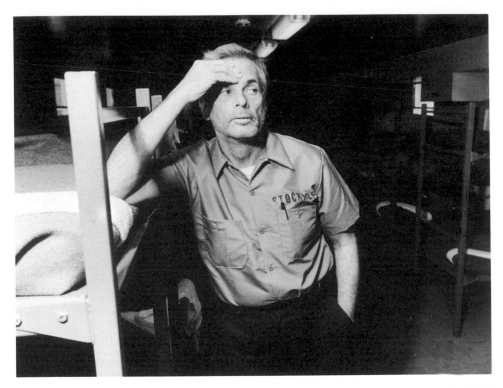

Rasheed was free, but I was in jail. While the protesters marched in the sunlight, I was growing weary in the dank jail. My protest beard had already begun to sprout. *(Wide World Photos/Bill Cooke)*

Leaving jail the third and final time after thirty-seven days in custody for refusing to allow Erinn Abramson's murderer to tell an elaborate lie to a jury. *(Wide World Photos/Bill Cooke)*

The magnificent central courtroom in Miami's Federal Courthouse. Beneath the stunning mural, I've defended everyone from stylish kidnapper Charlie Johnson in 1952 to one of the cocaine-corrupted "River Cops" in 1988. The huge painting illustrates how the law is interwoven with South Florida's diverse population and lifestyle. *(Michael Carlebach)*

Lisa Keller at age thirteen, the year her father began teaching her how to satisfy a man.

Morris Keller holding the fish. The burly ex-sailor's sadistic sexual habits exploded out of the darkness and into Florida's conscience late in the summer of 1986.

Lisa Keller in handcuffs at age twenty-nine, charged with murder and facing the electric chair. The frail, timid, and sickly woman was chained to a table during some of her courtroom appearances. The abuse had taken a new form. (The Miami Herald/*Pete Cross*)

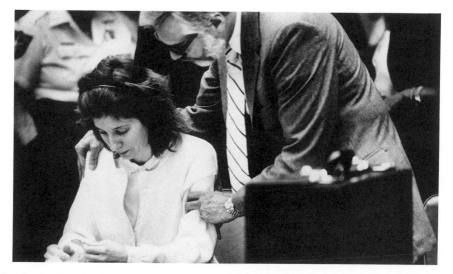

Comforting Lisa after her emotional reaction to the horrifying pictures of her father's battered face. (The Miami Herald/*Pete Cross*)

Superstar prosecutor Kelly Hancock. In the courtroom, Hancock appears as the absolute embodiment of law and order—the handsome, heroic protector of you and me and everything we hold dear. He wanted the death sentence for Lisa. (The Miami Herald/*Pete Cross*)

While a hushed courtroom fought to hold back sobs and gasps, a trembling Lisa describes the sixteen years of shame and degradation that led to her violent explosion. "She is suffering from the same disorder as a war veteran would have that was brutalized in Vietnam." (The Miami Herald/*Pete Cross*)

Lisa's younger sister, Vicky, testifies how her father often treated Lisa. (The Miami Herald/*Pete Cross*)

The Mother—Dorothea Keller cringes outside the courtroom following Lisa's testimony. "Lisa never told her mother. But, typically, that's the way these things are." *(The Miami Herald/Pete Cross)*

The Verdict. History is made. Women can protect themselves. The world may someday be a kinder and gentler place. *(The Miami Herald/Pete Cross)*

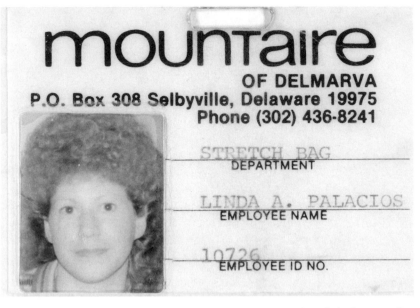

A Nightmare in Delaware. The discovery of Linda Palacios' cold, nude body in a trailer bathroom ignited a mystery that almost destroyed her boyfriend, his sister, and their family.

The jury visits the trailer. I wanted each of them to enter the tiny cardboard bathroom that was being promoted as the scene of a vicious fight to the death. *(Gary Emeigh)*

With co-author Dary Matera. The former journalist's detective work cracked open the case and exposed a questionable police investigation. *(Gary Emeigh)*

Elsie prays while her daughter Doris looks grim. Even though Doris ramrodded the defense of her brother, her untimely emotional outburst in the gallery nearly destroyed his chances. *(Gary Emeigh)*

Charles, flanked by his sister Doris *(left)* and his aunt Catherine *(right)*. His grandmother Mabel leaped out of her seat when the verdict was read, raised her arms to the sky, and screamed "Thank you, Jesus, I knew he was innocent . . ." *(Gary Emeigh)*

Deputy Attorney General M. Jane Brady. She's no doubt telling me again how she's going to kick my city slicker butt all the way back to Miami. *(Gary Emeigh)*

11

PRENTICE RASHEED AND THE TUTTI-FRUTTI DEFENSE, PART II:

The Not-So-Grand Jury

BRINGING PRENTICE Rasheed's case before the public was easy. The media kept calling, requesting interviews. The story grew bigger with each new report. Rasheed eventually appeared on such national programs as "60 Minutes," "The Today Show," "Larry King Live," "Nightline," and even "Oprah." He handled himself well, and needed only minimal coaching. My son Mark decided that he should continue to wear his baseball cap during every appearance. The television producers kept asking him to remove it, but we insisted that it remain. The hat established an identity, a "Famous Amos" look that photographed well.

Along each stop of the campaign trail, the support for Mr. Rasheed was overwhelming. The *Miami Herald* conducted a poll and found that three out of five responding readers believed people should be allowed to use deadly force to protect their property. That was a radical departure from existing laws in virtually every state that prohibit the taking of life to protect property.* I can understand such a reaction in Miami, where crime is a problem, but when we left the big cities and ventured into the rural areas, the feeling was even stronger.

Prentice Rasheed had touched a nerve. Most people felt they had the right to protect what's theirs any way they saw fit. They were sick of robbers and burglars stealing their possessions, and were quite angry about what the state was trying to do to Rasheed for fighting back. We received letters of support from across the country. Many contained checks for Rasheed's defense fund. The contributions, which we had never requested, ranged from one dollar, sent by a woman in Hawaii, to $1,000, from an oil company president in Kansas.

This is not to say we didn't face opposition. Criminologists and liberals were quick to condemn Rasheed's actions from an intellectual standpoint. The liberal *Miami News* and *Miami Herald* wrote editorials calling for his prosecution. (*The Wall Street Journal* editorialized against charging Rasheed.) The best opposing view, however, was expressed by Detective Spear, one of the first officers on the scene at Rasheed's store:

"We can't have everyone setting traps in their homes and stores," Spear warned. "What happens if a police officer has to break in? They could be seriously hurt or killed. My brother is a fireman, and I'd hate to see him go into a building to put out a fire and get killed by someone's trap."

Good point.

When both sides offer solid arguments, the debate tends to rage on. Rasheed was big news, and there were more supporters than detractors. The *Herald*'s poll found that 73 percent of its readers felt he shouldn't be prosecuted.

Actually, what was saving Rasheed's hide was a big dose of blind luck. I'm reminded of the classic comment that rich businessmen from blue-blood families make when asked how they achieved their wealth: "I chose my parents well." Similarly, Prentice Rasheed "chose" his victim well. The man who fell into the trap had the classic "rap sheet a mile long." Odell Hicks was one bad dude. He had a history of burglary and robbery arrests, and had been con-

---

*As of 1989, only Colorado and Louisiana have enacted so-called "make my day" laws that allow home and store owners to shoot burglars.

victed of a brutal rape. That last offense won over the women's vote right out of the gate. Everybody in the area surrounding Rasheed's store knew Hicks. They described the twenty-six-year-old drug addict as an arrogant SOB who often boasted about the stores he had ripped off and the women he had sexually assaulted.

Circuit Court Judge Ellen Morphonios also knew Hicks. "Maximum" Morphonios—a tough, no-nonsense judge, who was featured on "60 Minutes" for her one-woman war against crime—thought she had sent Hicks away for good in 1977, when she handed down a life sentence plus thirty years.

"He wanted the world to know he was the friendly neighborhood rapist," Morphonios told the *Los Angeles Times.* "He bragged that he had raped seventy-five or one hundred women. . . . He went to a wash house and he got one woman's laundry and he spread it out like you'd spread out bread crumbs for a duck. The woman went along picking it up. When she got to a bushy area, he grabbed her."

Hicks's sentence was appealed by his public defenders and was later slashed to eight years. He served his time and was released.

Carl Hiaasen, a columnist for the *Miami Herald,* summed up Hicks's death in a single line: "His contributions to society will not be missed."

What also helped Rasheed's case was the medical examiner's findings that Hicks had been smoking crack and drinking the night of the burglary. The cocaine in his system may have combined with the minor electric shock to give Hicks his final high.

The confusion over how Hicks entered the store without being shocked, and then couldn't repeat the trick on the way out, had a simple explanation—greed. On the morning of Mr. Hicks's demise, police found piles of freshly stolen clothing, jewelry, watches, and shoes in the alley behind Rasheed's store. The property was just outside the security bars protecting the back door. Hicks apparently didn't put the portable stereo out there with the other booty because he couldn't fit it through the bars, or he was afraid another crook would come along and steal it while he was escaping through the roof. Maneuvering the large, stolen radio through the grate may have activated the deadly electric current that his rubber tennis shoes negated when he entered.

He was also doomed by his own stupidity. Once safely inside the store, Hicks could simply have unplugged the trap. The booze and cocaine were probably factors in that fatal oversight.

* * *

WHILE RASHEED and Mark were hitting the talk-show circuit, the pressure was building on State Attorney Janet Reno to decide whether to file the manslaughter charge or drop it. I called her a few times, expressing my concern, but saying only, "This is a tough call. I hope you do the right thing." As I expected, Reno did what all prosecutors do when faced with a hot potato. She tossed it to a grand jury. Usually, this is nothing more than a shell game designed to shield the prosecutor's office from an unpopular decision. It's an effective technique because ninety-nine times out of a hundred, the grand jury does exactly what the prosecutor wants.

Grand juries are probably the most misunderstood body in our legal system. When a grand-jury indictment is handed down in a big case, the media jumps on it and spreads the news far and wide that an important decision has been made. The impression the public receives is that this super-duper jury has found someone guilty. That's not the case at all, and such misleading pronouncements can prejudice future jurors. Far from being a superior entity, a grand jury is actually less important than a regular jury. It's the regular jury that decides guilt or innocence, life or death, jail or freedom. Grand juries actually do little more than look over the police's shoulder and tell them whether they made a good arrest.

Consider the facts: A grand jury consists of eighteen to twenty-three average citizens who meet in a room in the local courthouse to decide whether there is enough evidence or "probable cause" to indict someone for a crime. In a grand-jury hearing, there are no defense attorneys, no defense witnesses, and no defense evidence. All of which adds up to no defense. The state attorneys bring in the evidence supporting their side, call their witnesses and their experts, and present their case in secret, without opposition, before the citizen jurors. Faced with this one-sided presentation, the panel invariably rubber-stamps what the state attorney asks. (In Florida, as in most states, the state attorney is the legal adviser to the grand jury.)

An English professor concerned with proper syntax, or an innovative newspaper editor wanting to better inform the public, should start a drive to clarify the misconception about grand juries. They can start by giving this not-so-grand jury a more descriptive name, like "sub-jury" or "minor jury." I like "rubber-stamp jury" myself.

Along with the advantage of profiting from being able to present a one-sided case before a supportive jury, state attorneys have another technique they use in the grand-jury process. Sometimes the state sends the accused a letter "inviting" him to testify. Those who feel they are innocent usually leap at this opportunity to set the record straight. Even the guilty often jump at the chance to defend themselves.

Guilty or not, the accused often leaps right into his own grave.

The prosecutor's invitation almost always includes the killer clause, "You will be required to waive immunity and testify truthfully under penalty of perjury." The translation: "Our skilled prosecutors are going to hand you a long rope made from the finest hemp. Then, as if by magic, they will get you to hang yourself without your knowing it."

Prentice Rasheed was eager to testify. He was innocent, so why not tell everyone? Hell, it was working in the media. It worked on "Nightline." It worked on "The Today Show." Surely it would work before the grand jury, Rasheed reasoned. He consulted the attorney who did his business finances and was advised that he should indeed testify. He was told that it was a dangerous mistake not to testify, and that passing up this opportunity would make it appear that he was guilty.

I told him to forget it. He was naturally upset.

So was I. The prosecutors had a rope knotted and bowed like a Christmas package, waiting for Mr. Rasheed.

"Mr. Rasheed," they would ask, "did you test your contraption before using it?"

"No," he would say.

"Are you a skilled electrician?"

"No," he would say.

"Did you study the effect of electricity on the human body before plugging in your device?"

"No," he would say.

"Did you post any warning signs around your death trap to scare off little children, curious young boys playing on the roof, or even a burglar?"

"No," he would say.

"Did you ask the police to inspect it? Did you have an electrician check it out? Are you aware of the Florida statute that prohibits the use of booby traps?"

"No, no, and no," he would say.

They'd slice and dice him with a dozen or so additional questions and build a textbook case for "the negligent taking of human life." That's the definition of manslaughter. It would be all she wrote for one Prentice Rasheed. His Warholian fifteen minutes of fame would be followed by fifteen years of obscurity behind bars.

Rasheed, aided by the sterling advice of his bookkeeper/attorney, was determined to walk into this trap. I reminded him of his promise to follow my orders, but he wavered. I detailed the above scenario, explaining that the only way they could prove negligence was to get it from his own mouth. I also told him the stories of one of my clients, Dorothy Wright and Alger Hiss. Wright was a young woman who was forced at gunpoint to shoot someone. She begged and I allowed her to walked into a grand jury expecting to be cleared, and came out with a murder indictment. Hiss has the most famous grand-jury case. He was a State Department official who helped write the United Nations Charter and was with Franklin D. Roosevelt at Yalta. His world came crashing down when Whittaker Chambers, a former avowed communist, accused him of being one too. Hiss was "invited" to respond before Richard Nixon's House Un-American Activities Committee. Despite being advised not to go, and despite being a brilliant, Harvard-educated lawyer himself, Hiss bent to public sentiment and chose to "clear his name" by testifying. He did, and denied the charge. A federal grand jury took notice and invited Hiss to testify. Again he accepted. But the federal grand jury also invited Chambers. Hiss was not only a communist, Chambers sang, but they were comrades from the same communist cell.

Two men. Two stories. One of them committed perjury before a federal grand jury. The federal grand jury concluded it was Hiss. A regular jury agreed, and Hiss was thrown into prison for five years.

The moral here is that Hiss was not jailed for being a communist; he was jailed for committing perjury. It's not against the law to be a communist. It *is* against the law to lie to a federal grand jury or to a congressional committee. Had he kept his mouth shut, the charges would have blown over. By responding to the invitations, Hiss hung himself, big time.

After these lessons in American history, Rasheed finally got the message.

With that settled, I could then deal with Rasheed's well-founded concern over how his refusal would look. After all, we were trying his case in the court of public opinion, and ducking a grand-jury invitation wasn't going to look good on the street. But I had that covered. I told Rasheed to tell everyone he would be happy to testify, but it was his lawyers who were the "bad guys" and wouldn't let him. We would then show up the morning of the hearing, and I'd take the heat.

We arrived early, giving ourselves enough time to accommodate the mob of media. Rasheed looked sharp in his sport jacket, slacks, and maroon baseball cap. When it came time for him to testify, he was handed "the letter." He promptly gave it to me as I had instructed. I glanced at it, saw the words *waive* and *immunity*, and handed it back to Janet Reno.

"I can't let him testify without immunity," I said.

"I thought so," she answered, then convened a meeting with her assistants. They met for an hour or so, apparently discussing whether to grant Rasheed immunity. They decided not to, and rescheduled their party without the guest of honor.

The media mob tried to interrogate Rasheed about not testifying. Mark and I shielded him.

"He wanted to, but we refused to allow it," Mark explained.

Naturally, the mob turned on me. I don't know what it is about me, but the nastier the reporters get, the more I enjoy it. There was no sense in trying to educate them about the grand-jury system; I've been trying to do that without success for years.

"You write your stories, I'll practice law," I said to the sea of pens, pads, cameras, lights, wires, and disembodied voices.

The hearing was delayed another week. Then we all gathered again at the same place.

While Mark and I jousted with the media mob outside, things were going our way in the grand-jury room. Behind the walls, the crucial testimony was coming from two experts. The first was Agustin A. Recio, professor of electrical engineering at the University of Miami. The second was Dr. Joe Davis, Miami's nationally respected medical examiner. Not surprisingly, the two men contradicted each other on the dangers of electricity. Dr. Recio, a man who has worked with electricity most of his life, downplayed the danger. Dr. Davis, a man who has worked with dead people most of his life, warned of its danger. Such contradictions are typical of expert testimony. You talk about what you know, and if what you know are thousands of electricians who have been shocked by high voltages and survived, you downplay it. But if what you know are hundreds of people who were shocked by sometimes low voltages and ended up on your autopsy slab, you take a more cautious view.

Typical of Dr. Recio's view was this exchange with Assistant State Attorney Leonard Glick:

> GLICK: If this [cord] were to be attached in the wall right now, could I tell by looking at it which wire, which end of the wire has the . . . current flowing through it?
> RECIO: No.
> GLICK: How would I be able to find that out?
> RECIO: Touching it.

That was a rather interesting instruction, especially considering that Dr. Davis had testified that one small pop of electricity could instantly stop the heart and kill you on the spot.

Fortunately, I think Dr. Recio had the most effective, and certainly the most colorful, testimony. After melting everyone's minds with the technical aspects of electricity, he told some "war" stories:

> I grabbed the two wires, and it was 480 volts, and I knew exactly what was happening. I guess I danced the strangest dance in my life because I was, my hand clasped, you know, fist clenched, really into the two conductors. . . . I couldn't command my muscles to open. I couldn't. I was kind of dancing . . . the only way I had was to bend myself and place a foot on top of one of the conductors and pull away, disconnect myself from that conductor . . . the individuals who were watching me at a distance thought I was monkeying around, playing around. In reality, I was being electrocuted by 480 volts! . . . My hands were slightly burned, very slightly burned, and I recuperated without assistance from anybody.

Even more dramatic, and also heartrending, was Dr. Recio's "Tutti-Frutti" story.

> We have a ferret, Tutti-Frutti. It's a beloved animal of my family. . . . One night we were watching TV and . . . we heard a noise in our room. . . . A minute later, seconds later, the noise is a little faster pace and like little legs. . . . I said to my wife, "Hey wait a moment." I rushed. She [Tutti-Frutti] had bitten the . . . extension that was connecting the fan . . . her fangs had pierced the thermoplastic material of this insulator. She made contact through her teeth with 115 volts, and apparently she could not open her mouth because of the contractions and because of her jumping. She got tangled in the wire . . . there was no way she could free herself! I pulled the plug and removed her from the cord. The animal was scared to death . . . but she survived! A little animal like that.

The point was that the 115 volts that little Tutti-Frutti took square in her mouth for "a full minute," was the same voltage Prentice Rasheed had hooked to his grid. If it couldn't kill a glorified rat, how could Rasheed have guessed it would kill Odell Hicks?

Dr. Joe Davis explained how. He said it had something to do with "ventricular fibrillation" and "dysrhythmias." In English, he translated that the heart has its own tiny electrical system, and any foreign electrical intrusion can interfere with the natural order and cause it to shut down. It's not so much the voltage as how it travels through the body. If the current goes in your finger and out your elbow, you're okay. If it hits you in a way that it passes through your chest, you could be history.

I don't think that the average person has any real concept of the dangers of electricity, how little it takes, really, in just the right phase of the cardiac cycle, to kill. I don't think people realize that, because most people have had shocks. They survive, and you can go down to Home Depot right now and you can buy, for minimal dollars, electric fence attachments. Now, the average person, what do they know about amperes, about voltage, so forth?

Dr. Davis had his own "war stories" to relate:

We've run into these cases of sexual aberrations [in which people attach] electrodes to the genitals and you find them [dead] in unusual positions, so these things have happened. . . . Those who get a fatal shock have up to ten seconds to do things. We have a collection of famous last words by these people, such as, he's standing in front of a mirror, gets a shock, and says to a fellow worker, "Look, I'm turning blue!" or "I'm all right," or "Get me out of here." . . . That ten seconds of consciousness that you have . . . is residual oxygen . . . in the brain to keep you going.

Dr. Davis added that although the crack in Hicks's system could have been fatal in its own right—it was for University of Maryland basketball star Len Bias—he didn't feel it played a part in the burglar's death.

Despite Dr. Davis's harsher view of the dangers of electricity, I don't think his testimony was damaging. His warnings about electricity caught everyone by surprise, and he himself acknowledged the public's ignorance on the subject. Both factors worked in Rasheed's favor.

In all, the grand jury met twice and heard thirteen hours of testimony. Even Rasheed's neighbors were called to the stand. But

"Tutti-Frutti" and the two doctors had made the biggest impression. When the testimony ended, the decision was placed into the hands of the grand jurors.

That's where our strategy of trying the case in the court of public opinion took hold. Normally, the jury would have followed the prosecution's lead and ruled to indict, but the prosecutors had been unusually balanced in this investigation. Because of this, and because the case had received so much publicity, I felt that the grand jurors might, for once, act on their own. Grand jurors are regular citizens, taken from all walks of life. Most of them probably knew Rasheed's story before they entered the courtroom. Their husbands, wives, children, and grandchildren no doubt had opinions on such a hotly debated case, and no doubt expressed their opinions to the family member sitting on the grand jury. Family members do things like that. They're not supposed to, but try to stop them.

At the close of each day, the judge admonishes the jurors, grand or regular, not to "talk to anyone about this case, or read any newspaper stories, or watch television reports." Despite that edict, it's a rare human being who can shoulder the burden of deciding the most sensational case in town without succumbing to the temptation to peek at the paper, glance at the television coverage, and/or run the facts by a best friend or trusted relative.

The Rasheed jurors deliberated for two days—giving them a full night to go home and let Aunt Zelma and the gang throw in their two cents' worth.

For Rasheed, Mark, and me there was nothing to do but wait. Waiting is the toughest part. For a good man like Prentice Rasheed, a man with no criminal record and no criminal intent, the pain of waiting is intensified. The body practically goes numb with fear. Would the nightmare be over or just beginning? Would Rasheed's decision to fight back against criminals result in his being considered one? The mind spins. You wait. You think. You fear. And the tension eats at you.

On October 28, 1986, two days short of a month after Odell Hicks's death, the Dade County Grand Jury reached a decision. Rasheed, Mark, and the media horde were all packed in my office. As the judge read the verdict in court, a television news producer radioed it to his reporter holding a walkie-talkie in my office. We heard the producer say that the grand jury had found that there was "no true bill," meaning there would be no manslaughter indictment against Prentice Rasheed. He practically leaped to the ceiling when we explained that he'd been cleared. Hell, I almost did too.

"I'd like to say to the American people, *Allah al-Akbar,* God is the greatest," Rasheed told the reporters. "I also want to say that I am very, very sorry, deeply sorry, that the life was taken of young Mr. Odell Hicks."

Did our strategy of trying the case in the court of public opinion make a difference?

"The only reason he got off was the public sentiment," declared Detective Spear.

The wording of the grand jury's decision reveals how close a call it was:

> Prentice Rasheed used deadly force . . . he was not justified in doing so. However, we find no evidence that Prentice Rasheed intended to use deadly force to protect his property. We find no evidence that he intended to kill or cause great bodily harm. . . . The deceased was electrocuted by a current of 115 volts. That is the current in our homes. Each of us has been shocked by such a current. None of us were seriously hurt by such shocks. The experts agreed that the majority of citizens would expect a shock from the device arranged by Prentice Rasheed, but would not expect it to cause death or great bodily harm. As average citizens, we agree with this finding . . . this grand jury feels very strongly that intentional killing solely to protect property . . . should never be tolerated. Deadly force is permitted and should only be tolerated when it is necessary to protect oneself or others from death or great bodily harm.
>
> We caution citizens who would protect either their persons or property with electrical devices such as rigged by Mr. Rasheed. We have learned just how dangerous a household current can be. Everyone is on notice that electrical devices designed to jolt you can kill you, and laws against such devices should be reviewed and enforced.
>
> We understand and share Mr. Rasheed's frustration with crime in our community. But the answer does not lie in taking the laws into our own hands. The answer lies in improving the capability of the criminal justice system to prevent crime and to take forceful action against crime.

All of which sounds noble and fair, but as I mentioned earlier, the only thing that saved Prentice Rasheed was the criminal record of the man he trapped, and possibly the color of Odell Hicks's black skin. Had Rasheed trapped Detective Spear's brother, a white fireman, you can bet he would have been indicted. And he may have been convicted of manslaughter or possibly second-degree murder in the subsequent trial. Therein lies the problem with blind traps and similar efforts by the public to fight back. The next Prentice Rasheed isn't going to have it so easy.

The grand jury's decision does tell us something good about our legal system. Under the law, the criminal background of Odell Hicks was not to be considered. Under the law, Prentice Rasheed's guilt or innocence should have been judged no differently had he trapped Charles Manson or Billy Graham. But the citizens of the jury were able to see through the "blind justice" and render their decision based upon exactly what happened.

Although courtrooms are filled with eloquent lawyers and wise judges, the most important cases continue to be decided by the average citizen.

EPILOGUE

Prentice Rasheed's celebrity continued for an unusually long time following the grand-jury verdict. Many of the television appearances, such as those on "60 Minutes" and "Oprah," came after the decision. He was awarded the honor of serving as the Grand Marshal of the King Mango Strut parade in Coconut Grove, and ran unsuccessfully for the Metro Dade County Commission. Someone even wrote a rap song about him.

As long as he wears his hat, he's widely recognized around South Florida. His store has become something of a landmark, and business has picked up. Rasheed, ever the businessman, has decided to capitalize on his small measure of fame by designing and marketing a burglar-prevention device.

He was burglarized again shortly after the verdict—someone shattered the storefront window—but as of 1989, hasn't been seriously robbed since.

Ironically, a few months after the grand jury rendered its decision on his case, a less favorable decision was reached on mine.

Rasheed was free, but I was going back to jail.

12

THE JAILING, PART II

There is an extremely difficult ethical problem here. We did the best we could.
—Judge Phillip Hubbart, Third District Court of Appeals, Florida

UNLIKE PRENTICE Rasheed, any attempt to plead my ongoing contempt case in the court of public opinion would have been fruitless. There wasn't a single area of the entire appeal process in which I would face a jury, grand or otherwise. The *Miami Herald* could have taken a poll and discovered that 100 percent of its readers believed that I shouldn't be prosecuted in the Sanborn case, and it wouldn't have mattered. Judges were deciding my fate, and I had disobeyed the orders of a member of their fraternity.

And judges usually don't care what their Aunt Zelma thinks.

On December 27, 1986, two days after Christmas, the Florida Supreme Court decided not to hear my contempt case at all. That enabled them to avoid the whole issue of attorneys being ordered to present false testimony, and they were able to do so without comment. When a state supreme court, or even the U.S. Supreme Court, decides not to hear a case, it's not obligated to explain why.

A month later I was back in the booking room, watching the flotsam and jetsam of society parade before me. Closer study of my fellow lawbreakers revealed that many were more dead than alive. Unlike last time, when it was all new and horrifying, I began to feel compassion. Those of us who were blessed with caring parents and opportunity know nothing of what it's like to grow up without either.

One of the first problems I encountered was that no one knew whether my crime was a misdemeanor or a felony. Contempt of court is hazy. The corrections officer called Judge Shapiro. He told them to book me as a felon. That meant I would be sent in with the murderers and rapists and other fun types. Shapiro was getting burned in the press once again for his insistence upon jailing me, and apparently was going to make me pay for it. If he could have found a way, I'm sure he would have ordered me to spend my thirty days on death row, in a cell with mass murderer Ted Bundy (which probably wouldn't have been all that dangerous, since Bundy had once asked me to represent him).

I was given another blue prison uniform and handed a toiletry kit provided by the Salvation Army. That's the most valuable possession a prisoner has. The kit contains soap, a plastic razor, a toothbrush, toothpaste, talcum powder, shaving cream, and after-shave lotion. I wouldn't need the razor and shaving cream. I decided to let my beard grow as a protest against a legal system that jailed an attorney for refusing to permit perjury.

I wasn't the only one protesting. Outside the Dade County Courthouse, Prentice Rasheed, Watergate burglar Frank Sturgis, and a young man named Angel Jorge had organized a rally. About forty people showed up, many waving signs saying FREE ELLIS RUBIN, and THIRTY DAYS FOR HONESTY? A second group picketed the jail. Overhead, an airplane circled the courthouse trailing a streamer that read, LET OUR LAWYER GO.

What was interesting was the makeup of the picket lines. There were blacks, WASPs, Latins, Italians, Jews, and Haitians standing together, forming a rare blend of Miami's cultural variety. The chanting protesters made great video for the television news shows, but it didn't help me much. Judge Shapiro was determined that I was going to do every second of thirty days. Even a personal appeal from my rabbi, nationally known Jewish leader Dr. Irving Lehrman, failed to elicit any mercy from the judge.

Shapiro was not without his own supporters, especially in judicial circles. "Rubin's personal view that the decision . . . is erroneous quite obviously cannot excuse his disobedience," agreed Judge Daniel Pearson of Florida's Third District Court of Appeals.

When it became apparent that this would be a real jail sentence, and not an in-and-out cup of coffee like last time, the reaction in the media intensified.

"It is the most bizarre episode yet in a stormy legal career spanning thirty-five years," wrote Charles Whited, the *Miami Herald*'s respected columnist. "And I, as part of the jailhouse press crowd, wondered at the necessity of clapping a veteran lawyer behind bars on rather flimsy cloth."

The next day, the *Herald* ran a lead editorial under the headline "No Good Cause to Jail Mr. Rubin":

> To see the Miami lawyer behind bars as a prisoner of conscience surely gives most folks in South Florida an image of justice gone awry. . . .
> It may be legal for a lawyer knowingly to assist in perjury, but it's not right. It's asinine . . . there is no good cause—none—for ordering a lawyer to suborn perjury.
> Something is dead wrong when blind obedience is called upon to govern the conduct of a lawyer over any other consideration—including principle. At a time when felons are often sentenced to house arrest or given light probation, locking up a lawyer for refusing to suborn perjury certainly sends the wrong signal to society.

The *Fort Lauderdale News/Sun-Sentinel,* which had written a supportive editorial the first time I was jailed, echoed similar sentiments in a second editorial published the same day as the *Herald*'s:

> A Miami judge has inexplicably found room to imprison an attorney whose only crime was to recognize that his duty to represent his client was outweighed by his duty to uphold the state's and his own code of ethics. . . . Rubin does not belong behind bars; his presence there mocks justice.

I was ordered to mock justice in a barracks at the Dade County Stockade. My new home had about forty bunks. On one end was a bathroom with showers, plus an area for watching television. On the other end was the guard and another television set. One TV broadcast in English, while the other was frozen on the Spanish station. The television sets blasted about twenty hours a day. The lights were on twenty-four hours a day. The only way anyone could sleep was to get a Walkman-type radio and play soft music through those spongy earphones. That, and wrap a towel around your eyes to keep out the light. Anybody walking through the prison at night and seeing cell upon cell of prisoners with earphones in their ears and towels wrapped around their heads would get the impression that some kind of laboratory experiment was going on. Actually, it *was* an experiment. An experiment in survival.

While there were methods to combat the noise and light, there was nothing to do about the smoke. Virtually everyone in the jail smoked. The thick haze hung in the air as in a scene from Dante's *Inferno.*

On the positive side, my fellow inmates treated me well. In fact, they were overprotective. From the first day I was there, the toughest black prisoner and the toughest Cuban prisoner took bunks to my left and right. When I showered, they stood guard and didn't allow anyone else inside. They never said why they did this, and I never asked them. I suspect that my history of championing both black and Cuban causes in Miami for nearly four decades must not have gone unnoticed, even among the prisoners.

The food was plentiful and wasn't that bad. It was the hours that were the killer. We ate breakfast at 3:30 A.M., lunch at 10:00 A.M., and dinner at 4:00 P.M. They gave you ten minutes to eat, no more, no less, and made you eat everything with a plastic spoon, including spaghetti. A fork or a knife could be used as a weapon.

I got into a brief scuffle with a prisoner over the use of the telephone. He went over his allotted ten minutes and I was getting pretty testy. The other prisoners broke it up before any damage was done. That was fortunate. A sixty-two-year-old attorney has no business taking on a prison-hardened man half his age.

I was taken out of the prison a few times to attend hearings on my ongoing cases. Like everything else, that too was a lousy experience. The corrections officers put me on a bus where I roasted for hours in the hot sun before it filled up and was allowed to leave. At the courthouse I was put into a holding cell while my colleagues wandered by to visit their clients. Many were startled to see me in the little monkey cage. The majority of my fellow attorneys wouldn't even look at me. Apparently, seeing me behind bars exposed their own shame for putting clients on the stand they knew were lying.

I was in court one morning for a pretrial conference regarding the Yahwehs, an eight-thousand-member black religious group who wear white robes and consider themselves to be the true Semites. They believe their leader, Yahweh Ben Yahweh, is the son of God and the long-awaited Jewish Messiah. The local Jews, of course, are appalled by this big, blue-eyed black man who claims to be their Messiah. Actually, Yahweh Ben Yahweh is a personable man with firm convictions. He's taken in people with no hope and no self-esteem, and given them a purpose. Whatever one feels about Yahweh Ben's claims, he and his followers have done wonders in the area of urban renewal. They've purchased acres of rundown ghetto property, chased out the drug dealers and muggers, rebuilt and refurbished the areas, and created profitable enterprises. The vandalism and burglary that blights other depressed-zone businesses, like Prentice Rasheed's, doesn't affect the Yahwehs. That's because everyone is scared to death of them. A former Yahweh member was convicted of murdering some people who refused to see the light during one of their restoration projects. The man then turned around and accused some Yahwehs of chopping off the heads of their enemies, adding to their menacing image.

I appeared that morning before Judge Ellen "Maximum" Morphonios, of all people. Appropriately, I stood in front of her wearing handcuffs. Instead of applauding my condition, she took one look and ordered my keeper to immediately "take those damn things off of Ellis!" She toughened up again when I asked for a delay in the upcoming trial because of my circumstances. She refused to grant it, and ordered me to interview witnesses at the jail. That wasn't a pleasant thought. The poor Yahwehs had a bad enough public image without having to truck down to the Dade County Jail to confer with their felonious attorney.

I was also escorted before Judge Ted Mastos for another hearing regarding the Yahwehs.

"How much longer is Sidney going to keep you there?" Mastos wondered. "He's made his point. This is uncalled for."

BACK AT the stockade, my first job assignment was to reorganize the prison law library. I took to that with a passion. Inactivity is the worst enemy of prisoners, and most take to their jobs with interest and dedication. My task was to sort through the partial sets of Florida law books that had been donated to the jail. I was given some assistants, and together we alphabetized and stacked the books. After that, they assigned me to teach history, English, and reading. Many of the prisoners couldn't read, which was doubtless one of the major reasons they were there to begin with. I enjoyed the teaching, and my classes were well attended. A great many of the men longed to make it on the outside without having to resort to crime. It was sad.

In contrast to the rest of world, prisoners dread the weekends. During the week we had our assigned jobs to keep us busy. On the weekends we were locked down and forced into dreaded inactivity. The weekends dragged on, and I began to long for Monday so I could get back to work. What a difference from the Monday-morning blues on the outside.

During our exercise periods in the yard, some of the prisoners played volleyball. The "Violators" were pitted against the "Perpetrators." I was the referee. In the middle of one game, a prisoner sidled up to me. He spoke out of the side of his mouth to avoid detection.

"You the lawyer?"

"That's me," I answered in a similar, side-of-the-mouth fashion.

"Do you defend murderers?"

"Sometimes."

"Will you defend me?" he asked.

"Did you kill someone?" I inquired.

"No, but when I get out, I'm gonna jack up two people."

"Get outta my face," I said, using the proper prison lingo.

Next to the surreal horror of the prisoner booking area, the most interesting place in the stockade was the visitors' room. That's where the prisoners and their visitors attempted and perfected every creative form of undetected public sex they could get away with. Bending down to pick up a dropped pen would reveal some startling pornographic sights under the tables. The soulful kissing also served another purpose. Women would transfer packs of cocaine from their mouths to the mouths of their beaux. Two were arrested for that while I was there.

After receiving my first visitors, I realized why the prisoners were so intent on getting the most they could out of the visits. The penalty for having a visitor was severe. Following every visit, the corrections officers would force us through an extensive strip-search. They poked and probed every orifice in our bodies. It was terribly degrading. After the first time, I called my family and said there would be no more visits. I'd rather be alone for a month than go through that again. Fortunately, I was able to have my wife added to the defense team. That enabled me to see her without subjecting me to the post-visit rape. Irene took advantage of the situation by hiding Hershey bars in her bra and smuggling them in to me.

We never tried the kissing method.

With all the smoke, coughing, strange hours, dangerous inmates, and what not that could have placed me in peril, it was something as simple as air conditioning that eventually did me in. The prison was freezing. People have different tolerances for temperature. What's comfortable for one person is deadly for another. This lesson in physiology explains why control of the thermostat is one of the most fiercely protected domains of inmate society. In the Darwinism of the prisons, the cold-weather forces have evolved into the winners. I'm a hot-weather person, so the relentless frigid air blowing upon my body began taking its toll. By the second week I was getting sicker and sicker. I called my doctor, Jay Levine, described my symptoms, and he became alarmed. He said I probably had pneumonia. He called the prison officials and told them I needed treatment. They said they would take me to Ward D, the prison unit at Jackson Memorial Hospital, the county's huge public medical facility. Ward D makes the booking room look like Club Med. The only thing worse than going to Ward D was going to the electric chair, and that's debatable because the electric chair is quicker. I refused, and they called Judge Shapiro. At first he said it was Ward D or nowhere. Then, apprised of my critical condition, he finally relented and allowed me to go to the Miami Heart Institute at my expense—and on my own time. That meant the clock stopped while I was in the hospital. When I was better, I would have to resume my full sentence with no time credited for the hospital stay. I was in the hospital a week, thus increasing my thirty-day sentence to thirty-seven days.

When I was ready to resume my sentence, they sent me to the North Dade Detention Facility to keep me from infecting the general prison population. There I had a choice of rooming with the trustees or going into an isolation cell. The trustee cell contained six men and was filthy. The temperature was about forty degrees. I figured I'd last one night in there. I chose the isolation cell. I could use the peace and quiet, I thought.

I was brought to a dismal room about ten feet long and nine feet wide, with a cot, a sink, a chrome toilet, and a steel mirror. When the door slammed behind me, it was pitch black. The only thing I could see was a sliver of light coming through the food tray slit in the door.

In a black cell, you have nothing to do but let your mind wander. It gave me an opportunity to think over my life and career and many of my past cases. It gave me a chance to try to determine who I was, what made me the way I was. As I sat in the dark, I remembered things I hadn't thought of in years. But one thing that really came back was being alone.

This wasn't the first time I was ordered into isolation. There was a small boy, more than a half-century before, who had suffered the same fate. And his only crime was being imperfect.

13

LOCKJAW

ONE OF my earliest childhood memories is of peering out a hospital window in Syracuse, New York, watching Dr. Harry Kallet drive up in a black Ford Model A sedan with tall, white tires. I was four years old, so it must have been sometime in 1929. It was snowing that afternoon, and the roads were icy. Dr. Kallet was always in a mad rush. Not surprisingly, his car entered the hospital grounds at a greater speed than the other cars. As I stood at the window, I saw the doctor's car slide across the road and careen off the shoulder, crashing into a sycamore tree. Dr. Kallet jumped out, grabbed his black bag, and walked briskly toward the hospital.

Dr. Kallet was our family doctor. He had come to the hospital to see me, and was standing in my room in a matter of minutes. As he examined me, I watched with fascination as bright red streaks of blood dripped from his bald head, rolled down his forehead and over his nose, into a bushy brown mustache that was slowly turning crimson. Although the doctor occasionally dabbed at the cut on his head with a white handkerchief, it was obvious that he paid little heed to the injury and the accident. He was far too busy to trifle with any interruption of his tight schedule.

I had been in the hospital for nearly a week, suffering from scarlet fever. The fever finally had broken, and Dr. Kallet hurried over to say that I could go home. He snapped his bag shut, turned, and dashed off, still bleeding from his bald head.

When I returned home, I couldn't talk right. In fact, I couldn't talk much at all. I'm not sure whether I had the problem before I went to the hospital, but for some reason the two events are associated in my mind.

I couldn't talk because I had a severe stammer, a disability often confused with stuttering. Stammerers frequently become stutterers, but in its purest form, stammering is by far the worse of the two. A stutterer repeats sounds machine-gun-style before the word comes out. For example, "house" becomes "hou, hou, hou, house." A stammerer can't even make the "hou" sound. Using the example just given, when the stammerer comes to the word "house" in a sentence, the face contorts, the mouth moves, and nothing, not a sound, emerges. It's a total block that stops speech dead.

For a stammerer, learning to stutter to get through a sentence is a step up.

Among the words I blocked on, "Ellis" was the most frequent—and the most frustrating. For virtually my entire childhood, up to adolescence, I was unable to say my own name.

My condition was a shame to my parents. They didn't understand what was wrong and kept bringing me to Dr. Kallet, a general practitioner. In the early 1930s there were few speech therapists. Most parents took their stammering or stuttering children to medical doctors whose understanding of the handicap was limited. (Even today, medical science hasn't found a definite cause, or a positive cure.) Dr. Kallet did his best to help, but his attempts at finding a cure now appear barbaric.

The worst of these was when he persuaded my parents to send me off to a farm where I would be isolated from my family and forced to live like a monk in a world of silence. The theory was that I needed to rest my throat and facial muscles and escape the environment that was supposedly causing the problem.

My parents dutifully located a middle-aged farm couple who lived in the frozen boondocks of upstate New York. They were complete strangers and had advertised for help, or boarders, in the Syracuse newspaper. These strangers were to be my new "parents" for a year. My mother packed my little blue suitcase, bundled me up in corduroy knickers, black earmuffs, and dark red mittens, and led me to our Buick.

I felt like an unwanted dog being taken to the pound.

We drove three hours in the snow to reach the farm. I was bewildered by it all, but my inability to talk made me too ashamed to stammer out a protest. After arriving at our destination, my parents chatted awhile, handed over my things, and got back into the car to drive away. I ran out to them, clutching my mother's leg in a death grip and screaming hysterically. My mother, fighting her own tears, picked me up and handed me to the farmer. She climbed into the car again and they drove away. Although my parents explained that I was only going away for a "long visit," I knew something was wrong and suspected that I would never see my father and mother again.

That night I was placed into a gray room that contained little more than a small bed. I cried myself to sleep.

All that's left in my memory regarding the farm couple are a few fleeting images of a husky man in a red checkered shirt and an equally sturdy woman in a white apron. I rarely said anything to them, and they didn't talk much to me. In fact, they didn't talk much to each other. I can't remember whether they were mean or nice, just that they were quiet. I was the only child on the farm, and I don't remember any visitors ever coming by. The atmosphere was bleak and isolated.

Life on the farm consisted of getting up at dawn, collecting chicken eggs, milking cows, shoveling out the barn, chopping down trees, gathering firewood, and remaining silent. Each day seemed to last a hundred years. I was only five, so I don't know how big a tree I could have chopped, or how much help I was, but I remember working from sunup to sundown.

The animals were my only friends, but I quickly learned not to become too attached. I was horrified when one of my friends, a chicken, pig, or turkey, was slaughtered for dinner.

I didn't attend school, and although my mother wrote letters, I didn't speak to my parents the whole year. I don't know whether the couple had a phone or not, but it didn't matter. I was afraid of telephones and was unable to say one word into the receiver.

Despite the slow passing of the days, the seasons eventually ran their cycle. In late fall, just as the maple trees were becoming bare, my parents drove up. I was thrilled to see them, and was overjoyed when they said they were taking me home.

When I returned to Syracuse, my parents were crushed to discover that I still couldn't talk. In fact, I was worse than before! The year in isolation had accomplished nothing. That night, fearing a return to the farm, I gathered up my things in a small wooden wagon and ran away. I made it to the fire station, where a beefy fireman with a big smile figured out what I was up to and called me over. I couldn't talk to him, but somehow he learned my name and address and took me home. My grandfather gave me a spanking.

I was so angry I set fire to an empty field of tall, dry grass near my house. The fire grew into a sweeping blaze that required two fire trucks to extinguish. I was quickly fingered as the suspect and my grandfather beat me again. After the fire trucks left, I grabbed a broom and went out into the field to beat out the smoldering chunks of grass. That only fanned the flames and started the fire again. Back came the fire trucks, sirens blaring. My grandfather spanked me for the third time that day and locked me in the garage, where I was forced to spend the night on the floor.

Life was going from bad to worse, and it was all because I couldn't talk right.

My parents continued to seek Dr. Kallet's advice. I went through a series of "cures," all of which would bring nightmares to anyone who has suffered a similar speech impediment. I was told to think before I spoke, to think out every word, every sentence. That merely increased the fear and the stammer. I was told to take a deep breath and talk only as I exhaled. That was silly.

I was instructed to tap my toe as I spoke, to get some kind of rhythm. It didn't help.

My parents were instructed to purchase a metronome, and I was supposed to speak in time with the ticking. That may have helped Liberace learn to play the piano, but it did nothing for me.

My family eventually moved from Syracuse to Binghamton, and I escaped Dr. Kallet and his "cures."

As I grew older, my mind began to develop its own solution. Stammerers develop a "tic" or "starter." That's a word or sound used as a crutch to get us through a sentence. These are the common words and phrases—"you know," "really," "right," "know what I mean," and "uh"—that infest many people's language, even those without diagnosed speech impediments. Stammerers also develop keen vocabularies. When the tongue freezes, the mouth says "uh" while the mind searches its memory bank for a synonym to replace the blocked word. After a while, a stammerer can get very good at hiding the problem.

For example, if someone asked my name, my answer would be, "My name is, El, uh, uh, Rubin. And my first name is, El, Ellis."

I also began to go to the library and read everything I could about stammering and stuttering. To my dismay, I learned that the doctors of the time believed there were four main causes:

1. Scarlet fever having burned out some of the nerve connections.
2. Being forced to become right-handed, as was the practice with left-handed children in those days. The rationale for the stammering being that screwing up the brain-to-hand connection also damaged the brain-to-tongue pathways.
3. Suffering nerve damage as a result of having been delivered with forceps.
4. Suffering a head injury.

Besides the bout with scarlet fever, I was a left-handed forceps baby who had suffered a head injury from falling out of a moving automobile. And I had been forced to learn to write with my right hand.

This discovery made me believe I was physically a mess, and further increased the fear.

Yet, as I continued to grow, I began to notice some strange aspects of my handicap. When I was ten, I realized I could speak clearly and without hesitation into a telephone—as long as I held the hook down with my hand. The second I released the hook and heard a human voice, my mind froze and my tongue scrambled. When I put the hook back down, I was as articulate as President Roosevelt.

I could also speak when alone, and to my mirror image, but couldn't talk to people. Reading aloud to others was impossible.

My relationships with schoolmates and neighborhood children were naturally strained. Stammerers and stutterers probably face more abuse than those with any other handicap. If a child is blind or crippled, there's a natural sympathy. If a child talks like Porky

Pig, or Roger Rabbit, it's open season. To escape the taunts, I buried myself in sports and literature. I was drawn to books about great lawyers and politicians, people who were outstanding orators. I envisioned myself in their place, giving rousing speeches to cheering throngs.

Unfortunately, I couldn't spend all my time playing ball and hiding inside my imagination. I had to face the outside world. This led to the inevitable humiliation that is burned into the memories of all stammerers and stutterers. Describing these painful moments never captures the embarrassment one feels. One incident stands out in my mind.

When I was twelve, my father gave me a Flexible Flyer sled. He sold them at his army-navy store, so he brought one of the expensive toys home. The Flexible Flyer was the Cadillac of sleds. Most sleds were made from rigid steel and went straight. The Flexible Flyer had joints and rivets that allowed it to be steered. Not only that, it would fly like you wouldn't believe! I ran out to the big hill where all the kids used their sleds and zipped down a few times, weaving in and out and feeling like a million. Then a dark cloud named Shibley Hyder appeared. I remember his name to this day. He was an Armenian brute who was the neighborhood bully. We were about the same age, but Shibley was twice as big. He and his gang of mini-thugs knocked me down and took my sled.

"Don't worry about Ru, Ru, Ru, Rubin," he said. "He can't even te, te, te tell anybody who ta, ta, ta, took it!"

Everyone laughed. I ran home crying, as much from the humiliation as from losing the sled. I told my father what happened, and he drove over to the Hyder home that evening and retrieved the Flexible Flyer.

I had my sled, but I couldn't go to the hill anymore. Shibley vowed to dismember me for telling on him.

In junior high, there were two kids who constantly taunted me. Their names are also burned into my memory—Billy Aykroyd and Robert Pierpont. They ridiculed my speech impediment by calling me "Lockjaw."

I had only two close friends. As I mentioned in the introduction to this book, one was Rodman Serling. He would grow up to become a great author and screenwriter, and the producer and creator of the classic television series "The Twilight Zone." My other friend was another boy who lived nearby, a big Polish kid named Steve Skomskie. Steve had the bright idea to have me challenge Billy Aykroyd to a boxing match. I did, and Steve set the date for a month away. Steve had two pair of boxing gloves, a heavy bag and a speed bag in his basement, so he became my trainer. His training consisted of beating me senseless every afternoon after school. Rod also took an interest in the fight and would stop by to offer eloquent words of encouragement. Rod additionally took it upon himself to spread exaggerated tales of my boxing prowess around, a strategy aimed at sowing fear in the mind of Billy Aykroyd.

When the day came for the fight, I was petrified. I wouldn't get out of bed, and Steve and Rod had to come get me. They practically dragged me to Steve's house.

"If you don't show up, you'll be worse off than before," Rod exclaimed. "Everyone will think you're a coward. You have enough problems already. You shouldn't have to deal with that too!"

Thanks, Rod.

When I arrived at Steve's house, I discovered that he had built a ring and surrounded it with chairs. Seated in the chairs were twenty kids. Steve was charging five cents a head for ringside seats, a nice piece of change for a child in 1937.

We waited and waited, but Billy Aykroyd never showed. I was thrilled. Steve and I put on an exhibition, but without the element of hate, the audience screamed for their nickels back. Steve refused, and things got ugly. Rod and I slipped away before the riot.

The next day at school, I was a hero and Billy Aykroyd was taunted for being a coward. For a few days, I could even talk some. It was the damnedest thing. Unfortunately, as the memory of the non-victory faded, the fears returned and my tongue twisted up.

Back to the library I went, reading about lawyers and stammerers. I read somewhere that the great Athenian orator, Demosthenes, had been a stammerer or a stutterer and had cured his problem by putting pebbles in his mouth, going to the Mediterranean shore, and shouting speeches over the crashing sound of the waves. I began putting marbles in my mouth and speaking to my mirror image. I practiced that way and actually made progress.

Then came high school. That standard rite of passage has rocked the self-esteem of millions of teenagers. Whether the cause is an ill-timed plague of acne, a nose grown huge overnight, weight problems, an inability to deal with puberty and the opposite sex, paralyzing shyness, physical or emotional immaturity, or any of a hundred others, high school can be brutal. With me, these typical hurdles combined to tangle up my tongue as never before. High school became a nightmare of dodging teachers' orders to read out loud, skipping classes when I was supposed to give speeches, and burying myself in the library. Sports continued to provide a physical escape and boosted my sagging confidence. I was especially good at baseball and track. But still, high school for a stammerer was the pits.

When I was a senior, I had another humiliating experience. I was working in my father's store, and wasn't paying attention one day when my father suddenly appeared with some business friends. Stammerers and stutterers spend their lives anticipating situations either to avoid them or prepare set speeches to handle them. This time I was caught off-guard with an unexpected introduction.

"And what's your name, young man?" the stranger said.

I completely froze up. I couldn't say "Ellis." Seventeen years old, and I couldn't say my name. I panicked and began to sweat. I ran to the rest room, sobbing. My father was terribly embarrassed. I decided I was going to leave Binghamton forever the day I graduated.

Within a week, I inadvertently found the way out. My old boxing coach, Steve Skomskie, decided to catch a train to New York City to take the qualification exams to become a navy fighter pilot. He asked me to accompany him on the trip. When we arrived at the recruiting post at 90 Church Street, Steve said, "You might as well take the tests with me, Ellis." I did, and found that all those years hiding in the library paid off. I scored high and was accepted. Ironically, Steve was found to have sugar in his urine, and failed.*

When I returned home, my father couldn't believe it. It was 1943. America was in the middle of World War II. There was much concern in the Rubin family about how America was faring if the navy was so desperate that they accepted me into officer candidate school.

*My friend Steve Skomskie cured his medical problem, went to the U.S. Naval Academy at Annapolis, and achieved his dream of becoming a fighter pilot. In the 1960s, Steve took a test flight from the Key West Naval Air Station. He flew into a cloud over the Bermuda Triangle and was never seen again. Not surprisingly, Rod Serling based many of his television programs and written stories on pilots disappearing into clouds. He also wrote one of the most famous boxing stories of all time, *Requiem for a Heavyweight.*

"How can you give orders?" my father asked. "You can't even talk. What if you have to radio for help?" His question became my incentive.

After I graduated from high school, the navy sent me to Trinity College, an Episcopalian school in Hartford, Connecticut. At Trinity, an amazing transformation occurred. When I put on the crisp white navy uniform, most of my stammer vanished. The uniform and the authority that came with it were the ultimate "tic." I could memorize orders and shout commands without missing a beat. I still had to duck out of general curriculum classes that involved oral readings or speeches, but when placed in a position of command, I could communicate. Some call that raising the "necessity level."

Halfway through the term, the navy found itself overstocked with pilots. The eight hundred men in training at Trinity would be given a test. The top 10 percent would remain in college and become deck officers, while the rest, 720 men, would be shipped out to the fleet immediately. It was 1944 and the war was raging. When the test results were posted, eight hundred men crowded around the bulletin board. I could smell the nervous sweat in the air.

Once again, those years hiding in the library paid off. I finished seventy-eighth, just squeezing under the eighty-man limit.

The navy transferred me to Holy Cross, a Catholic college in Worcester, Massachusetts. Aside from giving me a general education and a military education, the navy was giving me a well-rounded religious education as well.

The pressure to succeed at Holy Cross remained intense. Each Friday the officer candidates were given tests on the information dispensed that week. Fail one test, and out you went to the fleet. No consideration was given to a stammerer ducking classes to save himself from embarrassment. I was forced to learn a new trick. I discovered that if I memorized pages in the textbooks, I could repeat them from memory without blocking up. For some reason, the route from the memory banks to the tongue bypassed whatever my problem was. It was a tremendous amount of work, but I memorized and survived.

In fact, I began to memorize my entire life, like an actor memorizing a role. Dates, social activities, sports—everything I did was planned. When I told a date, "I love the way your eyes sparkle in the moonlight," it came from the script. When I said, "Nice shot, Chuck," to a guy on the basketball court, it was playacting. It was a bizarre way to live, but it beat the alternative.

I graduated from Holy Cross on June 20, 1946. It was my twenty-first birthday. I became a college graduate, an ensign in the navy, and earned the right to vote all on the same day.

By that time the war was over, and America was paring down its armed forces. I served on LST 861—"LST" standing for Landing Ship, Tank.

My plan was to remain in the navy for life, forever hiding my handicap behind the stripes on my shoulders and memorized commands. It wasn't to be. There were simply too many soldiers with no war to fight. This time I couldn't beat the cut by taking a test. The postwar navy had the luxury of weeding out everyone but Annapolis-trained officers. I was assigned to the reserves and shipped home to Binghamton.

No longer able to hide behind a uniform, and back at the scene of my worst memories, the stammering demon once again possessed me. The naval officer in the smart white duds was a memory. In his place was the stammering boy who was made fun of by everyone.

After moping around for almost a year, I decided to escape Binghamton and use the GI Bill to pursue my lifelong dream of becoming an attorney. I had licked the stammering problem before by focusing my mind on a greater purpose. Maybe I could do it again.

I chose the University of Miami law school for a number of reasons. It was new, class attendance was secondary to passing tests, and graduates weren't required to pass the state bar exam. The class-attendance waiver was crucial. That enabled me to do my dodge again, ducking out of public-speaking classes and hiding my handicap. I located a speech therapist on the campus and began secretly taking classes. By then, however, it was apparent that my problem was psychological. It was a blush that publicly exposed my feelings of shyness and low self-esteem.

I survived law school and graduated in 1951. As I mentioned in the introduction to this book, the great New York attorney Sam Leibowitz gave a stirring speech at my commencement, inspiring me to ignore my handicap and go after my dream of becoming a trial lawyer. Miraculously, the stammering and stuttering all but vanished when I stood before my first jury.

They have never returned.

* * *

IT'S DIFFICULT to analyze accurately the factors that sculpt one's own life, especially when that life was molded by a struggle with a handicap. That's a job for psychiatrists and psychologists. Still, as I lay in the darkness of the isolation cell in the North Dade Detention Center, I tried to determine what effect my early life had upon me.

My navy training had a direct correlation with my imprisonment. The navy had instilled in me an unwavering sense of right and wrong, an attribute that, even before my jailing, had forced me into conflict with the often crooked world of American law. My multifaceted religious training was also a factor. Whenever I faced a routine ethical or moral problem, I recalled the Navy's simple honor code at Holy Cross:

"I will not lie, cheat, or steal, nor will I tolerate it in others."

One can't begin to imagine how difficult it is for a lawyer to hold on to that credo.

The lingering effects of my long battle with a speech dysfunction run even deeper. The two things a stutterer or stammerer fears most are public speaking and confrontations. The ultimate fear would be a public confrontation. As an outspoken defense attorney, I've spent the last thirty-eight years speaking publicly and being involved in heated confrontations. And I've taken it far beyond the courtroom. I've been grilled under the hot camera lights by investigative journalists from such television programs as "60 Minutes," "Nightline," "West 57th," and "Good Morning America." I've been involved in heated debates on virtually every major television talk show, including "Oprah," "Donahue," "Larry King Live," "Today," and "Good Morning America."

For some reason, I find that I now relish the opportunity to do the exact thing that terrified me as a child and young adult.

My wife feels I'm compelled to test myself continually under intense pressure to make sure that the stammer isn't lingering inside, waiting for an opening to return. Perhaps. But I'm reminded of the great athlete Glenn Cunningham. Cunningham's legs were burned in a schoolhouse fire when he was a child, and he was bedridden for nearly two years. He came close to losing the ability to walk. After willing himself out of bed, he began not only to walk, but to run. He ran and ran, until he could run a mile faster than any human ever had before him.

I'm sure that Glenn Cunningham was fueled by the memory of a sick little boy with withered legs, lying helplessly in bed, just as I can never forget a lonely, silent little boy on an unfamiliar farm, collecting chicken eggs on a freezing morning.

AS MUCH as the stammering problem and the navy experience affected me, they only formed the foundation of my life. The structure was built by my subsequent years battling in court, and the endless string of bizarre cases that fate tossed my way.

Continuing my forced introspection in the jail isolation cell, I turned the dial of my small radio and picked up the broadcast of a National Basketball Association game on a distant station. I heard the announcer mention something about the game being blacked out on local television.

Sports blackouts. Now there was a memory.

14

BUSTING THE BLACKOUTS, PART I:

Don Quixote and King Alvin I

ON A quiet Saturday afternoon in April 1970, I received a call from a local newspaper reporter.

"Ellis, the Orange Bowl Committee just voted to lift the blackout of next year's game."

I sat up in my chair.

"They claim you had nothing to do with it," the reporter continued, laughing. "Can you believe that?"

That evening on the news, the chairman of the committee, W. Keith Phillips, looked into the camera and said, "In the overall picture, Rubin's action had no effect whatsoever in the decision."

I couldn't help laughing myself. For the previous three years I had hounded the Orange Bowl Committee to lift the local television blackout of the annual college football game. I filed unsuccessful lawsuits. I organized fan groups and card and letter campaigns. I spoke before a half-dozen area city commissions and persuaded them to pass anti-blackout resolutions.

For three years the committee stood firm. The Miami taxpayers who paid for the Orange Bowl Stadium, and their counterparts all over South Florida, remained the only football fans in the nation who couldn't watch the sold-out New Year's Day game on television.

Then, suddenly, the committee had a change of heart—one day before I was scheduled to debate the issue with them on television.

Feeling victorious, I was ready to retire my anti-blackout activities on a high note. But when I told my family the news, my thirteen-year-old son Mark was not impressed.

"Daddy, you've got to lift the Super Bowl blackout next."

Coincidentally, the 1971 National Football League championship game, Super Bowl V, was set to be contested in Miami's Orange Bowl Stadium.

That promised a confusing scenario.

On January 1, millions of South Floridians would be able to turn on their televisions and watch in blackout-lifted glee as the University of Nebraska attempted to overpower Louisiana State University in the 1971 Orange Bowl.

Sixteen days later, when the Dallas Cowboys and Baltimore Colts took the field for Super Bowl V, the televisions were once again slated to go black.

Same stadium. Same sport. Same oblong-shaped, laced-up leather ball.

Different TV rules.

From the fans' perspective, it didn't add up.

THE ORANGE Bowl Committee members were choirboys compared to the exclusive fraternity of twenty-six arrogant multimillionaires who owned National Football League teams and ran the professional league. Aside from their wealth and business acumen, this coterie of macho men had the good sense to hire a man who is widely accepted as being the best sports commissioner ever—Alvin Ray "Pete" Rozelle. Tanned, silky smooth, and always impeccably dressed, Rozelle is a public-relations genius. He is given much of the credit for the tremendous growth in power, wealth, and popularity of football. Sportcaster Howard Cosell, in his book *I Never Played the Game*, observed about the recently retired NFL chief, "Never in my lifetime in sports has anyone commanded and controlled the media like Pete Rozelle."

The NFL owners wanted their precious blackouts in place, and media darling Pete Rozelle was their champion to keep them. A quick perusal of the law books revealed that suits dating back to the early 1950s had been filed in various cities, trying to lift the NFL blackouts. All had failed. The courts ruled that the NFL was considered a private enterprise that had the right to operate as it saw fit. The NFL's argument was that the live, paying crowd at the stadium would diminish if the local team's home games were shown on television for free. Even if the stadium was sold out, the NFL felt that lifting the blackout would cause fans to stop buying tickets to future games and instead gamble that it would be a sellout and end up being televised.

My argument was the same one I offered concerning the Orange Bowl. The Super Bowl had become an event of such magnitude that it transcended the sport. The game would forever be a sellout. The NFL's great success with its championship game had outdated the need to shut out the local fans to protect the live gate.

The NFL didn't see it that way.

Realizing that I could expect little help from the courts, the only hope I had was to attack Pete Rozelle in his area of greatest strength—public opinion. And this time it was going to take more than a handful of resolutions from South Florida city commissioners.

I was on active naval reserve duty in Charleston, South Carolina, when the game plan developed. Meandering through a sporting-goods store, I ran across the most beautiful pair of white leather track shoes I'd ever seen. I tried them on and they felt terrific.

An idea lit up my brain like the proverbial lightbulb.

Returning to Miami, I took out a map and charted a course from the Orange Bowl east to U.S. 1, and north seventy-five miles up the Gold Coast of Florida. My calculations took me near Riviera Beach, a small community north of Palm Beach. The seventy-five miles was the radius of the television blackout.

I was forty-five then, but thanks to the naval reserve training, I was in good shape. I began running every morning and afternoon until I could do five miles without stopping.

In midsummer I announced my plan to jog from North Palm Beach to the Orange Bowl to gain support for lifting the Super Bowl blackout. Volunteers, including my four children and my ever-present wife, Irene, would fan out over every city and community along the way and ask people to sign petitions. The plan quickly fell into place. Three North Miami Beach high school football players, Ronald Book, Jeff Mell, and Steve Kortvese, offered to run with me. People called from Jupiter, Lake Park, Palm Beach, Lake Worth, Lantana, Boca Raton, Delray Beach, Fort Lauderdale, Hollywood, North Miami, and elsewhere to assist with the petitions.

On the morning of the kickoff, the media were out in force. Miami's CBS affiliate assigned reporter Ike Seamans and a camera crew to follow me part of the way. (Seamans won an Associated Press award for conducting his interview while running beside me. He later became an NBC correspondent.) Local reporters and camera crews met me at almost every stop.

Although I limited my running to five miles each morning, and another five each evening, the pace was killing me. The Florida summer heat, even in the off-hours, was blistering. During my training, I didn't anticipate the effects of running on concrete or that the crowds and interviews would sap my strength. Besides, I couldn't ease up because the cameras were often pointed at me.

I nearly collapsed, but refused to give up. The support along the way was encouraging. Cars honked, people cheered, everybody wanted to see the Super Bowl. Finally, a week after starting, I made it to the Orange Bowl, clutching the petitions. A crowd was waiting, and the police opened the locked gates to allow me to jog in. Once inside, I looked around, half-dead from exhaustion, and realized there was no one to present the petitions to! None of the city commissioners, and certainly no one from the NFL, was fool enough to be there waiting to receive them. I ended up presenting the petitions at the next city commission meeting. The jog, along with a simultaneous mail-in campaign, resulted in close to 75,000 signatures.

The NFL hung tough. Miami Dolphins owner Joe Robbie was particularly vehement in his pro-blackout comments. The consensus was that I could jog straight to hell for all the NFL cared; they weren't going to lift the blackout. What they failed to understand was that it wasn't Ellis Rubin they were fighting. The "Ban the Blackout" movement was mushrooming and included the NFL's most vital support group, the "couch potato" television sports fans.

When it was convenient for the NFL, even Pete Rozelle publicly admitted the importance of the television fans. In a 1982 letter to Cosell, reprinted in the sportscaster's book, Rozelle defended the New York Giants' move from New York City to New Jersey by stating that "ninety percent or more of the Giants fans continued to follow their team in the same manner as before—on television. This is true of all our other NFL suburban moves."

What Rozelle didn't say was that these television fans put billions of dollars in the NFL owners' pockets by enabling the commissioner to negotiate huge contracts with NBC, ABC, and CBS. Yet, when it came time to return the favor by lifting the local blackouts of sold-out Super Bowl games, Rozelle turned his back on these very same fans.

It didn't make sense, from a business or public-relations standpoint.

I continued to receive calls and letters encouraging me to keep fighting. The most touching of these came from people in hospitals, shut-ins, and sailors stationed on ships, including the crew of the USS *Calcaterra* at Key West. I instructed everyone to send letters to Pete Rozelle at league headquarters, 410 Park Avenue, New York, and to write the owners of every NFL team.

As the game approached, I devised a compromise. I promised Rozelle that in return for lifting the blackout, South Florida television viewers would contribute one dollar each to a fund to buy any unsold Super Bowl tickets. If the game was a sellout, which it would be, the money would be donated to Variety Children's Hospital and the NFL Players' Pension Fund.

Sick children and battered NFL veterans. Rozelle couldn't turn his back on them.

He did. The hospital and pension plan donations were rejected.

I then began to ask questions. I wanted a precise breakdown of who actually were offered tickets to the NFL's premier game. Some sportswriters followed up and investigated. It turned out that a huge batch went to the owners, and similar blocks were offered to politicians ranging from city commissioners to the governor and senators. Most of the remaining tickets went to corporate fat cats. It turned out that the good old American blue-collar sports fans who supported the teams during exhibition games and the regular season were booted from their seats and left to peer through a knothole in the fence when it came to the Super Bowl.

This revelation didn't sit well with the bread-and-butter fans. When the news of who was filling the seats at the Super Bowl was released, the "Ban the Blackout" movement reached new heights.

There were other sticky questions to consider. Why did the NFL have an antitrust exemption? How much did the television networks pay the NFL? Even the players wanted to know the answer to that. I was pounding away, making the NFL executives hot under the collar.

But still, they refused to budge.

As the game neared, I filed two lawsuits based upon the Sherman Antitrust Act. The federal and state courts ruled that I wasn't a proper Sherman Antitrust plaintiff because I couldn't show any monetary damages resulting from being prevented from watching the Super Bowl on television. Such legal rulings are virtual step-by-step directions on how to refile a suit. I explained my plight to the media, and sure enough, a motel owner from Fort Lauderdale named Rubin called and asked to be the plaintiff. He said that because of the blackout, his customers deserted his lodging for motels outside the seventy-five-mile blackout zone in order to see the game on hotel TV.

Bingo. He could show monetary damages directly relating to the blackout.

I filed suit on behalf of the motel owner, naming Pete Rozelle and the television network as defendants. The case came before Arthur Franza, a state circuit court judge who had just been appointed. It was Franza's first case. The emergency hearing was set for the Saturday morning prior to the Sunday game.

Despite gaining a hearing date, I still had a big hurdle to overcome. Rozelle had to be served with papers to appear. That wouldn't be easy. The commissioner spent the early part of Super Bowl week in New York. When he arrived in Miami, he was advised of my desire to serve him, and made himself scarce. I knew that every Friday before the Super Bowl, Rozelle gave a "State of the NFL" press conference. He would have to surface.

Deputy Constables Joe Reitmeyer and Al Carballosa were in charge of serving the subpoena. They tried to crash the press conference at the Americana Hotel, but were prevented from entering by two huge ex-NFL players guarding the door. When the event ended, the NFL guards momentarily retreated and Carballosa darted inside. He made a beeline for Rozelle. The guards spotted him, as did a third behemoth protecting Rozelle.

"These three monsters came charging after me," recalls Carballosa, now a Dade County police detective. "I jumped over one table and up on another to get away from them. I mean, I'm a big guy, six-two, two hundred pounds, but those goons were each about six feet five, 280 pounds. Their necks were the size of my thigh. I'm hopping tables and the crowd is scattering, people are screaming, pens and pads are flying, and reporters are being knocked down. I tell you, it was something! I kept one eye on the gorillas and another on Rozelle. The commissioner was trying to duck out a back door. I was determined to get to him before he made it. I did, and handed him the summons.

"Afterwards, I was pretty pissed," Carballosa continues, voice rising. "I was a law-enforcement officer, an officer of the court. They were obstructing justice. Who is Pete Rozelle? He doesn't have any special power over the law. That was, what, eighteen years ago? Well, I'm still pissed!"

Rozelle wasn't too happy either.

An extremely annoyed Alvin Rozelle appeared in court the next morning. So did the Super Bowl media horde. Accompanying Rozelle was a choir of attorneys. He had NFL attorneys, network television attorneys, assistant attorneys. It was like a bar convention. When the judge arrived, he asked to see us in his chambers. We packed into the room, Rozelle and his army of legal muscle on one side, and me on the other.

Judge Franza appealed to Rozelle's generosity. He pointed out that the game was sold out and that the Super Bowl had become such a big event it would always be sold out. He asked Rozelle to voluntarily lift the blackout.

The commissioner huddled with his legion of lawyers. He emerged looking grim. Rozelle explained to the judge that he had no option but to uphold the desire of the owners, and the owners were adamantly against lifting the blackout. He said his job would be in jeopardy if he went against their wishes. The judge would have to rule.

Judge Franza offered alternative solutions, asking Rozelle if he could show the game on a delayed basis, starting the televised version one to four hours after the game started. Rozelle said he couldn't do it.

We must have stayed in the judge's chambers for two or three hours, trying to work out a compromise. Rozelle stood firm. South Floridians were going to see the Super Bowl over Pete Rozelle's dead body.

Judge Franza gave up and ordered us back into the courtroom.

We proceeded to argue law, none of which seemed to apply either way. Our forefathers certainly didn't consider television when they wrote the Constitution, nor did they anticipate a new national holiday called Super Sunday. Even so, I was sure Franza was going to rule in my favor. He could have been the biggest hero in Florida and could have carved out a place in judicial history by making a monumental ruling in his very first case. To my dismay, he ruled that although the blackout violated the Sherman Antitrust Act, he didn't have jurisdiction to rule on a federal issue. There were audible groans in the gallery.

Round One went to the NFL. The Colts beat the Cowboys 16–13 on a last-minute field goal that 2.5 million potential television viewers in South Florida didn't see. Channel 7 in Miami showed its audience a forgettable cowboy movie called *The Outriders* instead.

All wasn't lost. Dave Anderson, the talented *New York Times* sports columnist (and a fellow Holy Cross graduate), wrote a sympathetic article on my efforts, under the headline "Don Quixote and King Alvin I." The amusing image he created of me waving my sword at the windmills of Alvin Rozelle's NFL fortress was appropriate.

ROUND TWO was fought in New Orleans. I was invited by a hotel owner named Johnny Campo to fight the blackout of the 1972 Super Bowl in his city. I resurrected my jogging campaign and charted out a seventy-five-mile course from Baton Rouge down the banks of the Mississippi to New Orleans. I figured that had to be better than U.S. 1. I was wrong. Louisiana is probably the only place where you can run through mud and still get dust in your eyes. But Louisiana is prime football country, and the support along the way was enthusiastic. The anti-blackout fervor was especially hot in Baton Rouge. That football-crazy city is the home of Louisiana State University, a college football power. LSU fans were hellbent on seeing the Super Bowl, and applied heavy pressure on the NFL. They pounded the first chink into the NFL armor and gave me my first victory. A new measurement was taken, and someone discovered that Baton Rouge was actually eighty miles from Tulane Stadium, the site of Super Bowl VI. That fired up the locals like never before, and damned if the NFL didn't decide they were out of the blanket of darkness. The blackout was lifted in Baton Rouge.

The NFL forces retreated and stood their ground in New Orleans. The local courts tossed out my lawsuits, and the game stayed off the New Orleans tube.

Round Two was a draw. At Tulane Stadium, the Dallas Cowboys crushed the Miami Dolphins 24–3 as happy Baton Rouge fans watched in the privacy of their homes.

ROUND THREE was the NFL's Super Bowl Waterloo. The 1973 Super Bowl VII shifted to Los Angeles, the nation's number-two television market. The Los Angeles Coliseum blackout radius encompassed a huge potential audience of 10 million viewers, comprising a mega-source of advertising revenue for the local and network TV stations. Blacking out such a colossal market would actually hurt the NFL. The blockbuster ratings of the Super Bowl, increasing every year, would be hamstrung by throwing a blanket over the nation's second-largest television audience.

Even the television networks were beginning to chew on the Super Bowl blackout bit.

"A ban on blackouts will be a great relief to guys like me," CBS sports director Bill MacPhail told *TV Guide.* "The Super Bowl always is an awful headache because no other game is played that day and eighty-eight phone operators can't handle all the screaming complaints from local fans."

I was invited by a group of Los Angeles attorneys to try to relieve the network executives' headaches by leading the fight in L.A. I made a preliminary trip in April 1972 and found that they had a smooth operation ready to blast off. Television interviews and radio talk shows were already scheduled, as were meetings with volunteer fan groups. They even had my jogging route charted.

This time I came up with a new wrinkle. NBC was televising the game that year. We wrote the network and followed up with calls reminding its executives that the NFL wanted to black out the nation's number-two audience market. We then contacted the companies that had purchased advertising at $210,000 a minute, which at the time was the highest rate ever charged on television. We informed these companies that, despite their unprecedented payments, their messages would go unseen by 10 million Southern California consumers.

I didn't jog a step that year. After our contacts with the Super Bowl sponsors, a message came down from Mount NFL in New York that the Super Bowl blackout in Los Angeles would be lifted on a one-year, experimental basis.

No Super Bowl game has been blacked out since.

Round Three went to the couch potatoes.

But before that historic moment, there would be a series of sensational skirmishes on the opposite coast involving the playoff games leading up to the 1973 Super Bowl.

15

BUSTING THE BLACKOUTS, PART II:

Tricky Dick and the Redskins

> *The next time that Florida dude opens his mouth about*
> *lifting the blackout, I'm going to sue* him.
> —Don Hubbard, president of Louisiana Sports, Inc., in
> *Sports Illustrated,* September 4, 1978

AFTER YEARS of football futility, the 1972 Washington Redskins had been built into a contender under the guidance of their eccentric but inspirational coach, George Allen. With the Redskins' improvement came renewed fan interest. Washington's Robert F. Kennedy Stadium is a small park by NFL standards, seating a cozy 53,000. The entire stadium was sold out years in advance to season-ticket holders.

Senator John Pastore of Rhode Island, chairman of the U.S. Senate communications subcommittee, was unhappy to discover that the majority of Redskins fans were not only unable to attend the games; they couldn't watch the team on television because of the blackout of regular season home games. These fans were totally shut out. Pastore decided something was amiss, wrote an anti-blackout bill that covered all games, and called a congressional hearing on the issue in early October. (Senator William Proxmire of Wisconsin tried to pass a similar anti-blackout bill after my 1971 campaign in Miami but was unsuccessful.) I was invited as one of the first speakers and was scheduled to appear right after Pete Rozelle. On October 4, Rozelle and I argued our positions.

The senators appeared receptive, or at least were cognizant of the vast body of blacked-out voters I represented. Even so, the congressional anti-blackout forces were beaten by the clock. The 92nd Congress adjourned the following month without ruling on Pastore's bill. The inaction killed it.

Round Four went to the NFL.

But the fight was far from over. Like General MacArthur, I would return.

THAT DECEMBER, the revamped Redskins won their first divisional title in twenty-seven years, earning them a spot in the playoff hunt for the Super Bowl in Los Angeles. The team consisted of a grizzled collection of mercenaries known fondly as the Over-the-Hill-Gang. Coach Allen had taken a sad-sack group of perennial losers and quickly developed a winner by trading paper—future draft choices of untested college players—for experienced veterans. Allen's catchy slogan was "The Future Is Now."

The nation's capital responded to Allen's handiwork by going berserk over the colorful team.

Despite the Super Bowl anti-blackout victory, the preliminary matches leading up to the big game remained banished from the local television airwaves, pursuant to NFL rules. That didn't sit well with the frenzied Washington fans. They ached to see their beloved Redskins' two playoff games on local television, especially the contest against the despised Dallas Cowboys.

I was invited to lead the charge by Robin Ficker, a Silver Spring, Maryland, attorney who was president of the Redskins Fan Club. Ficker was so involved in battling the blackout that he quit his job as assistant general counsel for the National Soft Drink Council. When I arrived in Washington, the city was in the throes of football fever. Everywhere I went, people recognized me. From the minute I stepped off the plane I was greeted with cheers, hugs, and handshakes. The whole Maryland, Virginia, and D.C. Beltway area was of one mind: the damn blackout had to go.

The tactic in Washington was to fight strictly in the courts. No gimmicks in the land of the lawmakers. The first lawsuit was filed in U.S. District Court for the District of Columbia. The plaintiffs were Ficker, a fan named Connie Stevens (no relation to the actress), and Stevens's daughter, Delores Henheghan, a cheerleader at Federal City College. Our new angle was that the game was being televised by a station in Baltimore, only forty miles away. That enabled some, but not the majority, of the fans in Washington and surrounding Maryland and Virginia to see it. In our opinion, that was roughshod discrimination that clearly violated the Federal Communications Commission's rule banning censorship of an indiscriminate portion of the viewing public. The rich folks with big antennas could see the game. The poor folks with rabbit ears were out of luck.

The hearing was scheduled before Judge Joseph Waddy on the Thursday before the Sunday game.

The day before the hearing, December 20, 1972, we received an unprecedented boost. President Richard Nixon made a direct appeal to Pete Rozelle to lift the blackout! It seems Nixon's Pennsylvania Avenue residence fell inside the blackout zone.* In addition, Nixon, a pigskin devotee known as "the nation's number-one football fan," was planning to spend the Christmas weekend at his Southern White House in Key Biscayne, Florida. Aside from the Redskins–Green Bay Packers match, he also wanted to see the Miami Dolphins–Cleveland Browns playoff, which was blacked out in South Florida.

Nixon dispatched the nation's top law-enforcement officer, Attorney General Richard Kleindienst, to go eyeball-to-eyeball with Rozelle on the President's behalf.

I figured that was it. Forget the lawsuit. This was a request from the single most powerful man on earth.

Pete Rozelle didn't blink. He turned the President down flat.

The embarrassing rebuff made front-page news around the country. Reporters flocked to Washington to determine whether

---

*President Nixon had his own way of beating the blackout. He had Redskins games piped directly into his White House television set. His concern in 1972 was for his fellow D.C. fans.

Nixon was going to nuke the NFL headquarters in New York. Suddenly, the attention increased tenfold and became focused upon my hearing. Not only were the hopes of the Redskins fans riding upon my shoulders, but it seemed as if the honor of the presidency was at stake as well.

And all I was being asked to do was accomplish something that had stymied the President of the United States.

That evening, the mayor of Pittsburgh, an attorney named Pete Flaherty, flew in and offered to join us at the counsel table. The Pittsburgh Steelers were also in the playoffs that Sunday, and would be facing their most bitter rivals, a rowdy band of black and silver demons known as the Oakland Raiders. Mayor Flaherty's constituents were climbing the walls with anticipation.

We paraded into court the next morning. At the opposite table were Pete Rozelle's henchmen, an even larger corps of high-priced legal talent than before. Missing was Rozelle himself, who claimed other commitments. That was a heady move. I don't think King Alvin I would have made it through the Washington airport alive.

In the gallery behind Rozelle's crew sat an ominous figure, the late Edward Bennett Williams. Williams, another Holy Cross grad, was arguably one of the greatest lawyers of all time. He was unquestionably a man I deeply respected. He also happened to own the Washington Redskins and was therefore in favor of the blackout.

So much for respect. I subpoenaed Williams to appear.

Surrounding Williams was a noisy group of colorfully attired Redskins fans who fought with the media for seats.

The legal fireworks never got off the ground. Judge Waddy dismissed the suit on a technicality. I had listed the CBS Washington affiliate, WTOP, as one of the defendants instead of the CBS network itself. Since WTOP was the only CBS station in the country blacking out the game, it seemed logical. Waddy ruled that CBS had to be listed. Normally, such a minor point can be taken care of at the bench with a few strokes of a pen. Waddy ruled that the whole suit would have to be refiled.

Ficker, Flaherty, and I went to work and had the new suit ready by that afternoon. Waddy rescheduled the hearing for the next morning.

We gathered again, same faces, same positions, same colorfully attired fans interspersed with the reporters.

Both sides offered their familiar arguments. Waddy threw out the suit again. This time he decreed that Ficker, Stevens, and Hen-heghan showed no "irreparable injury" resulting from the blackout.

I wondered if President Nixon's dignity counted, but he wasn't a defendant, so I held my tongue.

The Circuit Court of Appeals, District of Columbia, was upstairs in the same building. That is the second-highest court in the land. Anticipating the negative ruling, we had already typed the appeal. We rushed upstairs and found staff members of the appeals court waiting to help us out. They obviously didn't have tickets to the game. The court set a hearing for the next day, Saturday. That was a miracle. An appeal on that level can take years. And what judge on any level would agree to a hearing on a Saturday two days before Christmas?

U.S. Court of Appeals Judges George E. Mackinnon, Carl McGowan, and Malcolm R. Wilkey did just that.

The local radio and television stations were airing blackout bulletins almost every hour, updating the community on each new legal maneuver. The following morning, the same cast of characters regrouped before the three smiling appellate judges. After both sides offered arguments, I was confident that public sentiment would carry me to victory this time. How could I lose? Why would the judges have scheduled an emergency, Christmas-weekend hearing just to shoot me down?

They fired a bazooka. The law simply wasn't in our favor. The judges ruled that the blackouts could only be lifted by an act of Congress.

One could almost hear the collective wailing and rending of clothes by Redskins fans throughout the area. Congress was not in session. The President had been rendered powerless. But we had one last card up our sleeves. Ficker dialed the Supreme Court and asked to have the clerk call him. It was Saturday, and the clerk, attorney Michael Rodak, was unavailable. No one knew where he was. Ficker appealed to the media. The radio and television stations put out an SOS. By chance, Rodak heard the report on a Baltimore television station while attending a Christmas party in Maryland. He called. Ficker asked if there was any way to expedite an appeal. It was a bold request of our nation's highest court. Rodak didn't bat an eye. He explained the procedure, gave Ficker his home number, and advised the young attorney to notify him the moment the papers were ready.

Rodak, a big Redskins fan, didn't have a ticket to the game.

As Ficker began readying the appeal, we received another unexpected boost. Ed Garvey, executive director of the NFL Players Association, had taken a vote of player representatives and determined that the players themselves were in favor of lifting the blackout.

"The Washington, San Francisco, Miami, and Pittsburgh fans deserve the opportunity to see their teams perform in these championship games," Garvey announced.

Ficker worked most of the night preparing the complicated Supreme Court papers. He typed them on a manual typewriter. By 3:00 A.M. he was wrung out. He drove to the Supreme Court and gave the hastily prepared briefs to a night security guard. Chief Justice Warren Burger sent a chauffeured stretch limousine to pick them up.

The chauffeur was rooting for us. His television had rabbit ears.

For the rest of the morning, practically everybody in Virginia, Maryland, and Washington, D.C., stayed glued to their televisions and radios waiting for Burger's decision. How could we lose? Burger had sent his own limo in the wee hours of the morning to fetch the papers. The thought of the sleek limousine pulling away with the appeal pumped us full of adrenaline. We were so wound up, anticipating the thrill of victory, we could hardly sleep.

Burger read the papers over breakfast.

When the decision was reached, the clerk called.

"I'm sorry," he said, genuinely saddened. "The writ has been denied."

There was no further explanation. Apparently the long line of precedents from previous courts was simply overwhelming. The Redskins fans had lost out.

Round Five was an overwhelming victory for the NFL. We were left dazed and bloody, hanging onto the ropes—but still standing.

That afternoon, in the agonizing television darkness, the Redskins crushed the Packers 16–3 before 53,140 cheering fans, the largest crowd in Robert F. Kennedy Stadium history. Henry Kissinger, Maine Senator Edmund Muskie, and baseball great Joe Di-Maggio watched from Edward Bennett Williams's private box.

I wasn't invited.

In Pittsburgh, with five seconds left in the game and the Steelers losing 7–6, Steeler quarterback Terry Bradshaw launched a desperation pass toward running back Frenchy Fuqua. The pass apparently bounced off Oakland defender Jack Tatum, waffled back ten yards, and mysteriously ended up in the hands of Steeler full-back Franco Harris. Franco sprinted sixty yards for the winning touchdown as time expired. Franco's "immaculate reception" remains the most dramatic finish of a playoff game in NFL history.

"A miracle sent from heaven," said Bradshaw.

The Pittsburgh fans in the stadium were the only ones who shared in the heavenly event.

In Miami, the Dolphins stayed unbeaten by grinding down Cleveland 20–14. No one on Key Biscayne, including President Nixon, saw a single play.

In San Francisco, Dallas Cowboys quarterback Roger Staubach threw two touchdown passes in the last eighty seconds to lead the Cowboys to a thrilling come-from-behind victory over the 49ers. Owing to the blackout, only San Francisco fans with tickets were forced to suffer through Staubach's heroics.

The following week, the Dolphins beat the Steelers and the Redskins stomped the hated Cowboys. Everybody saw the games on television except the exasperated fans in Washington and Miami.

Then, like magic, out of the darkness came the cathode ray light. In sunny L.A., the results of our earlier victory in Round Three went into effect. Ten million Southern California sports fans curled up in front of their television sets and watched as the undefeated Dolphins beat the Redskins 14–7 in the nearby Coliseum. The highlight of the game was a comedy of errors ignited by the littlest fellow on the field, a baldheaded Cypriot named Garo Yepremian. The Dolphins' jovial, foreign-born place-kicker attempted a pass-to-nowhere when a field goal attempt went awry. Yepremian's classic "pass," which was more of a super fumble, was intercepted by Redskins cornerback Mike Bass, who scurried down the field for the team's only touchdown.

Yepremian became an instant national celebrity.

IN COURTROOMS, as in all aspects of life, a shattering loss can sometimes pave the way to eventual victory. Washington wasn't about to forget what happened with the Redskins in 1972, nor would President Nixon forget King Alvin Rozelle I.

I didn't forget either, and I wasn't content to wait for Congress to act. Back in Miami, I continued to fight the blackout of both sold-out playoff and regular season games. I again targeted the corporate advertisers, organizing pickets at the local branch businesses.

The "Ban the Blackout" forces picketed Firestone tire outlets, Ford, Chrysler, and General Motors dealerships, high-tech companies, beer distributorships, anyone who advertised during NFL games. The pickets spread to other parts of the country. The companies weren't pleased. After spending millions to advertise during NFL games, they found themselves being cast as Great Satans who were keeping the NFL, and their own advertisements, from the fans.

I also advised "Ban the Blackout" club members in New York, Chicago, Cleveland, Green Bay, Los Angeles, and New Orleans, as well as unorganized fans around the country, to keep the pressure on their congresspeople and senators.

On Thursday, September, 13, 1973, just as the new football season was about to kick off, both the House and the Senate passed a bill calling for an immediate end of the blackouts of all NFL games sold out seventy-two hours in advance. Nixon signed the bill the next day.

Under the banner headline, "Congress Gives Home Fans Free Pass," the *Washington Post* wrote: "The House of Representatives and Senate found seats for millions of ticketless pro football fans yesterday by passing a bill to end home television blackouts of sold out National Football League games."

The vote in Congress was 336–37. The Senate took a voice vote.

In a concession to the NFL, the bills were designated as a three-year experiment.

Three days later, eight NFL games were televised to the home fans.

Miami almost remained black that Sunday. In the eighty-thousand-seat Orange Bowl, Dolphins fans fell 818 tickets short of a sellout before the seventy-two-hour deadline. Robbie relented and allowed the game to be televised.

At the end of the three-year test period, and for years afterward, the NFL owners made rumbles about reinstating the blackouts. They never have.

Round Six, and the come-from-behind knockout victory, went to the couch potatoes—with a big assist from Richard Nixon, Senator Pastore, Senator Proxmire, Richard Kleindienst, Robin Ficker, Mayor Pete Flaherty, Congress, and sports fans around the nation.

The blackout battles actually owe much of their success to simple tenacity. I lost every single court case, eleven in all, and we still managed to win the war. If there is anything that epitomizes the cliché, "If at first you don't succeed, try, try again," this has to be it.

The long fight also symbolizes what a single, determined individual can accomplish. My quixotic campaign against the titans of the Orange Bowl and the NFL has had a direct effect upon the lives of hundreds of millions of people. In some cities, such as Washington, Denver, and New York, all the games are sold out before the season begins, so the television fans never miss a play anymore.

Ironically, with the exception of a few big games a season, the Miami Dolphins rarely sell out. The seventy-two-hour rule probably did less for my hometown fans than for those in any other NFL city.

After the blackouts were lifted, I continued to butt heads with Dolphins owner Joe Robbie. I had little choice. Every time the fans became upset with the obstinate Dolphins dictator, my phone would ring continuously until the problem was solved or the fans were satiated.

The next confrontation came in 1974, when Robbie, like many NFL owners, decided to force season-ticket holders to purchase tickets to the lousy pre-season exhibition games. The fans howled and began dialing my number in droves. We sued, based upon an illegal tie-in, and lost. The courts ruled, in essence, that if Joe Robbie wanted to, he could force season-ticket holders to purchase tickets to sit and watch the paint peel on the stadium girders during the off-season.

After that episode, Robbie decided I wasn't welcome to see his games anymore—pre-season, regular season, or playoffs. He refused to renew the five season tickets I had faithfully purchased since the team's inception in 1966.

"He doesn't have to force his money on me any longer," Robbie told the press.

I can't really blame him, but it wasn't fair to punish my family for the sins of the father. I sued on the grounds that I was being discriminated against. The precedent for that kind of suit was not favorable. After trashing a number of plays, *New York Times* drama critic Alexander Woollcott was denied access to the Shubert Theater. Even when he had a ticket, they refused to let him in. The *Times* sued and won, but had the decision reversed by a higher court. The appellate court ruled that a ticket is not a contract but a license that can be revoked at the will of the seller. In English, that means the Shubert Theater had the right to ban anyone it pleased, including a venomous critic, as long as it didn't ban entire races, religions, or sexes. Similarly, the Florida courts ruled that Joe Robbie could prevent anyone he wanted from seeing his team, which amounted to one person—me.

This time my children, taking a page out of their old man's book, mounted their own media campaign. Mark, seventeen, wrote an impassioned letter to Pete Rozelle saying he and his brother and sisters were being unfairly punished. Mark promised that he and his siblings would work to earn the money to pay for the tickets if Robbie "doesn't want my father's money." The letter was published in the *Miami Herald.* Mark, Peri, sixteen, Guy, fourteen, and Kim, twelve, then picketed the Dolphins ticket office, holding signs saying DON'T NIX OUR TIX and ROBBIE UNFAIR TO KIDS. The story ran on the national news wires and made the pages of *The New York Times.*

Robbie relented, agreeing to sell my allotment of tickets to Mark. It ended up being much ado over nothing. Mark went to Stetson law school, passed the bar, and has continued the Rubin tradition of suing the Dolphins on behalf of the fans. His brother, Guy Bennett Rubin, also earned a law degree from Nova University Law School in Ft. Lauderdale, FL. It is a very proud father who is able to relate that both sons followed their dad in winning their first jury trials—both criminal cases.

In 1975, the Orange Bowl's artificial turf was a mess. The players hated it and complained bitterly that it was like playing on concrete. They claimed it ruined their knees and shortened their careers. At the same time, studies were being published that backed up the players' contentions. It was proven that there were considerably more injuries on artificial turf than on natural grass.

The fans could understand the need for phony grass inside domed stadiums, but in an open-air stadium in sunny, rain-soaked Miami? That was absurd. As a taxpayer and ticket holder, I sued the city and the turf manufacturer, claiming that the injuries to the players were depriving me of full return for my tax dollars and ticket price. It was a giant leap of legal logic, but shortly after the suit was filed, the horrid artificial turf was ripped up from the Orange Bowl gridiron and replaced with something called Prescription Athletic Turf, which is a fancy way of saying natural grass with water pipes running underneath. (I was interviewed during this crusade by a fledgling local sports reporter named Roy Firestone, now an award-winning ESPN broadcaster.)

In 1978, I was invited back to Louisiana to fight the four-state, two-hundred-mile blackout of the Muhammad Ali–Leon Spinks heavyweight championship rematch in the Louisiana Superdome. That was the blackest of the blackouts. The promoters somehow persuaded ABC to shut down all of Louisiana and parts of Mississippi, Alabama, and Florida. By then, my reputation as a blackout buster must have been formidable. The promoters had fits from the moment I arrived. Louisiana Governor Edwin Edwards publicly told me to go home. Don Hubbard, president of Louisiana Sports, Inc., was moved to utter his line about suing "that Florida dude." I had to call off a planned protest rally at the Superdome after we received threatening calls promising to break the legs of the protesters.

The threats were unnecessary. The courts "broke the legs" of my lawsuit, throwing it out.

Ali had better luck. He sent poor Leon on a literal one-way ticket to Palookaville and regained his title for a record-setting third time.

Meanwhile, the Miami Dolphins have been as successful on the field as in court. They've played in five Super Bowls, won a pair, and remain the only team in NFL history to finish undefeated when they went 17–0 in 1972.

That's all I ever wanted. A competitive, healthy team, respect shown toward the loyal fans who pack the stadium and pay the freight, and, if the arena is sold out, fun and excitement for the television viewers at home, especially shut-ins and kids.

EPILOGUE

In 1987, Joe Robbie opened a new football stadium to house his business. (He modestly named it Joe Robbie Stadium.) The friendly but aging Orange Bowl Stadium didn't have the giant video scoreboards, luxury "sky boxes," or other perks offered by today's modern sports complexes.

When longtime Dolphins season-ticket holders were reassigned seats in this magnificent new sports palace, many were dismayed to learn that their locations had been downgraded and they weren't as close to the action as before. They raised a fuss. As with most stadiums, seating priorities are based upon longevity. Those who renew their season tickets year after year work their way into the best seats.

The fans who felt slighted accused the Dolphins owner of

giving their hard-earned, primo seats to his friends, business associates, and high rollers. In return, the diehard fans who had supported the team for twenty-two years felt they were given the shaft.

The Dolphins' publicity folks insisted that no favoritism was intended, and explained that the configuration of the new stadium was such that there weren't as many seats between the forty-yard lines as in the Orange Bowl. Plus, they explained, because of the much-improved sight lines in the new stadium, the fans' "downgraded" seats were actually just as good as their old Orange Bowl positions, or even better! Although this logic raised a few eyebrows, it was, for the most part, accepted.

Then Joe Robbie made a mistake. A few days later the *Miami Herald* ran a story noting that Robbie had moved my family's seats from the forty-yard line into the dreaded end zone. Miami sports fans had a good belly laugh. All over town, people were saying things like, "I got bounced to the twenty, but, hey, at least I ain't in the end zone with Ellis Rubin!" When the laughter died, everyone began looking at their own tickets again. The anger returned, hotter than before. The feeling was that if Robbie had willfully banished Ellis Rubin to the abyss of the end zone, as everyone suspected, then the line about non-favoritism and stadium configuration was a bunch of baloney.

The next day my office was flooded with calls from fans wanting to sue Robbie for playing a shell game with their tickets. It may seem petty, but such issues are life-or-death to rabid sports fans. Since I was pretty peeved myself, I gathered their names and made noises about filing suit. The Dolphins relented after Mark and I met with their legal counsel, and nearly everyone who had contacted my office, including the Rubin family, gained better seats. (We ended up on the forty-eight-yard-line, primo seats.)

The irony is if Robbie hadn't tried to banish me into the end zone, the fans probably would have accepted the Dolphins' explanation. But Joe Robbie couldn't pass up another opportunity to stick it to Ellis Rubin.

AS I remembered the football duels, I began pacing in the small prison isolation cell. It occurred to me that no one in Miami could be more happy with my incarceration than Joe Robbie. He doubtless felt I belonged right where I was—permanently.

16

THE JAILING, PART III:

Dark Thoughts from a Black Cell

How can you tell when a lawyer is lying? When you see
his lips move.
—Old joke

I DON'T KNOW if it was the result of being locked up or what, but I was growing increasingly bitter about my profession. Sure, I'd won some big cases, but the memories of the ones I'd lost were starting to consume me.

I was in jail for refusing to let a murderer lie. A rich Arab thumbed his nose at the law, kidnapped four children, and escaped justice merely by flying away. A fifteen-year-old boy was imprisoned because no one could understand his brand of insanity.

Prosecutors disobeying the law to advance their careers. Defense attorneys up to their eyebrows in deception. And everyone plea-bargaining human lives as in some kind of cattle auction.

Friends suing friends. Neighbors suing neighbors. Personal injury attorneys getting rich preying upon the misery of others. Lawyers advertising, giving the public the impression that if someone dents your car fender, it's as good as hitting the lottery.

What happened to truth, ethics, and integrity?

There seems to be a new meaning for the phrase "blind justice." Instead of being blind to prejudice, race, wealth, or religion, justice has become blind to its own moral rot. And because of this, the American judicial system appears to be in a race with our public schools to see which one melts down first.

Our criminal justice system is under siege—not by criminals or crooked cops—but by lawyers who condone and even create false testimony, perjury.

Nowhere is the need for a moral reawakening stronger than in the legal profession, where "win at any cost" prevails today. It is time that lawyers get on a first name basis with the truth and join those few who are honest, who have compassion and who serve people and causes rather than worship at the altar of higher fees and winning statistics.

Dark thoughts from a black cell.

AFTER A day in isolation, I was sprung from the tiny cell and returned to the prison community. As the final weeks of my sentence dragged on, my view of the legal profession grew even more cynical.

Trial by jury is supposed to be a search for truth. Actually, trial by jury has become a gigantic lying contest. The jury selects a winner depending upon who lied the most convincingly, the prosecutor or the defense attorney.

And, far from being a revelation, many attorneys openly admit as much.

Harvard Law School professor Alan M. Dershowitz is a legal authority whose every utterance is greeted with unquestioned acceptability by the media as well as legal journals. Thousands of lawyers and hundreds of law professors quote and cite Professor Dershowitz as the ultimate authority on legal knowledge, appellate strategy, and trial tactics. In other words, Professor D. is the role model for a majority of the members of the American legal profession.

In the March 1984 issue of the *Trial Diplomacy Journal*, a teaching manual for trial lawyers, there was an interesting interview with Professor Dershowitz. In it, Dershowitz revealed his winning secrets for criminal defense attorneys:

Let's face it, in reality it's the prosecutor's job primarily to bring out the truth and it's the defense attorney's job primarily to suppress the truth. Those are completely different functions. If I am right, and I have never heard any defense attorney disagree with this, the vast majority of criminal defendants that we defend are guilty. Obviously, then, it's our job to make sure that the truth, the whole truth, and nothing but the truth does not come out.

Can you imagine this sign over Professor Dershowitz's chair at Harvard: "We who teach here seek only to suppress truth?" Or how about this over a judge's bench: "We who labor here seek only to obscure the truth."

What a contrast to the traditional courtroom motto, "We who labor here seek only truth."

F. Lee Bailey, writing in a July 1988 edition of *USA Today* magazine, offered this view:

> The sanctity of an oath aside, witnesses lie with astonishing regularity to attain their own ends, and courts tolerate that practice apathetically. Witnesses who give false testimony should be punished severely, and the lawyers who facilitate and attempt to profit from this corrupt evidence deserve permanent disbarment. I have never seen a major trial which lacked significant perjury, and I have yet to see that perjury punished.

Even the television show "L.A. Law" produced an episode that backed off its previous moral stand. In Chapter 8, I explained how the "L.A. Law" scriptwriters borrowed from my case and had attorney Michael Kuzak (Harry Hamlin) go to jail instead of letting a witness lie on the stand. In a subsequent episode, Kuzak faced the dilemma again. This time he offered a weak protest then allowed a juvenile murderer to tell the jury a series of prepared lies. Apparently, even in the heroic world of fictional television, the "L.A. Law" writers have smelled the coffee and given up.

All these statements and developments are linked by one word: arrogance. It's the arrogance of lawyers and judges who have come to believe that they *are* the legal system, and thus can control it as they see fit.

That's not what I was taught thirty-eight years ago.

I was taught that the public is our legal system—that it always has been, and should always remain so. The jury is the most important aspect of any trial. They seek the truth. Lawyers are ministers of justice—to gather the truth and present it to the jury. It has been said repeatedly that the jury is the cornerstone of American justice and thus of American democracy. But how can juries operate properly if we attorneys lie to them?

The law was never designed to enable high-priced attorneys to get their guilty clients off scot-free. I know it happens, and it's a cliché even to talk about it, but that makes it no less an abomination. And being a lawyer is not about being consumed with building a winning record and a bulging bank account. Being a lawyer is about serving justice. That's not only our greatest calling, it's our *only* calling.

Only very few lawyers practice this anymore. I was told by a judge to allow Sanborn to knowingly lie to a jury.

Court-ordered perjury is wrong, and ten thousand judges and ten thousand lawyers swearing on twenty thousand Bibles won't make it right. When you allow a client to commit perjury with court approval, you are tipping the scales of justice so far out of balance that you have no justice. If we don't have a system based upon truth, we have none at all.

BY THE third week of my stay at the "Dade County Hilton," I seriously began to consider calling it a career. I didn't feel I could face the lies and corruption anymore. The depression that envelops all men in prison was taking hold of me.

During the last days of my sentence, I could hardly stand it. I was inches away from rattling a tin cup across the bars, as in old prison movies, and screaming, "Let me out, let me out." How did the other prisoners tolerate it, caged in a sordid prison for five, ten, fifteen, or twenty-five years? For life?

By day twenty-nine, I was certain that I'd had it with the law. I'd retire to my condo on the bay, let my sons carry on, and go quietly into the night.

A funny thing happened on my way to freedom. As I walked out of jail with my protest beard in full bloom, my mood began to brighten. There's nothing like the Florida sunshine to wash away depression. I was met at the gate to freedom by several friends, clients, and, of course, Irene and the kids. The memories of those whose lives I had helped began pushing aside the images of the failures. Charlie Johnson. Prentice Rasheed. NFL football fans. Johnny Brown. The countless others.

Actually, I didn't have much time to mull over my vow to retire. I was scheduled to plunge right back into the legal arena a few weeks after my release.

A young woman stood in the shadow of the electric chair. A young woman who had once been a tortured little girl. It was another impossible case, another gut-wrenching example of a judicial system out of sync with the society it seeks to serve.

It presented me with a perfect personal crossroads. I could quit and escape the mental anguish of another probable defeat, a defeat that I knew would devastate me more than all the others combined.

Or I could fight.

One last time, I thought. One last time. If I lose this one, I'm history.

17

THE CONDO MURDER, PART I

AT 10:35 P.M. on Tuesday, September 2, 1986, legal secretary Marilyn White left the air-conditioned comfort of her South Florida condominium to take her dog, Snickers, on his nightly walk. About ten minutes into the leisurely stroll, White heard two "masculine" screams and two loud cracks. Snickers perked up his ears and looked in the direction of building 1526. That confirmed White's suspicions as to where the noise had come from.

White waited a moment or two, but heard nothing else. She didn't see anyone run from the nearby building, so she and Snickers continued walking and returned to their apartment.

At 3:15 A.M. the body of Morris Keller was found sprawled on the manicured lawn between buildings 1526 and 1528. Keller, seventy, was almost unrecognizable. His skull was crushed to such a degree it looked as though the top of his head had been blown off with a shotgun.

Broward County Medical Examiner Larry Tate was on duty

that morning. A Vietnam veteran with a Purple Heart and a chunk of shrapnel still lodged in his throat, the gravelly voiced doctor had worked in the Miami medical examiner's office during the late 1970s, when Miami reigned as the nation's murder capital. Much of the daily carnage was the result of the vicious territorial wars that pitted the "cocaine cowboys" of Colombia against each other and all the other aspiring drug barons.

As he walked in the darkness across the lawn of Morris Keller's condominium building, Dr. Tate figured he had seen it all.

"It was a nasty thumping on the head," Dr. Tate deadpanned in a way only a medical examiner can. "The attacker completely flattened Keller's face. The free-floating bone fragments gave his face the consistency of a bean bag. Somebody was really pissed off at the guy."

Dr. Tate determined that Keller had been struck at least sixteen times with a blunt object, and called it one of the most brutal bludgeonings he had seen in more than a thousand deaths. A number of the responding police officers, veterans of numerous grisly murder scenes, had to turn away at the sight of this one.

Keller, a retired Scarsdale, New York, cabbie and treasurer of his condominium association, was found with his wallet in the back pocket of his white shorts. His Rolex watch was missing, and so was a wad of cash he was said to carry in his front pocket. The untouched wallet gave homicide detectives the first clue that would eventually lead them to his assailant.

Morris's savage murder sent shock waves throughout and beyond the sixteen-building Whitehall One section of the expansive Pine Island Ridge complex. Shaken residents in the four-hundred-unit community talked of starting a civilian patrol and escort service to complement the armed security force. They collected more than $1,000 to offer as a reward for information on the beastly murderer. Sheriff's Captain Frank LeBlanc held a town meeting to calm the residents and followed up by appearing at the association's next board meeting.

The police effort helped, but fear and grief continued to spread through the complex like a sawgrass fire. Morris Keller had been a popular fellow. Born in Poland, Keller came to America with his family when he was four. He joined the navy and served on a submarine during World War II. After fighting New York traffic for thirty-five years in his yellow cab, he sold his home and $70,000-

taxi medallion in 1982 and retired to Florida. He had three daughters who were grown and gone, and he shared the new $60,000 condominium, just west of Fort Lauderdale, with his petite wife of forty-two years, Dorothea. He spent his time tallying up the condominium association's finances and actively participating in various condo clubhouse activities. He played pinochle on Monday and Friday nights, poker on Thursdays, canasta in between, and was a fixture at the community dances. He was well liked by virtually everyone.

Following his death, the flag flew at half-mast in front of the clubhouse. His daughter, Victoria, placed hibiscus blossoms on the grassy area between buildings 1528 and 1526 where he had died.

"It could just as easily have been any one of us," a shaken Teri Marder, the condominium's president, told reporters the morning of Morris's death.

Marder was wrong. It couldn't have been anyone other than Morris Keller, the "wonderful person" everybody loved. Morris Keller, the dapper dancer his friends described as "one of the nicest people in the world" and a man who "wouldn't harm a fly."

That was Dr. Jekyll. Inside Morris Keller lurked a Mr. Hyde with a secret that was about to explode upon the nation. Morris Keller, and men like him, would be stripped naked in one of the most harrowing and far-reaching trials in judicial history.

HOMICIDE DETECTIVE Philip Amabile, thirty-three, arrived at the scene of Morris's death that morning looking like a blend of Sylvester Stallone and Al Pacino. His black hair and thick black beard contributed heavily to the resemblance. Sergeant Richard Scheff, thirty-seven, arrived about a half hour later. Scheff also sported a full beard, though his was lighter and gave him a less intimidating appearance than his more physically imposing Italian partner. When they play the typical, good cop/bad cop roles, the Jewish Sergeant Scheff is the good guy. Amabile is the darkly brooding bad guy. Outside of this standard interrogation technique, the two New York transplants are friendly and personable. Beneath the hairy surface, both are men of intellectual substance. Detective Amabile is an adjunct professor at Broward Community College Police Academy. Sergeant Scheff is a verbose liberal whose opinionated views make him the polar opposite of a Dirty Harry–style detective. He's quick to defend the rights of even society's worst characters. "Our laws must protect the most disliked among us," he stresses.

That belief would come to play heavily in the investigation of the Keller murder.

RIGHT FROM the start, the two bearded detectives were suspicious of the theories offered by the condominium residents. The beating showed too much rage to have been committed by a stranger. In their experience, only friends, lovers, or family members exhibited such anger. In addition, whoever killed Morris Keller knew he carried his money loosely in his front pocket, and not in his wallet. That knowledge eliminated a random robber. As they inspected the scene outside, the detectives' suspicions focused upon an acquaintance or a relative. The latter option was narrow. The only family Morris had in town was his wife, Dorothea, and their twenty-nine-year-old daughter, Lisa. Lisa still lived in Scarsdale and had flown to Florida to visit her parents during the long Labor Day weekend.

When the detectives entered the Keller condominium to question the two women, their suspicions were shattered. Lisa was curled up on the couch under a blanket, trembling and visibly shaken. She was rail-thin and sickly, and wore a pacemaker to aid a bad heart. Paramedics had to be called to give the five-foot-seven-inch, 115-pound poet emergency medical treatment.

Dorothea was seventy, barely five feet tall, and weighed a frail seventy-nine pounds. When Sergeant Scheff walked into the living room, Dorothea clasped his hand in hers, looked into his eyes, and tearfully begged him to find the killer of her robust, 175-pound husband. She said she didn't know if she could survive without him.

Both women seemed genuinely distraught. Neither appeared physically or mentally capable of a brutal clubbing murder.

"At that point I was almost certain they couldn't have been involved," Sergeant Scheff recalls.

Lisa and her mother told the detectives that Morris had attended a board meeting that evening and had never returned. Thirteen people were at the meeting, ignoring a bad omen that dates back two thousand years to the Last Supper.

While talking with the two fragile women in the spotless apartment, the detectives noticed the latest edition of the condominium newsletter rolled up on one of the end tables. They didn't give it much thought at the time, but among the thousands of items found in a typical household, both Amabile and Scheff independently made a mental record of the newsletter.

The following day, a neighbor told the detectives that he had last seen Morris Keller at 9:45 P.M., walking home from the meeting to his apartment. Morris was only about twenty feet from his door, the neighbor said, and was holding a rolled-up condominium newsletter in his right hand.

That critical clue, combined with the time frame of the murder established by Marilyn White and Snickers, placed Morris Keller in his apartment following the meeting. It also meant that Dorothea and Lisa were lying. The newsletter, the neighbors' comments, and the missing hour exposed their story. Improbable as it seemed, the circumstances pointed to one of the women, or both, as being the beast that had all these people afraid to leave their apartments.

LISA AND Dorothea traveled to New York for Morris's funeral. They stayed with relatives until the end of the month, then returned to South Florida. Hearing that the pair were back in town, the detectives asked them to come in for further "routine" questioning. At the police station, Scheff and Amabile worked on Dorothea and Lisa for five hours. Lisa said the detectives told her that unless she confessed, they would be forced to arrest her mother.

"She won't last a day in jail," Lisa claimed the officers threatened. She also said she was told by the detectives that they knew Morris had been violent and was killed in self-defense. All Lisa had to do, they assured her, was confess. That way they could close the case and Lisa and her mother could go home. Regardless of whether the detectives actually made those threats and promises, which they deny, what happened to Lisa and Dorothea Keller is a textbook example of why everyone should demand a lawyer from the second he or she enters a police station. If people make this demand, the police must comply. If they don't, or waive their right, the police can bring out a psychological version of the bare lightbulb and rubber hose and turn the screws.

Two women in ill health being questioned for five hours without an attorney can lead to disaster for the defense and an air-tight case for the state, which is exactly what happened.

During the long, intense conversations with the detectives, Lisa began pacing the room and talking about her life. She related her love of mysteries and relayed one of her favorite stories. It was an "Alfred Hitchcock Presents" show in which a wife beat her policeman husband to death with a frozen roast, cooked it, invited all his police buddies over for dinner, and watched as they ate the murder weapon.

According to Detective Amabile, Lisa looked at him, smiled, rubbed her hands together, then spread them apart and said, "No evidence!"

The choice of that particular episode piqued the detectives' interest. Following Morris's death, police divers searched a nearby lake for a weapon. The weapon was never found. Dr. Tate said that he couldn't make a positive determination of exactly what the blunt instrument had been, but suspected it was a two-by-four. However, after an exhaustive microscopic search, the M.E. said he had not found a single fiber of wood in or around Morris's face and head.

Spurred by Lisa's strange Hitchcock story, Amabile and Scheff pressed on. They wore Lisa down and persuaded her to trust them. Fearing for her mother's safety, she finally broke. She stood in the interrogation room, walked to the far wall, turned her back to the detectives, and confessed. After going through her story once, Sergeant Scheff left the room to inform Dorothea and take her new statement. Detective Amabile stayed and had a shaken Lisa repeat the confession on tape.

In the taped version, Lisa said her parents had been arguing that afternoon over her increasing medical expenses. Morris, who didn't want to be responsible for the bills, began shoving his wife around. He stormed off to the condo meeting and promised to "take care of things once and for all" when he came back. He returned around 10:00 P.M., still spoiling for a fight. Morris assaulted his wife, and Lisa grew afraid. She decided to distract him to protect her mother.

> I told him that we'd settle this outside and he followed me out and he was very determined . . . he was very close behind me and he was calling my name and saying, telling me that "this was it." . . . When I had gone around the building a few days earlier I had knocked over a piece of wood, like a two-by-four, and it was still there. . . . I didn't really know what I was going to do, but he was behind me quickly and he grabbed ahold and I remember that thing was there and I took a—I swung at him hard and he started to scream. . . . I got scared because he didn't just fall, so I took another swing and then he fell but he was still moving and I was afraid to let him get up because if

he got up that would of been me there instead, so I took another swing and a few more after and then I walked away. . . .

. . . My mom had come around the corner about that time when he went to the ground and she froze, she wasn't really sure who was standing and who was laying until she—she just called out my name and if I didn't answer she would of, I don't know, run because he would have been crazy by then. But it was me who answered and she froze.

Lisa told her mother to return to the apartment and Dorothea complied without coming any closer. Lisa then removed her father's watch and the money wad from his pocket to make it look like a robbery. She tried to take his wallet, but abandoned the effort when she was unable to get it out of his back pocket. She went to a trash bin, found a garbage bag, opened it, dumped out the garbage, and dropped the watch, money, and stick into the now-empty bag. She walked to a nearby shopping mall and placed the bag in a dumpster behind a movie theater. She said that when she returned to the condo, she didn't say anything to her mother, and added that her mother just hugged her.

Detective Amabile asked her to repeat some statements she had made earlier about her father's abusive nature.

LISA: There are instances of my father who was abusive to my younger sister, and to my mother, to myself, some of them recorded in the hospital. Some of them witnessed by people, some law enforcement knowledge. . . .

AMABILE: And are those incidents what led up to the night of September 2?

LISA: Those incidents, many from when I was smaller, when I had nannies, when I was an adult, when I was in school. They were constant situations without any relationship to anything most times.

Prior to the taped interview, Lisa told the detectives that "he's been getting away with it for years." She wouldn't explain what "it" was, and grew silent when pressed.

When Sergeant Scheff informed Dorothea Keller of her daughter's confession, Dorothea's first instinct was to shift the blame to herself.

"Richard, please let me say I did it," Scheff quoted Dorothea in his report. "I can't let her go to jail. I'm seventy years old, she's my baby. I have to protect her."

Instead of letting Lisa go following her confession, as she said Detective Amabile and Sergeant Scheff promised, they booked her into the Broward County women's jail. According to Lisa, Amabile said it would only be for a day or so, until he could arrange a hearing. Shortly after the black iron bars had slammed in Lisa's face, Amabile and Scheff were appearing at a press conference to announce that they had solved the case. They charged Lisa with first-degree murder, and added that Dorothea Keller could, but probably wouldn't, be charged for assisting in the cover-up.

The news spread quickly through the Whitehall One condominium and the rest of South Florida. Whitehall residents were now doubly shocked.

"My heart is broken for Dorothea," neighbor Elsie Vlatofe told reporters who flocked to the condo for the reaction. "To lose a husband and then her child, it's horrible."

The next morning, a trembling, crying Lisa was dragged in handcuffs before Judge Mark Speiser. She was handcuffed to the defense table and was accompanied by a public defender. Lisa clutched her pacemaker monitor as the proceedings progressed. In Detective Amabile's probable-cause affidavit, presented in court, his written description of her confession deviated from her taped statements in one critical area. He wrote that "in a taped, post-Miranda statement . . . Lisa Keller further stated she hid behind bushes and waited for her father to walk past, at which time she snuck up behind him and struck him on the back of the head."

Lisa had said no such thing. In fact, it was Amabile who mouthed those words. From the confession tape:

> AMABILE: . . . did you hide behind the bushes in between the two buildings and wait for him?
> LISA: No, he was in clear view of me.
> AMABILE: Okay.

The mistaken line in Amabile's report laid the foundation for premeditated murder and destroyed Lisa's claim of self-defense.*

---

*According to the detectives, Lisa confessed twice. Only the second confession was taped. The detectives said Lisa made the statement about hiding in the bushes in her first confession, then reversed herself when the tape was turned on. Amabile said that when Lisa denied it during the taped confession, he meant to get back to the subject and clear it up, but forgot. Then, when filing the arrest report, he said his memory went back to the first confession and he mistakenly attributed to the taped version the remark about her having hidden behind the bushes. Both Amabile and Scheff feel that Lisa was calculating enough to change her story when the tape was turned on.

Lisa maintains that she never said anything about hiding in the bushes. She said her father was right behind her the entire way, and she didn't have the time or the inclination to conceal herself.

That line helped keep the sickly woman in jail without bond for the next eight months, providing still another example of the danger in talking to the police without an attorney. For Lisa, the abuse she thought she had escaped was merely continuing in another form.

Because the Whitehall condominium was near the Broward-Dade county line, the press coverage was intensified threefold. The major newspapers in Fort Lauderdale, Miami, and Hollywood (Florida) considered it a local story and jumped upon every new development—a situation that grew to be a considerable problem. On the morning of the hearing, all three papers published front-page stories taken from the detectives' press conference the previous evening. The articles described how Lisa "hid in the bushes" to "ambush her father" and club him to death. The reports poisoned the minds of potential jurors all over South Florida and virtually assured an unfavorable result at the hearing.

That same day, Paul Shannon of the *Miami Herald* discovered a talkative source in Lisa's younger sister, Victoria Marron, twenty-seven, a former emergency medical technician. Fortunately, Vicky's remarks supported her sister and helped counter the police statements. Speaking by phone from her home in Dobbs Ferry, New York, Vicky described Lisa as a timid "mouse" who had been a sickly, reclusive teenager who stayed in her room writing poetry. Vicky said her father never liked Lisa, called her "stupid" as if it were her name, and was a "very, very powerful man. He was always saying he could kill someone."

"Lisa was always the weakest one," Vicky continued. "She was a chicken. You push her and she falls to the floor."

Armed with this new angle, Shannon went back and requestioned Morris Keller's neighbors. A different picture began to emerge. Words like "loud," "crass," and "tactless" replaced the glowing eulogies. Several neighbors shook their heads and commented that one never knew what went on "behind closed doors."

A few days later, Pat Curry of the *Hollywood* (Florida) *Sun-Tattler* rang up Vicky to get some additional insights. Vicky was even more accommodating. Under a big, black, front-page headline—"Like Living in Russia"—the *Sun-Tattler* exposed more horrors inside the Keller household.

"You've got to understand," Vicky confided to Curry. "If you saw her and you saw him and you knew him, you'd be afraid. If he hit you, he'd send you flying. If I was in the same situation [as Lisa],

I would have done the same thing. If I could take her place, I would. She's just a little mouse. That's all she'll ever be."

Vicky added that she often saw her mother bruised and battered while she was growing up, and later implored her mother to leave Morris and come to live with her and her husband.

"I said, 'Ma, come up here. We've got a house, we've got a dog.' She said, 'He'll be waiting.' I told her, 'So, let him wait. Let him wait a lifetime.' "

Vicky said that Lisa, for all her timidness, had protected her mother before by diverting Morris's attention.

"She was trying to be stronger. She said twice she ran out of the house to get him away from her. A toothpick going up against a bulldozer doesn't work," Vicky explained.

While South Floridians were buzzing over these new developments, I received a call from one of Lisa's relatives, asking me to defend her. I met with him and Dorothea first. They were both very evasive about what had happened. Dorothea was vague, and skipped around in her account. I could sense she was having a difficult time deciding what, and how much, she should tell me. I tried to reason with another relative. He took me aside and said he had to stay out of it. He didn't want the rest of the family to know he was on Lisa's side. These reactions were the initial rips in a family that would soon be torn apart.

One of the first steps I took was to rein in the outpouring of information to the media. I wanted it controlled, but not shut down. Most attorneys gag their clients. They claim this is done for the client's benefit, but the truth is that the majority of attorneys lack public-relations skills and therefore fear what they don't understand. They silence their clients for their own protection, not for the client's. In a sensational case in which the media hangs on every word, this circle-the-wagons mentality results in an onslaught of one-sided stories that convict the clients in the public arena before they get to court. If the accused gets a jury of illiterates and does get off, what kind of life have you given him? Everybody in town thinks he's guilty and just slipped through a crack. That can be as bad as going to jail.

I wanted the news coverage organized to counter what was coming from the prosecution. Prior to my arrival, Dorothea, as sweet a woman as one can imagine, was holding virtual tea parties for the reporters who were beating a path to her door. The newspapers were filled with such details as how she scrubbed her sink and kitchen counter. I didn't immediately bring Vicky under my wing because her comments had been helpful. This oversight almost proved disastrous.

After meeting with Dorothea a few times, I went to the jail to see if Lisa could shed any light on what had happened that night. I found her in the jail infirmary, where she had been placed because of her bad heart. She was huddled in the corner. She had on an ill-fitting prison uniform and her hands were curled up so far inside the sleeves that I couldn't see them. I was filled with both compassion and rage. Compassion for her, and rage toward the legal system that had imprisoned her. Thin, sick, and shaking with fear, a woman like Lisa should never have been placed in a violent prison. It was an outrage that she was there to begin with. Instead of understanding, the judicial system was piling their own abuse upon a nightmare that had haunted this woman her entire life.

Counting those whose case I've rejected and those I've plead out and tried, I guess I've interviewed more than a thousand accused murderers, and I knew right away that there was much more to this case than anybody suspected. Much more than just an abusive father who beat his wife and terrorized his daughter.

I had to handle Lisa the same way people treat a skittish park squirrel they are trying to feed. Hold the peanut out, talk softly, and stay frozen as the little animal creeps forward. The first few times, the squirrel invariably hears or sees something that makes it jump back. Eventually, if you're patient, it will learn to trust you and take the peanut. Emotionally, that described Lisa Keller.

The next morning I filed for an emergency bond hearing to try to get Lisa out of jail and into a hospital where she belonged. On top of everything else, her pacemaker was defective, causing her great pain. The hearing was set for two days later, Thursday, October 2. Lisa sat next to me at the defense table in a pink and gray sweater, black skirt, and white shoes. She was once again handcuffed to the defense table like a Mafia hit man. I appeared before Judge Speiser, outlined Lisa's grave condition, explained that she had acted in self-defense, and asked for her release to get proper medical care. I was quite emotional about it. So were Lisa and Dorothea. As I spoke, they both sobbed and shook. Lisa dabbed her eyes with a coarse brown paper towel. She was so weak-kneed she could barely stand. As we approached the bench for the decision, she stumbled and braced herself against my son Mark.

Judge Speiser wasn't moved. A jail nurse testified that Lisa was okay. Speiser refused to set a bond or allow her to receive outside medical care. He ordered a cardiologist to examine her in the jail and placed her under twenty-four-hour medical supervision until the grand jury hearing the following week.

Dramatic as these courtroom developments were, they were secondary in the next day's newspapers. Marci Richardson of the *Fort Lauderdale News* had gotten hold of the ever-helpful Vicky and squeezed out the first of a cluster of bombs that were about to be dropped. The headline, the biggest since the *Sun-Tattler*'s "Like Living in Russia" proclamation, said it all: "Sibling: Suspect Not Slaying Victim's Child."

Vicky had shared with Marci some startling information she had just learned from her mother. Lisa had been the product of a mid-marriage affair, and Morris had "grudgingly" raised her. Vicky said her father never hid his hatred toward Lisa, but until her mother's confession, the reason had been a mystery.

The revelation wasn't a total surprise. In her confession, Lisa had mentioned that Morris wasn't her real father, and she had taunted him with that fact to get him outside and away from her mother that night. But the details concerning the affair and Morris's resentment caught me off guard. While Lisa and Dorothea were acting tight-lipped with me, the reporters were having great success. Vicky's comments again helped my case, but I didn't appreciate having to get the information out of a newspaper.

The media were also having a field day with Lisa's poetry. She had published a small volume in 1981 under the now-chilling title *Temper of the Night.* The reporters scoured the book for Edgar Allan Poe–type verse, but found instead that it was mostly filled with sweeping imagery on nature, love, lost love, and loneliness. I'm no literary expert, but the material was stylish and moving.

I went back to the women's jail to see if Lisa could express herself as well orally as she had in her poems. This time I found her in a wheelchair, nearly doubled over from stomach pains.

Usually, my initial visits with a client consist of small talk. I rarely talk about the "incident." Once the client begins to feel comfortable, he or she generally tells the story without prompting. When it's done this way, the story is told with more depth and honesty than it would be if I had to pry it out. After a few visits, it was apparent that Lisa had no desire to volunteer her story—ever.

Although she began to feel more comfortable with me, my attempts to ease out the details were mostly unsuccessful. She did relate that the last argument that had led to Morris's death began over a glass of water. Morris insisted that the whole family drink out of a single glass during meals, and Lisa had rebelled against this disgusting tradition that night at dinner. Morris became enraged when Lisa set down her own glass, and he promised to "settle this once and for all" when he came back from the condo meeting. Lisa and her mother waited in terror for his return, clutching each other like kittens in a storm. He came back, started beating on Dorothea, and Lisa taunted him to lure him outside and away from her mother. Beyond that, Lisa wouldn't, or couldn't, open up.

On the positive side, Vicky's public descriptions about the Keller family home life were starting to take effect. Sympathy for Lisa and her mother was growing, especially among women's groups.

A grand jury met on October 8 to consider the charge against Lisa. She and Dorothea were "invited" to testify without my assistance, à la Prentice Rasheed. I declined the kind offer. Assistant State Attorney Kelly Hancock paraded sixteen witnesses before the grand jurors, including Sergeant Scheff. The detective repeated the story of how she'd hidden in the bushes to ambush Morris. Not surprisingly, the grand jury rubber-stamped the state's wishes and reaffirmed the charge of first-degree murder.

The next day we were back in court for another emergency bond hearing and medical treatment request. The first doctor the court had ordered to examine Lisa in jail wanted no part of the controversial case. He had his attorney raise a fuss, and Judge Speiser was forced to assign a second doctor. The new doctor determined that although she was in considerable pain from her pacemaker wires pressing against her skin, she had "no significant pacemaker problems" and "should be able to live a normal life." What the doctor meant was that Lisa's physical anguish wasn't life-threatening.

As I continued to fight for her release in the hearing, the next bomb blew up right in my face. Detective Amabile strolled to the stand and told the packed courtroom that Lisa had been investigated by the Westchester, New York, district attorney's office the prior April, regarding a plot to kill her father. Lisa had given a man she met in a Yonkers, New York, bar $5,000 for what she thought were poison pills. The guy sold her sugar tablets, and later squealed on her. Lisa was called in and questioned by an assistant district attorney, then let go. Amabile testified that the New York investigators felt that bringing Lisa in was enough to foil the plan and scare her into not devising another.

Apparently, no one thought to consider that Lisa's purchase might have been nothing more than a cry for help. The New York investigators should have determined why Lisa wanted to kill her father. They should then have requested Florida authorities to investigate Morris. Social workers could have made arrangements for Lisa and Dorothea to undergo immediate medical and psychiatric treatment. But prosecutors are in the business of putting people away, not saving them. Instead of coming to the rescue, they chose to help grease Lisa's way to the electric chair. After reading about Lisa's Florida arrest in the New York newspapers, the New York prosecutors called Detective Amabile and Sergeant Scheff and shared the previous investigation.

On top of that, they let the informant keep the $5,000 he weaseled out of Lisa.

Because Lisa hadn't been charged in New York, nothing had shown up on her routine background check. The poison plot was news to me, the kind of news that could have doomed her to death row. Fortunately, Kelly Hancock and Detective Amabile exploded this bomb at a minor bond hearing instead of holding it back for the trial. Had they waited, Lisa might have gone right to the chair.

I had a talk with my client after this incident. I explained that another such revelation would destroy what little chance we had. She apologized and promised that there would be no more surprises. Normally, a premeditation discovery of this magnitude destroys the defense. It would be plea-bargaining time, and one would be inclined to accept any offer short of capital punishment. But this wasn't a normal case. The poison plot, now that I knew about it, could be used as a further example of how desperate Lisa was to free her mother and herself from Morris's reign of terror.

What the revelation did, though, was shatter any remaining hope of getting Lisa out of jail on bond. There were too many men controlling her life who didn't care or didn't understand what a woman like her had suffered.

As the details continued to spring forth, the overall picture was becoming more and more disturbing from a sociological standpoint. Dorothea said she had been hospitalized up to a dozen times as a result of past beatings. Vicky had called the police once after her father struck her. Lisa's reclusive childhood and teen years should have caused someone—teachers or school counselors—to take notice. One former teacher described Lisa as "disturbed" and "a pathetic little creature." No one took the time to find out why. If that was too subtle, her purchase of poison screamed out that something was wrong in the Keller house.

But where was the help? Thirty years, and where was the one helping hand that could have prevented this tragedy? Why had it reached the point where Lisa had to club her father to death? And where was the help now? In the blind eyes of the judicial system, the refrain was, "It's too late." Lisa was now nothing more than a murderess.

It was becoming obvious, from the results of the hearings, that a defense based on the premise that Lisa had been fighting back against a lifetime of physical and verbal abuse wasn't going to work. The legal system pays too little heed to wife-beaters and child abusers. As I was learning painfully with Lisa, if a wife or a child fights back, she then faces the wrath of the law. If I was going to win Lisa's acquittal, I needed something else. And I knew what that something else was. Lisa was displaying all the classic signs of a woman who had been sexually abused as well as battered. The only question in my mind was to what extent. From her behavior, I felt it was severe. If I was going to save her, I had to know exactly how severe.

For some reason, jurors draw the line at sexual abuse. As jury thinking goes, a man can pound on his wife and kids—spare the rod and spoil the child, the saying goes—but he can't rape his daughters.

My solution was to hire a pair of private detectives. One, a woman, was instructed to befriend Lisa and find out what had happened to her. The other, John Kilroy, was assigned to document examples of Morris Keller's cruelty. It took months, but both detectives met with success. Lisa eventually opened up. As I expected, the sexual abuse both she and her mother had suffered at the hands of Morris Keller was shocking. Lisa confided that she had been used as a sexual plaything by her father from the time she was thirteen. He had frequently forced her to perform oral sex as well as intercourse, and was often sadistic. The timid "mouse" had grown so emotionally imprisoned by what her father subjected her to as a child that the sexual abuse continued beyond her teenage years and into her twenties.

After Lisa told her story, Dorothea was compelled to open up as well. Dorothea's ordeal hadn't been much better. She had been raped as a teenager, and already had four children when she met Morris. He forced her to give them up, then never let her forget it. He beat her frequently during their marriage, sending her to the hospital for "strokes" and "stumbles" and "dizzy spells" to cloak the abuse. Both she and Lisa lived in absolute fear of Morris. Over the years, the two women had bonded like condemned prisoners sharing the same cell. Even after Lisa grew up and was able to escape the home, Morris still kept Dorothea prisoner. It was Lisa's love for her mother, and Morris's hold over his wife, that forced Lisa not only to return home, but to continue to submit to him as she grew older. Every time Morris abused Dorothea, she would call Lisa for comfort. Lisa would come, and Morris would turn on her. The two women were emotionally powerless to break the chain.

Dorothea explained that she had briefly left Morris thirty years before, because she was tired of his abuse. She had an affair and became pregnant. During her pregnancy, she and Morris reconciled. Morris promised to treat Lisa as his own, but never did. What Dorothea didn't know was that when Lisa was thirteen, Morris's ill treatment took on a new form. He began to abuse his stepdaughter sexually and threatened her to keep quiet about it. From that point on, Morris was determined to make Lisa pay in kind for the sexual sin of her mother.

"These past thirty years we've been living with fear, and not just fright, but sweat fear," Dorothea said. "I'd lock myself in my bedroom, go to bed at seven o'clock so I wouldn't have any confrontation, so there would not be anything said.

"I feel, basically, if I had taken my girls and done anything but stay with him, this would never have happened to Lisa. But I was always afraid that he would find me and he would finish me for good."

The first thing I did after finally getting to the heart of Lisa Keller's case was to schedule Lisa for a psychiatric examination. I hired two of South Florida's best, psychiatrist Burton Cahn and psychologist Leonard Haber, a former mayor of Miami Beach. When Dr. Haber interviewed Lisa at the jail, she sat in a chair against the wall instead of in the chair at the table facing him. As she spoke, she played with her fingers and tugged on her sweater, exhibited "childlike mannerisms," and appeared to be hiding herself in her oversized clothing.

After careful study, both doctors concluded that Lisa was carrying deep psychological scars from a long and sustained period of physical and sexual abuse.

From all I had heard, it appeared that Morris Keller deserved every whack Lisa had given him. And it also clearly explained the viciousness of the assault. When Morris attacked her on the lawn, Lisa was finally forced to break through the emotional chains and summon up the courage to fight back. When this courage broke through, it brought with it dark memories of sixteen years of sexual cruelty. The combination forced her arm to keep swinging and swinging far beyond what was necessary to kill her stepfather.

The doctors termed it "the battered-woman syndrome." It is an innovative concept in psychiatric circles that was vividly brought to life by actress Farrah Fawcett in the famous television movie *The Burning Bed.* In the movie, based on a true story, Fawcett portrayed a woman who burned her abusive husband to death after he passed out drunk on his bed. The battered-woman syndrome is defined as a brief period of uncontrollable rage that explodes out of women who have been subjected to years of beatings and abuse.

To the cops and prosecutors, the battered-woman syndrome is just some psychiatric mumbo-jumbo. Blind justice called Lisa's actions murder. First-degree murder. Electric-chair murder. Sure, Lisa may have had it rough as a child, but so have many kids, the prevailing law-enforcement theory goes. That doesn't give them the right to kill one of their parents.

Defending Lisa in this climate, even with the factor of incest, wasn't going to be easy. It was a brutal murder. Lisa had confessed. She had admitted to previously buying the poison, thereby establishing a prior attempt and handing the state attorney premeditation on a platter. I went to my law books. As far as I could determine, no child had ever been acquitted in a jury trial for killing a sexually abusive parent. Most had pleaded out; others had been convicted of all degrees of unlawful homocide. Incredibly, in this merciful society of ours, there was no precedent upon which to hang a defense.

Once again, I would have to create my own.

18

THE CONDO MURDER, PART II:

The Depositions

THE LISA Keller trial was delayed five times, extending the trial date from December 1986 to the end of April 1987. For a while, it looked as if it was going to convene while I was in jail. However, delays postponed it long enough to let me serve my sentence.

Which is not to say things were quiet from October to April. There were enough new angles to keep the momentum building. But there was one aspect that didn't become public: I clamped the lid on the sexual-abuse disclosure. I didn't want it even hinted at publically until the trial. Unlike Hancock and the detectives, I wasn't going to reveal my hand to the media at some minor bond hearing.

Instead, Hancock and I battled for months over a pair of witnesses. The first was one of Hancock's stars, the guy who scammed Lisa with the fake poison. Apparently the man could also testify that Lisa told him she had tampered with Morris's medicine to try to kill him, and had supposedly hired a hit man who was going to make

Morris's death look like the result of a burglary. Under the circumstances, it's not surprising that Lisa dreamed up ways to rid herself of her father. Plotting revenge is one way the weak and oppressed deal with the psychological horror of their physical helplessness. However, the informant's information wouldn't look good to a jury. I needed to interview this mystery witness before he materialized in court.

Hancock couldn't provide him. He wasn't trying to be coy. The prosecutor was having trouble himself. The confidential informant was doing all he could to stay at home in Spring Valley, New York, and duck having to testify in sunny South Florida. I figured Hancock would eventually smoke him out just in time for the trial. Anticipating such a tactic, I moved to dismiss charges against Lisa, based upon this man's refusal to appear for a deposition. The judge, of course, tossed out my motion. He assured me I would be able to depose him before the trial.

The second witness was even more complicated. At the end of October, I consented to a request from the *Miami Herald* to interview Lisa in jail. It was part of my "condition the community" strategy, but the interview itself became the focus of the pretrial sparring and caused many of the delays. The actual interview was nothing special. Lisa told *Herald* reporter Christine Evans about the sorry conditions in jail and mentioned that she was under a twenty-four-hour suicide watch because of something she scribbled on a napkin: "I regret being forced to make the choice whether to live or die." Jail guards found the note and figured Lisa was contemplating killing herself. Actually, she was preparing for the trial and had written that down as a good answer to use when grilled by Hancock. The sticking point in the interview was Lisa's admission to killing her father and her expression of no regret.

"If I had to do it again, if I was in the same position, I would," she told Evans. "It came down to him or me."

The article's paraphrased headline—"Lisa Keller: I Don't Regret Beating My Father to Death"—was far stronger than her actual statements.

The prosecutors argued that this was an important confession made to another person, and that Evans was therefore obligated to appear as a witness. The judge agreed, noting that it was the only confession Lisa made to an unbiased party, and the journalist's testimony was vital. Hancock listed Evans as a prosecution witness.

It was getting close to the time I was scheduled to serve out my contempt sentence, and I wanted to get that over with before we went to court. Hancock's desire to call the newspaper reporter as a witness handed me the perfect delaying tactic. I immediately scheduled Evans for a deposition. I couldn't care less about talking to the reporter, but I knew it would get the *Herald*'s attorneys screaming. I figured throwing this wrench into the machinery would give me enough time to serve my sentence. I guessed correctly. Judge Speiser ordered Evans to appear for my deposition. The *Herald* appealed to the Fourth District Court of Appeals in West Palm Beach. The appellate judges ordered a delay in both the deposition and the trial, a delay that stretched on and on into late April. Not only was I able to serve out my sentence, including the extra week I spent in the hospital, but I had five weeks to prepare for the case after I got out. We still might be waiting to go to trial had we waited for the appellate judges to rule on the controversial issue of journalists testifying in court. Hancock gave up and agreed to waive Evans's testimony and get on with it. To pursue the ideal of speedy justice, I sacrificially agreed to drop my deposition request.

Even without the journalist, the pretrial deposition period produced fireworks. Morris Keller's brother Sam and sister Charlotte, both of New York, insisted that Morris did not abuse anyone. They called the accusations a big lie created by Dorothea. Sam said he couldn't even be sure of Dorothea's claim that Lisa wasn't Morris' child. (Morris is listed as Lisa's father on her birth certificate.) Charlotte termed the seventy-nine-pound Dorothea "a devious, lying, cunning woman" who dominated her husband, and described Morris as being "very timid."

"I do know that Morris wanted Lisa to move to Florida so that it would be easier to take care of her," Charlotte added.

Back came Vicky to the defense. She was my witness, so her deposition was with Hancock. She countered that her aunt and uncle didn't live in their house and therefore didn't know what was going on: "What were we going to tell Aunt Charlotte, that he's beating on Mom, so that when we get home she would get it worse? We didn't say anything. You can't.

". . . Mother had black and blue marks on her arms that go around the arms like somebody grabbed you. But she kept on telling me, 'Oh, she fell, she hit a chair.' And I said, 'I'm not stupid.' "

Vicky told Hancock her father had confided to her that "love is a useless emotion." He was "mean, rotten, cruel, and vicious" but he didn't mess with her much because she herself was "mean, rotten, cruel, and vicious." She added that he had punched her in the mouth once after accusing her of eating the last piece of cheese in the refrigerator.

"I don't even like cheese!" Vicky said.

Tough as Vicky was in fending off her father, she enlisted additional help. Her boyfriend and future husband, Eugene Marron, is a no-nonsense emergency medical technician and police dispatcher. While he and Vicky were dating, he said he once caught Morris and her arguing, and jumped in when Morris "attempted to swing at her."

"At the time I told him that if he ever did it again, I would rip his heart out and stick it down his throat," Marron told Hancock.

Morris, Marron added, didn't bother Vicky after that.

The most anguished relative appeared to be Lisa's older sister, Candace Herbst, forty, of Westport, Connecticut. Candace, who has a master's degree in library science, loved her father, mother, and sisters, and didn't want to get caught in the middle. She knew nothing about any abuse and didn't want to testify. Her description of seeing Lisa in the police station shortly after the confession is touching.

"I was very upset. I remember holding my sister and crying. . . . I asked her if she really did it and she said yes. And then I asked her if she really hated Daddy that much and she said yes. And she said that I didn't know what had been going on."

It was the doctors, however, who best described "what had been going on."

Dr. Cahn, the former director of a Broward County organization that aided battered women, was used to emotional encounters with abused women and children. Still, Lisa's case was so severe he was admittedly shaken. He described his interviews with Lisa as "a very heavy, very dramatic, very tense, very emotional type of experience, both for her and for me."

Dr. Haber, a clinical psychologist and former psychology professor at Hunter College in New York, was more descriptive in his pretrial testimony with Hancock. He painted a chilling psychological portrait of both the battered woman and her attacker.

> Lisa began as a battered child. She observed her mother as a battered woman. She became a battered woman . . . she was also sexually abused by her father, in my opinion, based upon the examination, from the age of thirteen until the age of twenty-nine. Sixteen years. An incredible history.

. . . He used to hover over her. And she got this sense that battered women and battered children get, a separate sense of the presence of somebody. It's almost like a spooky kind of feeling that he was there and she would awaken to find him there.

He was feeding her, and he was providing a shelter for her, and making a home for her. And she could and should and must repay him with these sexual favors. And he introduced her to sex . . . oral sex and sexual intercourse and other things of that type . . . if she didn't do it, he would beat her mother and he would beat her. And he would take off after her younger sister. And furthermore, he advised her that she ought to be thankful and happy that he was giving her this opportunity. . . . She didn't have to do what the other kids had to do, specifically, do it in public. The same things, but in the presence of other adults that would be friends of his, implying that not only might they watch but participate. But he wasn't going to make her do that. And she ought to be thankful that she was blessed with the privilege of the privacy of these acts.

. . . She never told her mother. Typically, unbelievably. But, typically. That's the way these things are.

. . . She also has what is an extremely clear case of post-traumatic stress reaction. She is suffering from the same disorder as a war veteran would have that was brutalized in Vietnam. And she is jumpy beyond belief, untrusting, recurrent nightmares retriggering all of that stuff . . . you carry it with you in the form of nightmares, perspiration, fear, overreaction, hyperactive sensitivity.

Dr. Haber also gave a vivid description of what happened the night Lisa killed her father—from the perspective of what was going on inside Lisa's mind:

The battered syndrome is a cycle of tension building to explosiveness. . . . It's almost like a manic depressive psychosis. You get your fingerprint, each one a little different. But the cycle is the same. . . . In her case, it may have been finally triggered by a heinous offense in their family. Brutalizing males tend to be arbitrary and domineering and demanding and capricious and insulting. This is the technique of intimidation they use to browbeat their women. Now, he had a rule that she violated. And the rule was only one glass of water was permitted to be served at the dinner table. And everybody must drink from that glass. And she wouldn't drink from his glass. I saw a film once on brutalization, in which in order to drink you had to drink like an animal, licking the liquid out of the hand of the brutalizer. I mean, that's taking it—degradation— to another level. This is only one step removed from that. This is mine, you want a drink, you come and ask me permission to drink out of this glass.

. . . He threatened Lisa. He's going to finish her once and for all. And when he came back he was going to take care of this matter. . . . She and her mother were hoping, as they always do. They're hoping maybe, maybe, maybe. Sometimes there is a distraction, something happens, and the guy comes back. He's in a good mood. He doesn't beat them that day. So they're spared that time. You don't know. Part of the terror is you never know what's going to happen. . . .

. . . Lisa found something, a stick, a wooden object, hit him with it. Struck him a blow. Stopped him. . . . She was now terrified of him, of herself, for her mother, for what was going to happen. And now she's additionally terrified that she had hurt him. And the one thing that battered women and children don't do is resist, let alone fight back, because it intensifies the beating that they get.

. . . And I would say that sometime in that time frame, from the time that she fell back and hit him the first blow when she was panicked to the time that she struck him repeatedly, I would say that in my opinion her mental state would have gone from terrified to berserk. . . .

Dr. Haber said the abuse and emotional shock may have continued at the police station:

I'm paraphrasing her again. Something to the effect that if she only told them [the detectives] and finished it, she'd be out sooner. She'd be released the next day . . . she wouldn't be prosecuted. . . . I've done so many hundreds of these. And I've heard so many stories. And these things do tend to happen. It doesn't mean it happened in this case. But, you know, police have their job and they, they're very good at it too. So what she was explaining to me in her own naïve way is a subtle process of intentional manipulation. . . . I mean, a person that's locked up and charged with first-degree murder and threatened with the electric chair and deprived of their freedom, this is another blow, another shock. And being told everything will be okay, "just tell us," and "Wasn't it this?" and "We can't finish until you give us the details." . . . You don't care where you end up and what difference does it make to you since you've told them everything anyway. So whatever they say, whatever they want to hear, you tell them instead of arguing and prolonging it. The idea is that a battered person doesn't want to prolong anything, even if it means they get punched in the face. They want to get it over with and get on with it. And that may be the psychology behind that subtle process of moving from the initial disclosure [confession] with gaps to a final story.

Regarding Dorothea, Dr. Haber's diagnosis was similar:

She went through her whole history. . . . He abused her sexually, forced sex on her. But basically beat her, intimidated her, verbally assaulted her, belittled her, berated her, humiliated her. These are terrorizing, intimidating tactics . . . here is a woman that doesn't go around telling any of her neighbors she is battered from pillar to post. . . . She is real chattel, in the biblical sense, and feels impotent to absolutely do anything about it.

In March, Hancock's evasive star witness, the bogus poison-pill salesman, was finally flushed out. The Westchester, New York, police kept asking the burly ex-con to come to the station and cooperate with the Florida authorities, and he kept refusing. Finally they followed his car and nailed him for failing to signal on a turn. They tossed him in jail and told him he would be on the next flight to Fort Lauderdale.

The guy turned out to be William O'Brien, alias Frank Russo, alias Joe Benedict, alias Frank O'Connor. He was sixty-one years old and admitted to past convictions for attempted armed robbery, gambling, conspiracy to commit bribery, and possession of a pistol. He had spent a third of his life in prison, including a stint at Sing Sing. (As an interesting aside, the career criminal told me he's now retired and receives Social Security, Medicare, and food stamps. As that Russian comedian says, "What a country!")

O'Brien said a friend of Lisa's told him about her problems with her father. O'Brien decided to take advantage of her emotional state by conning her into buying the phony pills. He received $5,000 in two payments and gave Lisa's friend $1,850 for tipping him off to such an easy mark.

In April 1987, a few days before the trial was to begin, Lisa tossed a bomb of her own. She decided, without notice, to fire me. I received a call from a Fort Lauderdale attorney saying he and a second lawyer from Hollywood, Florida, were taking over the case. He said Lisa had lost confidence in me. I knew why. Part of the reason was that I had been in jail the previous month serving my contempt sentence, and that made Lisa and Dorothea extremely nervous about my preparation. Another reason was that I abhor coaching witnesses, something many lawyers swear by. When you coach witnesses, they sound stiff and phony on the stand, and the jury sees right through them. I like my witnesses to be natural. I interview them enough to know what they'll say, but I stop at revealing the exact questions I plan to ask. Sometimes I don't know myself what the questions will be until I get a feel for the trial. This practice tends to make some of my clients uneasy. They expect long coaching sessions and become uneasy as the trial approaches and no such sessions are called.

Another reason is that that little boy who stuttered still resides inside me. While I could speak before an impersonal mass ten thousand people at Ft. Lauderdale's Yankee Stadium without blinking, or battle a mob of news reporters with relish, I'm still somewhat uneasy in direct, one-on-one conversations. That trait often makes me appear distant and uncaring to some of my clients.

While these were contributing factors in Lisa's decision, there was one final aspect that I felt may have spurred her decision. When Lisa explained her story to me in detail, she changed some things. She said her father had knocked her down and jumped on top of her and was choking her when she reached into the bushes, found the stick, and hit him. From her confession, it appeared as though she was standing up when she hit him. Lisa explained, as Dr. Haber had, that she was so intimidated by the detectives' threats to jail her mother that she told them anything they wanted to hear. During the previous week I had been rough on her because I was having trouble with her new story. The way she described it conflicted with the medical examiner's testimony of how the wounds were patterned and where Morris's eyeglasses had ended up. The first blow sent the glasses forward, and the medical examiner was prepared to testify that Morris had been struck from behind, and not from the front or side, as Lisa described. I knew Hancock was going to jump all over this, and such a discrepancy could lose the case. For three days I made Lisa reenact the struggle on the floor of the jail while I played the part of Morris. It continued to come out wrong. Lisa was getting upset, and so was I.

"If I'm surprised in the courtroom, Lisa, you die," I said.

Lisa couldn't understand that I was trying to protect her from Hancock and the medical examiner. The actual angles of the blows meant nothing as far as my defense went, because both of the doctors, Cahn and Haber, felt Lisa was justified in fighting back against her father's attack. The human brain has a protective mechanism that often blacks out the details of a terrible incident. Lisa was no doubt having trouble trying to reopen those doors. The problem was, if Hancock and the medical examiner could make her appear to be a liar at that critical stage in her story, the jury might feel she was lying about everything else.

I wasn't getting through, so I devised another strategy. I anticipated that Hancock would ask Lisa to demonstrate the attack in court.

"Don't let Hancock get you out of the witness stand," I said. "When you step out of the chair, you're dead."

I advised her to do exactly what she had done with me numerous times—say she couldn't relive it.

She agreed. But apparently she felt I didn't believe in her anymore. She made a few calls to Dorothea after I left, and they decided to hire someone else. Judge Speiser refused to delay the trial to give the new attorneys time to prepare. I told the judge I'd be there on Monday, ready to go, and if Lisa wanted to fire me then, she could. That evening, Dorothea called, apologized, and asked me to stay on. Lisa called minutes later, apologized, and made the same request. We were all one big happy family again.

WITH ALL we had going against us, it wasn't surprising that our courtroom adversary would be one of the fastest-rising stars in the Florida judicial system. Kelly Hancock, thirty-seven, is a blue-eyed, apple-cheeked blond who could serve as a poster boy for the armed forces. He epitomizes the all-American boy. In a courtroom, Hancock appears as the absolute embodiment of law and order—the handsome, heroic protector of you and me and everything we hold dear. Hancock had combined his looks with a sharp legal mind and the heart of a farm-mortgage banker to compile a nearly perfect 100–1 record, including 66–1 in murder trials. His only loss was to a man whose brother shot and killed a young law student following an altercation in a Fort Lauderdale nightclub packed with drunken college students on spring break. Hancock wanted both brothers to fall because the one who had nothing to do with the impromptu shooting had nevertheless driven the getaway car. The jury convicted only the gunman.

Among Hancock's convictions is Roswell Gilbert, the seventy-five-year-old from the famous "mercy killing" trial. Gilbert's elderly wife had Alzheimer's disease along with a second debilitating illness. Gilbert shot her because he couldn't bear to see her in so much pain. Hancock cut through the public sympathy and put the poor old guy away for life. (The incident later became a television movie, *Mercy or Murder,* starring Robert Young. Coincidentally, Sergeant Scheff was the detective who handled the Gilbert case.)

Hancock was showing a similar lack of mercy for Lisa. Invoking his prosecutorial power, he kept the electric chair as the stakes in her trial.

In addition to this hurdle, Scheff and Amabile had never lost a homicide case in their entire careers, either alone or working as a team.

When a star prosecutor and some hot detectives are on a roll as Hancock, Scheff, and Amabile were, the judge usually gets swept up in their momentum. Decisions go their way. They are the home team. The defense attorney is the visitor. The prosecutor's objections are sustained while his opponent's are overruled. The prosecutor owns the courtroom.

Judge Mark Speiser is a young Tom Selleck type. I found it ironic that Lisa Keller, abused all her life by a man in a male-dominated world, would be pitted against a group of men who looked like they could do a fashion spread in *GQ*. In the early rounds, the pretrial hearings and motions, Judge Speiser had rejected virtually all of my pleas and had given Hancock and his detectives anything they wanted, including keeping Lisa in jail without bond. Thankfully, once the trial started, Speiser proved himself to be fair and evenhanded.

THE LISA Keller trial started off with a bang. The biggest bomb of all was dropped during the normally mundane jury selection.

Prior to the jury selection, the first question I had to ask myself was, "Do I want a dumb jury or a smart jury?" This time, because so much of the defense rested upon the testimony of the psychiatrist and psychologist, I wanted a smart jury. That meant college-educated professionals. And in contrast to most cases, I wanted authority figures on this jury. Morris Keller, as a father, was an authority figure. I felt that those in similar positions—fathers, office managers, or other supervisors—would be angered by his abuse of power. I particularly wanted fathers of little girls. On the women's side, there would be some natural sympathy, but it went beyond that. From the depositions, I knew that Lisa's oldest sister, Candace, was going to testify against her mother and sisters. Candace had married into wealth and she had been Morris's favorite. While Lisa had been sexually abused, the older sister had been praised by her father and sent to college. Lisa and Dorothea were literally and figuratively the poor stepchildren who never got a break. I wanted women jurors who would identify with Lisa and Dorothea and not with the rich older sister.

Once I had set my parameters, I could then plead my case before the jurors—not after they were selected, but during the selection process. One thing lawyers often overlook is that the jury-selection process gives you a chance to get your side of the story in first. I needed to condition the jury to the defense I was going to present. This is done through carefully selected, open-ended questions. Many lawyers ask jurors "closed" questions—those that can be answered yes or no. For instance, "Are you prejudiced against blacks?" Or, more subtly, "Will the fact that the defendant is black affect your thinking in any way?" Those questions will elicit a simple negative and will tell you nothing, not even whether the person is prejudiced. Rarely does anyone admit that.

A lawyer needs to draw a juror into a conversation that brings out what you need to know about him or her. There's not much time, so the questions can't be wasted. Seven of my favorites are:

1) "What kind of pets do you have? If none, why?"

2) "What do the bumper stickers on your car say? Why don't you have any?"

3) "What does 'reasonable doubt' mean to you?"

4) "How do you feel the courts are dealing with criminals today?"

5) "What's the most important thing you teach your children?"

6) "How do you get news? TV, radio, papers? Why?"

7) "How do you spend your spare time? Hobbies, clubs, groups, politics?'"

The above questions can quickly reveal a person's religion, moral code, sympathies, lifestyle, political leanings, and prejudices.

After going through my routine questioning, I picked one specific juror to begin trying my case. He was an ex-marine and the father of several daughters.

"What do you think of a father who sexually abuses his thirteen-year-old daughter?" I asked.

"A guy like that deserves no sympathy at all," the prospective juror answered firmly.

There were ripples of noise throughout the courtroom. Prior to that question, no one had had a clue as to what my defense would be. There had been reams of newspaper and television stories about Morris's death and Lisa's arrest, but nothing had surfaced about the sexual abuse. Not a word. Up to that point, the story had been that Morris Keller had physically abused his wife and daughter, and Lisa had killed him either by design or in self-defense. When I asked the ex-marine my question, the whole course of the trial changed. The startled look on Judge Speiser's face is something I'll never forget.

I asked the other potential jurors the same question in different ways.

"What if the father says, 'I'll kill you if you tell your mother?'"

"Do you know what 'justifiable homicide' means?"

"How do you feel about incest?"

"Did you see the movie *The Burning Bed?*"

I was planting seeds and hammering away at my message.

I picked out a woman and asked her if she had ever heard of the battered-woman syndrome. Since she hadn't, I was allowed to explain it. In two hours of questioning, I had everyone in the courtroom thinking that Morris Keller had possibly sexually abused his daughter. They had arrived believing Lisa was a vicious animal, and were now viewing her with the deepest sympathy. If we could have taken a vote then, Lisa Keller may have been acquitted by the whole jury pool, 75–0.

I also sat the intelligent jury I wanted. There were eight men and four women, including a retired electrical engineer, a newspaper photographer, two bookkeepers, a computer operator, a pipefitter, a restaurant supervisor, a retired gas station owner, an insurance agent, an engineer, and a housewife. The male/female ratio was also planned. On the surface, one might think it would have been better to have more women on the jury. The problem with that logic is women tend to judge other women more harshly than men do. Women might be prone to think that it was somehow Lisa and Dorothea's fault for tolerating the abuse, and might not be able to understand why they didn't just leave the guy. From my experience, even a woman juror with an alcoholic, abusive husband waiting at home frequently fails to see her own weakness in others.

Men, on the other hand, understand the dominance factor. Somewhere in their family is a sister, daughter, or cousin married to a rotten jerk she refuses to leave. The male jurors would see Lisa and Dorothea as victims, and view Morris Keller as slime.

Unfortunately, we had an entire trial to go through before the men and women of this brainy jury would take their vote. Hancock would be given the time he needed to regroup and counterattack my defense. Still, despite the overwhelming odds against me, I felt the case was now mine to lose.

IN HIS opening statement, Hancock described Lisa as a calculating killer, and characterized the killing as "one of the most vicious homicides in Broward County history."

My opening statement continued to pound home the message that Morris Keller was a horrible beast who created his own killer. I described the lifetime of misery he had inflicted upon both Lisa and Dorothea.

"From the age of thirteen until August of 1985, Lisa was Morris Keller's sex slave."

The "sex slave" comment brought in the national press. That was part of the plan. If it was to serve any purpose at all, Lisa's case had to be tried in public. I wanted the whole community, and the whole nation, to know what Morris Keller had done, and what Kelly Hancock was trying to do to Lisa in return. I wanted the jurors' husbands, wives, sons, and daughters to know. To free Lisa, I had to set a legal precedent. To accomplish that, I felt I had to expand the courtroom beyond the walls of the courthouse.

In the following morning's *Fort Lauderdale Sun-Sentinel*, the trial coverage included sixteen paragraphs paraphrasing or quoting my opening statement.

There were three sentences devoted to Hancock's.

HANCOCK OPENED his case by calling Dr. Tate to the stand and displaying a series of grisly color photographs showing Morris Keller's brains literally oozing out of his caved-in skull. When Hancock brought the photos by for me to view, Lisa saw them and recoiled in horror. She began sobbing so loudly that Judge Speiser had to call a recess.

Hancock was just getting started. While the heart of his case centered around the savagery of Lisa's attack and the prior plot to poison her father, he reached into the netherworld and tried to paint Lisa and Dorothea as lesbian lovers. Throughout the trial he hinted at an incestuous homosexual relationship. The hints turned into headlines.

"Maybe it was Dorothea, not Morris . . . who was having a closer relationship than would be normal," Hancock quipped to a *Newsday* correspondent.

In court, Hancock used some of Lisa's poignant letters to Dorothea as his "proof." Lisa's poetic expressions of love were certainly beyond what most women would write, but they were nothing more than the heartfelt feelings of a woman who loved both her mother and the written word. I jumped all over Hancock for trying to dirty this beautiful mother-daughter relationship. I read a number of the moving letters to the jury. A few of the women jurors became teary-eyed at the loving sentiments Lisa expressed.

Hancock called a corrections officer to the stand to testify about the "unusual" things she had observed in Lisa's cell during her seventy-year-old mother's visits. According to her, Lisa and Dorothea hugged and kissed when they first met, and Dorothea had put her hand on Lisa's knee as they talked.

"What are you trying to say?" I demanded from the now-embarrassed officer on cross-examination. "What is your filthy mind trying to say?"

After a lifetime of sexual abuse, after claiming to have been tricked into a confession, after being kept in jail because of a detective's misstatement, after being denied outside medical care, Lisa was now being subjected to a public smear campaign of the worst kind.

Hancock's low-road tactic did cause me a moment of panic. One of the witnesses I had subpoenaed for Lisa was a longtime friend. She was to testify that Lisa was afraid of her father and had confided some of the ways he abused her. I had the woman flown in from her home up north. During a break in the trial, I was having lunch at a nearby restaurant that attorneys frequent. I heard a conversation coming from the booth behind me.

"Did you get a look at that witness Rubin's calling, Lisa's girlfriend?" one attorney said.

"Yeah," the other answered. "What a bull dyke! Kelly's really going to do a number on her. That's his case right there. I think I'll take off to see that."

I left my food half-eaten and raced down to the courthouse. I spotted Lisa's friend sitting on a bench in front of the courtroom. The woman was about six feet tall and had short-cropped hair and all the mannerisms of a man. She admitted she was a lesbian. I told her what I had heard at the restaurant.

"Oh my God," she said. "What should we do?"

"We should get you the hell out of here, fast!" I said. "I'm canceling the subpoena."

I asked Dorothea to take her down a back stairway and put her in a cab for the airport. I told her to stay at a friend's house when she got home, take time off from work, and not answer the telephone. Hancock would have to locate and subpoena her himself if he wanted her back.

It was perfectly normal that Lisa, an outcast in high school, would have befriended others who were unconventional. Nor was it unusual that a poet who traveled in creative circles would have many gay friends. There was nothing beyond friendship involved. But Hancock wouldn't see it that way. He tried to find the woman. During my entire defense, he kept asking me when I was going to call "Lisa's friend."

Meanwhile, the skittish William O'Brien made it to the trial. He almost had a cardiac arrest when he spotted the *Miami Herald*'s talented court photographer, Pete Cross, taking aim with his Nikon. O'Brien apparently was unaware that cameras are allowed in the courtroom in Florida. He begged the judge to let him wear dark glasses. After a conference, the judge announced that O'Brien suffered from photophobia, and granted his request.

The camera-shy ex-con told the jury that he'd gotten Lisa's phone number from the friend, called, then met her in Manion's Bar, an Irish tavern in Yonkers, New York. They'd met again in the lobby of the Crowne Plaza Hotel in White Plains, New York. According to O'Brien, Lisa told him that she'd hired a hit man to "have the old man wiped out," but the hit man took her money, $5,000, and skipped. Figuring she was an easy mark, O'Brien decided to rip her off for another $5,000 by offering to sell her a magic death potion that couldn't be detected by a medical examiner. Lisa bit and paid the money in cash. O'Brien gave her sugar pills. The con man then realized he could end up being charged in a murder conspiracy. So, after ripping her off, he went to the district attorney and ratted her out.

Normally, a defense attorney would try to discredit the witness by pointing out his criminal record and other unsavory qualities. In this case, I didn't feel I needed to do much of that. His actions spoke for themselves. Instead, I asked him why Lisa wanted to poison her father. He said Lisa told him that she and her mother had been put through "many, many years of abuse and degradation."

I couldn't have said it better myself.

Hancock then called Robert Neary, the Westchester County, New York, assistant district attorney to whom O'Brien sang. Neary said he questioned Lisa, but found her "too frail" to pose a threat to anyone.

Detective Amabile followed. He played Lisa's confession. A taped confession played in a packed courtroom is almost always the dramatic highlight of a trial. The hushed audience listens spell-bound as a killer breaks down and 'fesses up. You never see this on television because television is a visual medium that needs to have the action of the surprise witness leaping out of the audience and confessing. In the real world, taped confessions are the dramatic equivalent. Lisa's confession was as spellbinding as they come.

Typically, as the last words of a confession echo off the court-room walls, a good prosecutor heightens the drama by standing and announcing "Your Honor, the prosecution rests!" Bang the drums and cut to the commercial. Hancock played right to script.

But it was the wrong script. He rested his case on the biggest blunder of the entire investigation. Lisa had not confessed to hiding in the bushes and sneaking up behind her father. She hadn't con-fessed to any premeditation at all. The jurors had heard Scheff testify about her "crouching in the hedges" and Amabile testify about her "hiding in the bushes," and had heard Hancock orate on her sneaking up behind her father and pounding him with the club. Then, when the big moment came—they found she had said noth-ing of the sort. The detectives had misled them. Hancock had mis-led them. They treated the jurors the same way O'Brien had treated Lisa—like a sucker.

Jurors don't like being treated this way. And in case any of them didn't realize how they had been duped, my cross-examina-tion of Amabile brought it all out. The poor detective had nowhere to hide. He said Lisa had admitted the premeditation in the previous untaped confession, but he had written on the arrest affidavit that she had said all those things in the taped confession.

"She never used those words, you did!" I said.

RUBIN: Why didn't you just tape the whole session?
AMABILE: We just didn't.
RUBIN: Isn't it because there was no mention . . . of intent to kill?

The detective just hung his head in silence.

It was a terrible ending to the prosecution's case—and a great beginning for my defense.

19

THE CONDO MURDER, PART III:

The Defense

*The battered woman frequently, to escape being battered,
has to kill the batterer. That's what our society makes
them do.*
—Dr. Burton Cahn

MY FIRST witness was Dorothea Keller.

The tiny woman walked through a silent courtroom and climbed into a witness box that practically swallowed her. Her faced was framed by a halo of wispy white hair. She spoke in a soft, trembling voice and frequently dabbed her eyes. Her life story was one horror after another.

Dorothea said she had been beaten so often by her father that she was forced as a teenager to run away from home. She caught a ride to the train station from a family friend. He raped her on the way.

"I didn't know you were a virgin," she recalled him saying. "Your father told me you were a whore."

That evening, she stayed at her aunt's. The woman's husband came home drunk and tried to rape Dorothea himself. She escaped and was taken off the street by a friendly truckdriver who let her sleep in the cab of his vehicle. She took up with the man, Robert D'Orsio, had three daughters by him, but never married. She then met and married a soldier named John Curran and had another daughter. He deserted his wife, his children, and the military in a single dash and was never seen again.

Dorothea met Morris in 1945, when she caught him in bed with a friend of hers. He was a sailor, and invited her to follow him to California. She did, leaving her four daughters with her mother. Morris insisted that she forget about the children, and she complied, instructing her mother to put them up for adoption. They were placed with a wealthy family and remained together.

Things were okay for the first few years. Then Morris became violent. It reached the point where Dorothea was beaten on a weekly basis.

"I was used to it," she said. "It was a fact of my life."

The couple moved to the Bronx, New York. Dorothea had two more daughters by Morris, and Lisa in between by another man. Although they had lived together since 1945, she and Morris didn't marry until 1967. Dorothea said Morris held on to her by threatening either to kill her or to expose her past to her children.

Morris became increasingly violent, sending his battered wife to the hospital on several occasions. Once, while she was hospitalized, Morris tried to break into her room. The nurses moved her to another, and she heard him screaming through the corridors, "I'll find you and I'll kill you."

I introduced hospital records and police reports to back up that part of her story.

Dorothea continued. She said Morris often demanded that she perform oral sex, which she refused. After one demand, he hit her in the back and knocked her down the stairs.

"I laid there for three days. I didn't move for three days. He had to step over me."

Even when they both reached their seventies, neither Morris's abuse nor his sexual appetite let up. Dorothea testified that he refused to let her attend her one condominium activity, a weekly bingo game, unless she had sex with him.

"I told him I'd rather not go."

In 1981, Dorothea said she was severely beaten and took an overdose of Valium in a suicide attempt.

As Lisa matured, Dorothea said she also became a target of Morris's abuse. But Dorothea claimed to have known nothing about the sexual aspect.

I took Dorothea all through her painful past because I wanted to bring out all the "dirt" under my gentle questioning. I didn't want to leave anything for Hancock to attack, if he chose that course. A cardinal rule of trials is that you don't harshly interrogate pregnant women or little old ladies. As I anticipated, Hancock ignored it. He attacked Dorothea by painting her as a liar and as a heartless, immoral woman who had borne a litter of illegitimate children, then abandoned them for a man she hardly knew. Dorothea merely cried harder. That technique might work with an arrogant forty-year-old who shot her rich old husband for his money, but it alarms the jury when it's done to a shattered, elderly woman. I couldn't understand what Hancock felt he was accomplishing.

My next witness, on the eighth day of the trial, was Victoria Marron, Lisa's sister. Animated and sure of herself, Vicky vacillated between giggling and crying. Lisa, sitting beside me at the defense table, mirrored her younger sister's emotions. Vicky said her father had treated Lisa like dirt and explained how Lisa earned her nickname, "Stupid." Morris would sit the girls on the bed and ask them math questions. When Lisa hesitated, he'd slap her and knock her off the bed. After that, "Stupid" became Lisa's official name.

Vicky described the welts and bruises she often saw on both her mother's and her sister's bodies, and said Lisa called her once, screaming, "He tried to kill me! He tried to kill me!" Rushing over, Vicky found "hand rings, literally, hand rings around her neck. It was gross."

Vicky testified that she had called the police on her father during the cheese incident mentioned earlier, but her mother refused to confirm her story and the police were unable to do anything. Her mother, she said, was too afraid of being killed to speak out.

I asked the feisty Vicky why she didn't hit her father back.

"I would have been murdered. He would have beat the bloody daylights out of me."

She quoted her mother as saying, whenever she pleaded with her to leave her father, "He'll find me and kill me."

Vicky testified that when Lisa had her pacemaker implanted, Morris felt it was nothing but a way to get attention. Vicky found that incredible. "I said, 'Dad, you don't do this to get attention.'"

Vicky added that she married a Catholic man and had a Roman Catholic wedding. Her family is Jewish. Her father refused to attend the wedding and refused to allow anyone else in the family to attend.

"No one showed up," Vicky said tearfully.

THE DOCTORS followed. From the standpoint of legal history, their testimony was the most important. Both doctors, Cahn and Haber, were superb. Dr. Cahn, the former director of Women in Distress, was particularly engrossing.

"There's no question in my mind Lisa believed sincerely her life was in danger and her mother's life was in danger, and that hers was in imminent danger unless she ended her father's life," he testified.

"Nobody knows what goes on behind closed doors in the home or in the bedroom. No one on the outside has any idea of the abuse. . . . A battered woman, frequently, to escape being battered, has to kill the batterer. That's what our society makes them do. They have no escape."

Dr. Cahn estimated that 30 to 35 percent of American women live with abusive men. The abuse intensifies as time goes on. He said the women tolerate it for many reasons: they believe the man will stop; their pride prevents them from admitting they made such a lousy choice; they are afraid the man will hunt them down and kill them if they leave; they feel they are unskilled and unable to make it on their own financially, or are afraid to try.

The police, Dr. Cahn continued, prefer not to get involved in what they refer to as "domestic disturbances," and the beatings are often worse after the police officers leave.

Dr. Cahn said both Lisa and Dorothea showed the classic signs of the battered-woman syndrome, which he defined as years of physical beatings and emotional torment combined with an inability to escape the home for the previously mentioned reasons—fear, denial, love, pride, and/or economics. He further stated that Lisa additionally displayed the signs of a woman who had been sexually abused, a factor that occurs in one-third of all child-abuse cases.

It was by no means unusual that Lisa didn't tell anyone what her father was forcing her to do, the doctor said. He quoted Lisa as saying she was afraid her mother might think she instigated it, that she was ashamed, and that her father had threatened to kill her if she told anyone. These factors, the doctor testified, are frequently cited by sexually abused children.

Hancock attacked Dr. Cahn's credibility, pointing out that he had never testified about the battered-woman syndrome in court before. He repeatedly asked why the doctor didn't run to the police with his theories and discoveries about Lisa, and why he didn't try to find out why Lisa's story had changed from the original version she told the police.

"I felt Lisa was sincere with me, honest with me, truthful with me," he answered. "The feelings she was conveying you couldn't make up. I don't care how great an actress you are. . . . Lisa was so realistic, so believable that I would have believed Lisa in contrast to the police officers."

Dr. Haber supported Dr. Cahn's findings and focused on the sexual abuse. He turned out to be one of the most effective medical experts I've ever put on the stand. As he elaborated on his gripping testimony from his deposition, I was so captivated that I frequently forgot that I was supposed to ask him questions.

Dr. Haber described to the jurors how Lisa was forced to have sex with her father, sometimes two or three times a week, from the age of thirteen until she was twenty-nine. He quoted Lisa as saying that her father was "vile, insulting," and that he had made her feel dirty. Dr. Haber described Lisa as a woman with low self-esteem who had lived in fear of her father.

According to Dr. Haber, Lisa told her mother that she was afraid of the dark, and that was why her father spent so much time in her bedroom.

On day ten, I called Lisa Keller to the stand. I usually don't recommend that the accused testify. There's too much that can go wrong during the cross-examination, especially with a pit bull like Kelly Hancock. In Lisa's case, however, she had a story I wanted the jury to hear. Directly from her.

Shaking with fright and hiding under a bulky sweater, an ashen

Lisa spoke in a voice that cracked, quavered, and often broke down completely. She squeezed a tissue and clutched in her hand a small cardboard heart her mother had made for her. When things grew tense, she twirled the heart around her finger. Spectators in the overflowing courtroom strained to hear every word.

> He told me I was at the age [thirteen] where a girl changes from a girl to a woman. He told me I would have to know what my responsibilities were as a woman. He didn't want anyone else to show me. He put his hands into my clothes, over my chest. He put his hands in my pants. He said, "This is where men find pleasure in a woman. It's necessary for you to know that."
>
> He told me . . . I had to know what my obligations were . . . my mom wasn't fulfilling her wifely chores [by refusing to perform oral sex] and that I should be proud to do that for him.

Even when she was twenty-nine and he was sixty-nine, she had yet to awaken from this nightmare.

> LISA: He told me he wanted to play. I told him I didn't want to play, but I didn't really have much choice. I felt filthy. I felt like a tramp and I wasn't. I hated myself and hated him. I wished he would . . .
> RUBIN: Would die?
> LISA: Would die. So I wouldn't have to put up with it.

The scars of that upbringing could be seen in virtually every aspect of Lisa's life. She told the jurors that her best friend had been a car, a 1974 Volkswagen Beetle she named Cory Leslie Simon. The car was destroyed in an accident with a bus, and the brokenhearted Lisa held a funeral for it. Her mom attended. Her father didn't.

Lisa tried to commit suicide in college by slashing her wrists. After that, she spent eighteen months in a nonviolent utopian commune in Canada, trying to heal herself and rid her soul of the violence and degradation. But she couldn't shake the haunting memories of her mother continuing to suffer the brunt of Morris's rage all alone. She kept returning home.

When her parents sold their longtime home in New York, Lisa, Dorothea, and Vicky walked around the yard and embraced the trees and shrubs they had planted, watered, and nurtured, and said a personal good-bye to each one.

> I have one vivid memory of my tenth birthday. My mom was having a party for me and she bought me a birthday hat. It was blue and had

a yellow feather on it. My dad wanted me to wear a hat he had made out of newspaper like a crown. When I refused, he said, "I have a present for you." He brought over a [boiling] pot of coffee, off the stove . . . and he dumped it on [my mother's] lap, grains and all.

Lisa admitted that she bought the bogus poison from O'Brien, but said she flushed it down the toilet when she realized that she couldn't take someone's life, even her father's. On the night she did take his life, she had little choice.

But that story would have to wait. As if the trial weren't already dramatic enough, Lisa's Friday-afternoon testimony was interrupted by the lateness of the day. She had just started to explain how her decision to drink out of her own glass of water ignited her father's final rage. The effect was like a season-ending cliff-hanger on a television soap opera.

The weekend was a welcome break for everyone, including the jury and audience. It had been one of the most tense and fatiguing weeks in court I'd ever experienced. On Monday, everyone was fresh. That wasn't altogether good. I didn't want Lisa to be fresh when I handed her over to Hancock, yet she had to be strong enough to fend off his verbal thrusts. I slowly and painstakingly had her go through the story of the killing. I wanted her to relive every blow, every moment. I wanted the jury to be with her mentally and physically.

He was out of control. He was talking crazy. I was afraid for my life. . . . I'm sorry the way things turned out, but it was either him or me. I killed my dad because I was trying to defend myself. If I didn't, my father would be on trial for murder now instead of me.

Lisa broke down in tears. The mental strain from Friday quickly combined with Monday's ordeal to sap her energy and leave her wrung out. She had been on the stand a total of ten hours and had relived the darkest moments of a very dark life. There was little that even Hancock could do at that point. He gave it a shot, but his efforts weren't as venomous as before. He pointed out that Lisa was able to think clearly enough after the clubbing to take her father's watch and money and discard them, along with the weapon. He reminded her that she didn't call an ambulance and "didn't know how long he lay down there before he died."

He asked her to come down from the stand to demonstrate how

she attacked her father. I tensed up. Lisa refused, pleading that she couldn't relive it. Hancock didn't press her. I breathed a deep sigh of relief.

Hancock did his best, but Lisa was too frail, sickly, and drained to badger. After his last question, I rested my case.

The trial was far from over.

I expected Hancock to call as many rebuttal witnesses as possible. After the defense rests, the prosecution can bring previous witnesses back or call brand-new ones to refute the testimony of the defense witnesses. It's another gift the law gives prosecutors to help them carry the burden of proving guilt "beyond a reasonable doubt." It this case, I felt it didn't matter so much what the rebuttal witnesses had to say as how long it took them to say it. I suspected that Hancock wanted to put as many days as he could between the jury's deliberations and Lisa's stirring testimony. He certainly didn't want the jury to begin deliberating with Lisa's words still ringing in their ears. We were on the same wavelength. Hancock called six new witnesses, nearly as many witnesses as I'd used in my entire defense. They were mostly Morris's relatives, including his brother, Sam, and sister, Charlotte. They repeated their statements in support of their brother from the depositions.

Candace Herbst, Lisa's older sister, was Hancock's best rebuttal witness. She came out against her mother and sisters. Showing virtually no emotion—a startling contrast to the tearful testimony of her two sisters and mother—she said her mother gave her father a "very hard time" and could be alternately "loving and gentle" and "cold and manipulative." Candace described Lisa as verbally combative with her father, and said "each gave as good as he got."

Ironically, Candace said she left home for good when Lisa was thirteen, which was the point Lisa said her father began molesting her.

Overall, Candace's stance against her mother and sisters was a sad thing to observe.

THE TRIAL stretched on to Thursday. I had requested that the jurors be bused to the scene of the crime, and the judge agreed to allow it before the summations. I felt that the field trip was vital to allow the jurors to see how close to the building Morris had been killed, and how open the area was. It was not the kind of place where anyone would plan a murder.

In his summation, Hancock described Lisa and Dorothea as liars and actresses who had initially fooled the police and their relatives into thinking they knew nothing of Morris's death. Now, he said, they were trying to fool the jury.

"They should receive Academy Awards," he said.

I asked the jury to send a nationwide message "on whether women have the right to be free in their own homes from molestation by their fathers and battering from their husbands. . . . We have opened the door on a family not too different from what doctors have said has been going on in this country for many years. Your verdict is going to be significant in this country."

Hancock countered, "We're not here to free the women of the world. We're talking about a murder where a child killed her father." He added that the only one who was abused was Morris Keller—"in this courtroom and that night."

Both Hancock and I implored the jurors to study the gruesome pictures.

"She violently, viciously, coldbloodedly killed her own father," he said. "Look at the photos. Lisa Keller is the architect of those photos, and they show premeditation."

I countered, "What could Morris Keller have done to enrage his daughter to such a state of frenzy to perform the most brutal murder in Broward County history?

"I'm surprised she's alive," I continued. "If Mr. Hancock's dad did to him what Lisa Keller's father did to her, do you think he'd be a lawyer, a representative of the State of Florida? He'd be lucky to be alive."

I then compared Morris Keller to Dr. Jekyll and Mr. Hyde, noting that in Robert Louis Stevenson's famous story, "even Mr. Hyde didn't rape and torture his own child."

Over eleven days, there had been thirty-nine witnesses and seventy-one exhibits of evidence. Lost in it all was one final bomb I had saved for the closing moment of my summation. Among those seventy-one exhibits was a single-page, handwritten divorce agreement Dorothea had persuaded Morris to sign a few months before his death. She had pushed him to grant her a divorce for years, and he had finally relented and told her to write some kind of contract. The police found it during a routine search of the apartment and thought nothing of it. During the trial, I had submitted it into evidence with little comment. Hancock didn't object.

The conflict the jurors faced was to determine once and for all whether Morris Keller was a decent man or a perverted beast. We had heard testimony supporting both views. Were Lisa, Dorothea, and Vicky lying? Was Morris really a gentle soul, as his relatives maintained? I told the jury that Morris himself had provided us with the answer. To set it up, I asked the jurors to recall a scene from the movie *Patton*. During his battle against the Germans in North Africa, Patton was facing Field Marshal Erwin Rommel. Patton anticipated Rommel's moves and was able to ambush him. As his forces closed in on Rommel's tanks, Patton stood on a hill and shouted, "Rommel, you magnificent bastard, I read your book!"

I walked to the evidence table and picked up the divorce document.

"Morris," I said, "we read your book."

At the bottom of Dorothea's little contract, Morris had signed his name. But that wasn't enough. Under his signature, he had written, "This doesn't take effect until I get laid."

THE JURY was out for nearly fifteen hours, over two days. They had to decide whether Lisa was guilty of first-degree murder, second-degree murder, manslaughter, or if she was innocent. The three conviction options cut the odds of an acquittal considerably. If a jury is battling over a decision, it usually compromises on one of the degrees of murder.

Outside, the tension of waiting cut deep into the faces of Lisa and Dorothea. Lisa waited at the defense table for two days. As the hours wore on, she looked increasingly tired and pale. Dorothea sat on a bench outside, looking similarly exhausted and drawn. Knots twisted inside their guts, and in mine. If there was ever a case I wanted to win, it was this one. I was gambling my career on it. If Lisa was convicted, I would never practice law again.

On Friday afternoon, the jury announced they had reached a verdict. They filed in and handed the bailiff their decision. Dorothea Keller clutched her hands together and prayed.

"We, the jury, find Lisa Keller not guilty."

Cheers rang out through the courtroom. Lisa's face dropped and she nearly collapsed. She hadn't heard the word "not" and only heard "guilty." Sensing it, I quickly hugged her and said, "We won! We won!"

"Oh my God, I'm going home," she said.

Behind us, the courtroom was in chaos. Reporters rushed to capture every moment. The pro-Lisa forces were delirious. Morris's relatives, including Candace, were angry and tossed bitter quotes to the press. Dorothea made her way through the crowd and embraced her daughter.

Inside the jury room, an emotional war had been waged. There was a lot of pacing, battling, and division. A number of the women jurors took a dislike to Dorothea Keller and had to be reminded that it was Lisa, not Dorothea, on trial. Three jurors called me after the verdict and said the first vote had been 9–3 in favor of first-degree murder. Other jurors disputed that, saying the vote wasn't formal and they disagreed on what that first vote had covered, first-degree, second-degree, or manslaughter. But most agreed that the 9–3 split favoring a conviction was accurate, and that the nine were never as firm in their feelings as the three. Eventually, it came down to four jurors, two men and two women, who were determined to set Lisa free. They swung the eight others.

"It was the most tension I've ever experienced," said *Fort Lauderdale Sun-Sentinel* photo editor Henry Fichner, one of the three jurors who had supported Lisa from the start. "I had to go to the doctor after the trial for treatment. I had back spasms and my muscles were all tied up in knots. I took a few days off from work to recover. I really felt compassion for my fellow jurors. We went through a lot. I don't ever want to do it again."

In the days following the verdict, there was much speculation about Lisa's future. Dr. Cahn wondered if she could ever settle into a loving relationship with a man. Directors of social groups and women's shelters from around the nation offered hope and a helping hand, while suggesting that Lisa get psychiatric care. Actually, Lisa has survived quite well. She changed her name, returned to New York, and appears to be doing well.

From a legal standpoint, the *Miami Herald* referred to the decision as "what experts say may become a landmark victory for battered women and children."

However, in that same article, Sue Osthoff of Women Against Abuse—an organization that offers legal help to women who fight back—offered a word of caution. When asked how much impact she felt the Keller case would have, Osthoff said, "Unfortunately, not enough. Twelve people understood and that's terrific. [But] . . . when a battered woman is found not guilty, it's like, well, great, now we're starting at ground minus fifty instead of ground minus five hundred."

The usual cast of civil libertarians, police captains, and college professors railed at the verdict. They said it promoted a vigilante mentality and gave people the right to kill any SOB they didn't like. The names Prentice Rasheed and Bernhard Goetz, the man who shot four alleged muggers in the New York subway, came up again. One college professor, William Wilbanks of Florida International University, wondered in print if kids could now "gun down their parents because they might be spanked?"

Personally, I liked the reaction of *Fort Lauderdale News/Sun-Sentinel* columnist Gary Stein:

"For two weeks, it was the kind of trial that makes you just want to hug one of your own family members and be grateful if things at home are fairly normal."

EPILOGUE

The Lisa Keller case places prosecutor Kelly Hancock, Detective Philip Amabile, and Sergeant Richard Scheff under a harsh and possibly misleading light. I feel it's necessary to come to their defense. Cases like Lisa Keller's are rare. Ninety-nine times out of a hundred, Hancock, Amabile, and Scheff are the good guys who break their backs, and sometimes put their lives on the line, to fight the bad guys. They put in long hours at tough jobs so that the rest of us can live in a safe world. They're all highly skilled at what they do. They're just not perfect.

20

A NIGHTMARE IN DELAWARE, PART I

WHEN AUTHOR Dary Matera started shadowing me to research this book, I welcomed his presence. It's always good to have another person around as a sounding board, especially one with investigative skills.

Traditionally, lawyers depend upon private investigators to do their legwork. The gumshoes take orders and generally come up with the facts, figures, and other basic information. I learned that authors are that and more. They are fueled by a creative energy that goes beyond the desire to pick up a paycheck. Having Matera aboard proved to be an asset.

Most of the stories chronicled in this book occurred prior to Matera's involvement. These have been relayed and researched in the traditional coauthor/subject manner. But there were a few that we worked on together. The most important was the Charles Reynolds murder case. It turned out to be one of the most mysterious of my career.

* * *

CHARLES REYNOLDS, thirty-nine, crawled out of bed at 4:30 A.M. on March 30, 1987, and glanced out the window. It was dark, cold, and drizzling, a truly miserable Delaware morning. He dutifully folded his allotment of the *Delaware State News,* got into his rusting car, and delivered the newspapers along a rural route in and around the small town of Ellendale. He was home by 7:30 A.M., fixed his own breakfast, then spent the rest of the morning chopping and delivering firewood. After lunch, he retired to the workshed he had constructed fifty yards behind the family's mobile home and began crushing aluminum cans. He had designed a device specifically for that purpose, and was quite proud of it. A thousand crushed cans could be traded for about $10 at the local recycling center.

The three jobs amounted to a lot of sweat for little money, but it was enough. The Vietnam veteran was an outdoorsman with simple tastes. In Southern parlance, the rugged, brown-haired Reynolds was a "good ol' boy."

As was his habit, Charles took periodic breaks from his afternoon can-crushing and returned to the trailer. He would grab a beer or an iced tea and chat with Linda Ann Palacios, thirty-two, his attractive live-in girlfriend of thirteen months. This afternoon, he took a longer break at 4:00 P.M. because Linda was feeling frisky. They made love in the peculiar way Linda preferred for a half hour or so, then Charles returned to the shed. By 7:30 P.M. he was worn out from his long day. He came back to the trailer, saw the bathroom light on, and figured Linda was either taking a bath or was napping in her nearby bedroom. Charles plopped down on the living room couch, watched Bette Davis and Lynda Carter being interviewed on "Entertainment Tonight," then drifted off to sleep.

It was still drizzling when Elsie Reynolds returned home from her job as a private tutor at exactly 8:57 P.M. She remembers the time because Linda had left her a note on the kitchen table to call a neighbor. Elsie checked her watch to make sure it wasn't too late to call.

Elsie noticed her son sleeping soundly on the couch. That wasn't unusual, because the couch was Charles's bed. Elsie refused to let her son and his girlfriend sleep together. She owned the trailer, so she set the rules.

Elsie called the neighbor, discovered it was the wrong Mrs.

Smith, chatted for less than a minute, then went to use the bathroom. Entering the tiny, matchbox room, she was shocked to discover Linda lying face up on the floor, wedged between the commode and the wall—a space about a foot wide. Linda was nude, and her left leg was stretched up on the counter near the sink. There was a cut on the bridge of her nose and another over her eye, but neither were bleeding. Elsie shook Linda's outstretched foot in an effort to awaken her, then rushed to the living room to get Charles.

"Something's wrong with Linda!" she shouted, rousing her son from his sleep.

"Where's she at?" Charles asked, shaking the sleep from his brain.

Elsie pointed to the bathroom, and Charles walked down the narrow hallway to see what was going on. He figured his mother was overreacting.

His mind cleared instantly when he looked into the bathroom. "Linda, what have you done?" he cried.

Elsie watched from the living room as Charles carried Linda down the hall and into the bedroom. Charles shouted for his mother to call 911 for an ambulance. He lay Linda down on the bed and began giving her CPR, which he had learned in the army. He pinched her nose and began blowing air into her mouth. Elsie returned from the phone and stood beside her son.

After trying without success to revive his girlfriend, Charles moved her head. It was then that both he and Elsie first saw the slender pink string digging into the skin around her neck. It had been doubled and looped in a choker knot. The looped area to the left of her larynx was caught in her skin, keeping it from coming loose. Charles slipped his fingers under the string and heard a pop as the tension released. Charles then repeated his mouth-to-mouth resuscitation. There was no response. Elsie reached over and touched the two small knots on the end of the string that were barely extending through the loop. The knots slipped through and the string fell back behind Linda's head. Charles and Elsie both inspected it and discovered it was a fabric cord about thirty inches long and a quarter-inch wide. It was a common accessory found on a woman's blouse, often used as a string tie, as a drawstring on the sleeves, or as a lace down the front in place of buttons. Elsie had many similar strings in a basket in her room.

Elsie called 911 again, only now she was barely under control. A few minutes later, Charles called.

While they waited, Elsie and Charles returned to the bathroom to inspect the scene. Neither noticed any sign of struggle in the bathroom, and thought only that it was an accident or suicide. They looked at the ceiling to determine how Linda could have hung herself, but concluded that the string tie was much too short.

When the ambulance finally arrived at about 9:45 P.M., the fire rescue officer certified what Charles and Elsie already knew—Linda was dead. The police were called and the mobile home was soon swarming with uniformed officers and detectives.

The officers proceeded with their investigation, but were hampered that evening. Ironically, the body of another Delaware woman, Susan L. Riddleberger, eighteen, had been discovered in her yellow Chevrolet Chevette a few minutes after 8:00 P.M.

Riddleberger, a convenience store clerk, had been strangled.

FOR SOME inexplicable reason, police universally are loath to connect separate murders, even ones that scream out their similarities. Mass murderers such as Charles Manson, Ted Bundy, Christopher Wilder, Juan Corona, Bobby Joe Long, Wayne Williams, and John Gacy must leave a long trail of corpses before the police will admit they are dealing with a single madman. Thus, although Sussex County, Delaware, generally has only a dozen or so murders a year, finding two strangled young women a short distance apart in the same evening meant little to the investigators.

Since the Reynolds incident had initially been reported as a suicide, the detectives decided to dispatch their one mobile crime laboratory to the Riddleberger scene. After doing what little investigation they could in the trailer, the police asked Charles to come to the troop headquarters at 2:00 A.M. and make a statement. He repeated his story in detail. When he finished, much to his shock, he was arrested, and charged with murder. Two hours later, the police let him go for lack of evidence.

On the night of Linda's death, police investigators hadn't found a single scratch on Charles's body. Nor was there any other indication of a life-or-death struggle with Linda, a prison-tough wildcat of a woman who, at 125 pounds, weighed just ten pounds less than her short, wiry boyfriend. There were a few bruises on Linda's head and body, but except for some minor damage to one of the doors of the cardboard-like cabinet under the sink, there was virtually no sign of a violent battle in the tiny bathroom. A knickknack shelf hanging precariously on the wall above Linda's body was untouched. Even the taped-on toilet paper holder, inches above Linda's body, was undisturbed.

Investigators found a spot of blood on the sink, and a patch of blood on the bathroom wall. Charles's clothes, identified by his mother as the same he had worn that entire day, were sent to the FBI laboratory in Washington to check for traces of Linda's blood. Not a cell was found. Nor was any blood or printer's ink from Charles's newspaper-wrapping hands found on the long, pink cloth belt that police alleged to be the murder weapon.

Eleven days later, after failing to uncover any physical evidence linking Charles to Linda's death, the police arrested him again. This time for good.

In jail, a bewildered Charles was strangled into unconsciousness by one fellow inmate during a skirmish, and had his front tooth knocked out by another. But the physical pain was no match for the mental anguish. He was shattered by the death of his girlfriend, a woman he planned to marry. And he was tormented by the public accusation that he had brutally killed her.

IN 1979, Doris Reynolds, a tall, beautiful blond farm girl from Ellendale was accepted at the Delaware State Police Academy. Doris survived the sexist hazing and rigorous physical demands, graduated, and became a police officer in the small town of Laurel. Smart and tough, Doris was a good cop and was soon asked to join the prestigious Delaware State Police. Her career was slowed by her marriage and child-rearing responsibilities. A second pregnancy eventually forced her to turn down the state police offer. But surviving the academy and succeeding as a police officer filled her with confidence. In 1981 she moved to Coconut Creek, Florida, a community just west of Pompano Beach. She applied for a job with the U.S. Postal Service and was accepted as a mail carrier. She supplemented her income by working a few nights a week as a waitress at Crabby's Seafood Restaurant in Margate. The combined jobs brought in more than $40,000 a year, enough to support her three children comfortably. (The youngest child was from a second failed marriage.)

The same month Doris's older brother Charles was arrested for murder in Delaware, I sat fuming in my own cell. Doris followed my story in the *Miami Herald.* Not knowing what to do about her brother, she went back and reread *Herald* columnist Charles Whited's long, moving article about my ordeal. My stance struck a nerve. From her police background, she knew something was terribly wrong in the investigation that led to her brother's arrest. If anyone could fight the system that put her brother in jail, she became convinced that it was the jailed attorney in Miami. She pleaded with her family to pool their resources to help pay my fee. The family refused. They believed Charles was clearly innocent and the public defenders would prevail.

The public defenders ran up against a gale force by the name of M. Jane Brady, an undefeated Delaware deputy attorney general whose natural beauty was hidden behind a perpetual sour expression, icy blue eyes, and a heart of granite. Through the sheer force of her will, Brady convinced nine of twelve jurors that Charles was a cold-blooded killer. The remaining three, noting a total lack of evidence, refused to be swayed. The trial ended in a hung jury.

Brady wasn't pleased. She was now even more determined to erase the temporary smudge on her pristine record by putting Charles away for life in the retrial.

The public defender advised Charles that it was all but impossible to win a retrial. He begged his client to accept a plea of second-degree murder and cut his losses. Charles refused. He maintained his innocence. Virtually no one in Delaware, including the public defenders, believed him. Alarmed, Doris again pleaded with her family to chip in and hire me. This time they agreed, but came up well short of my minimum $50,000 fee for a first-degree murder trial. (I do get paid sometimes.)

Intrigued by the case, I lowered my fee twice, finally dropping it to $20,000. The family could only scrape up about half of that. I said they could pay the rest later. The money barely covered expenses in an out-of-state trial, but money has never meant that much to me. What Doris didn't know was that, like so many other cases, I may have taken this one for nothing. My gut feeling was that Charles Reynolds was innocent. And there's no greater crime in society than the jailing of an innocent man or woman.

DORIS, DARY Matera, and I hit Delaware like a storm. Before we had even arrived, newspaper stories told of how Doris had hired a "nationally famous" attorney to set her brother free. They viewed her as a hometown girl returning from the big city to rescue her brother. Matera was coming off his well-publicized best-seller, *Are You Lonesome Tonight,* about Elvis Presley's secret love. He was donating his services as an investigator to save an innocent man. Because of these juicy story elements, the second trial of the wood-cutter leaped from a few paragraphs buried in the back pages of the local newspapers to screaming headlines on the front pages of papers across the state. Correspondents and bureau staffers from both Maryland and Delaware flocked to Georgetown, the county seat of Sussex County, to catch the action. Night after night, the trial was the lead story on the local NBC and ABC affiliate stations. The NBC affiliate began its coverage with a lengthy feature on my career, referring to me as a "hired gun" and displaying an old *South Florida Magazine* article that hailed me as such. I was portrayed as the "nationally renowned" lawyer with more than 275 murder trials notched on my legal six-shooter.

It was a heady experience, and one for which I was unprepared. Nor was I prepared for the crowds that flocked to the 140-seat, Old English–style courtroom, including an endless string of attorneys who no doubt expected to see Clarence Darrow reincarnated.

If I was going to free Charles, I would have to be worthy of the comparison. I'd heard from a number of Georgetown lawyers and a judge not only that M. Jane Brady was undefeated, but there had not been an acquittal by a jury on a first-degree murder case in Sussex County, Delaware, in three hundred years. Although the story would later prove difficult to confirm beyond the past fifty years, the implications were staggering.

FROM THE moment the gavel sounded, I focused my attention upon the police officers. They had forgotten, neglected, or just not bothered to go to the trouble of collecting such critical evidence as fingerprints, tire prints, footprints, samples of the blood found on the bathroom sink and wall, or hair samples from the bathtub water. The inconsistencies strained belief. If there was a violent, life-or-death struggle in the bathroom as the police contended, the blood on the wall and sink could have been the assailant's. Did it match Charles's blood type? Linda's? Someone else's? Who knows? They never tested it. A towel hanging from the bathroom rack just twenty-five inches from Linda's body was still in Elsie

Reynolds's bathroom a year later when we visited. Did it contain the assailant's hair, after-shave, hair tonic, blood, saliva, fingerprints, makeup, lipstick, perfume, hair spray, clothing fibers, or any of a score of identifying substances? Maybe, but it was never taken as evidence. Ditto for the bathroom curtains hanging ten inches above Linda's head. They were still on the bathroom window.

"Haven't these Delaware detectives ever heard of Columbo, Charlie Chan, Jessica Fletcher, or even the Hardy Boys and Nancy Drew?" Matera commented.

The investigators also failed to perform any of a dozen routine police procedures, including making a scale drawing of the scene the night of the incident. Most of the responding officers didn't bother to take notes. Many of the policemen, from the uniformed patrolmen to the high-ranking officers, were taken to task on the witness stand. After the first day, the mood in the room where the cops waited to testify was reminiscent of a prison where the inmates are awaiting the executioner to call their name. One ranking officer was so unnerved that, by the time he took the stand, his voice cracked at my first powder-puff question.

By the third day, both Matera and I began wondering whether this might be more than just police bumbling. Although we never uncovered any evidence of intentional wrongdoing by the police, their investigative work was so haphazard that we had to allow for the possibility.

Evidence-tampering is one of the most serious charges that can be leveled against a police officer. Setting up the innocent to clear cases and earn promotions makes the drug profiteering of Miami's rash of crooked cops look like child's play. It's the kind of thing that, if exposed, would destroy careers and send cops to jail, a fate that might lead some police officers to do anything to avoid it. Including, we feared in our most anxious moments, dumping three agitators from Miami into the bitterly cold Atlantic.

That night at the Cape Henlopen Motel in Lewes, Delaware, our imaginations began to run wild. I told Matera about a Palm Beach judge who had been buried in the ocean in the midst of a big murder investigation. I explained how easy it would be for a couple of squad cars to pull up to the motel and drive us away, never to be seen again. Matera agreed, tossing in a few chilling stories of his own, from his days as a journalist. After we'd amplified each other's fears for an hour or so, we drifted off into an uneasy sleep. The next day we decided no longer to discuss the case on the telephone when we talked to our families in Miami. Matera's wife, Dr. Fran Matera of the University of Miami, was so unnerved by this edict that she tried to persuade us to come home immediately.

I decided to back off a possible police-corruption angle, but not out of fear. I didn't want to place the jury in a position where a not-guilty verdict for Charles would be construed as an indictment against their own police force.

Studying the photos of the crime scene, Matera kept harping about the items in the bathroom being moved around. I ignored him for a while, figuring he was confused by the different angles of the photographs. Crime scenes are set in stone. The police aren't supposed to move anything. But Matera kept insisting, and finally spread the photos on the defense table during a lunch break. I was dumbfounded to discover that he was right. Virtually every item in the bathroom had been shifted around. The towels on the floor, the ashtray, the cigarettes in the ashtray, a cigarette lighter on the floor, and the dislodged baseboard seemed to wander all over the place in successive photos. Even Linda's naked body on the bed had been slightly repositioned before the medical examiner arrived. The police aren't supposed to touch the body until the medical examiner completes the forensic investigation.

"Anyone who has ever watched an episode of 'Quincy' knows that," Matera marveled.

Actually, in Florida, it's against the law to move the body without the medical examiner's permission. And that law applies to police officers.

Continuing our study of the photographs, we noticed that the pink belt or "sash" identified as the murder weapon was in different places in different pictures. In some pictures, it wasn't there at all.

Confronted with this, the officer who photographed the scene and collected the evidence testified that it was his prerogative to move things as he did to search for further evidence. He claimed to have recorded the original scene with a set of establishing shots. However, many critical areas of the bathroom were missing from these photos. Others had no match, making it impossible to determine whether the scene depicted had been altered. Although the detective took more than one hundred photos, there were no photos of two of the most important pieces of evidence: the pink dress that matched the pink belt, and the clump of Linda Palacios's hair that was said to be found on the bathroom floor. There were numerous pictures covering every inch of the floor, but none showed the clump of curly brown hair that had supposedly been ripped from Linda's head during the death fight.

Charles and his mother swore to us that they never saw the clump of hair, nor had they seen the pink dress the police said matched the murder weapon. They also told us, separately, that the sixty-five-inch-long, one-inch-wide pink cloth belt in evidence wasn't the thin, pink string they saw buried under the folds of Linda's neck. I initially felt that they had to be mistaken. Where else could the hair and belt have come from?

I debated letting the explosive issue of the belt slide. The long, relatively wide belt in evidence actually helped Charles. There was nothing on it—newspaper ink, blood, or fingerprints—to connect Charles to Linda's death. However, it soon became apparent that the ligature would be the most critical item in establishing Charles's and Elsie's credibility. In his taped statement to the police, scheduled to be played before the jury, Charles said he hadn't noticed the "pink string" around Linda's neck when she was in the bathroom, hadn't seen it when he carried her into the bedroom, and even missed it when he first laid her down on the bed. Elsie told the officers the same story.

It was unfathomable that they wouldn't have immediately noticed the huge belt in evidence. It would have covered Linda's neck, and the two end strands would have hung down across her nude body to her waist. The jury would never believe Charles and Elsie.

As a final touch, the medical examiner testified that when she viewed Linda Palacios's body at the scene that evening, she hadn't seen a pink belt or a string tie.

The facts were starting to blur. Charles and Elsie saw a thin string tie. The police saw a fat cloth belt. And the medical examiner saw nothing.

We skipped lunch and searched through the photographs again. Matera, wielding a magnifying glass like Sherlock Holmes, homed in on the close-ups of the outline on Linda's neck. The autopsy shots, taken twelve hours after her death, showed little more than a bruise ringing her neck. But the photographs taken at the scene showed something entirely different. On the left side of Linda Palacios's neck, and at the front, were two unmistakable clues that proved Charles and Elsie were telling the truth about the ligature.

This made it clear to me that Linda Ann Palacios had not been murdered—by anyone! An attacker would have had to double the short string, place it around Linda's neck, push the ends through the choke-hold loop, and strangle her. Not even a professional hit man would have attempted such a difficult maneuver during a fight to the death.

Matera's sensational discovery helped, but if I was going to try to turn a small-town jury against its own state police force, I needed more.

21

A NIGHTMARE IN DELAWARE, PART II:

Advil, Asthma, and Autoeroticism

IT WAS nearly 2:00 A.M. on Thursday, March 24, 1988. The Atlantic Ocean was a block away, but it was dark and ominous instead of inviting. In the summer, Lewes, Delaware, is a resort town teeming with yuppies from Washington, D.C., and Maryland as well as around the state. But in March, on a twenty-eight-degree night, Lewes is a ghost town.

Matera and I had spent the evening trying to decide what to do about the ligature dilemma and when to spring his discovery. As we had done all week, we also argued possible scenarios, probabilities, and defense strategies in room number 2 of the deserted Cape Henlopen Motel. I finally slumped into bed, exhausted. Matera, a night person who jumps to life after midnight, remained sitting on the floor, furiously scribbling on his pad. Among the things he wrote and circled were the numbers "911." I had asked him earlier in the week to remind me to get a copy of the emergency police dispatch tape from Brady. Other issues had diverted our attention, and the trial was going into its fifth day. The next morning, Matera reminded me to get the tape from the prosecutor.

That afternoon we had lunch at the home of Charles Reynolds's eighty-four-year-old grandmother, Mabel. Charles's mother, Elsie, his aunt, Cathcrine Hudson, and his sister, Doris, were also present. After eating, I brought out the tape. I wanted to play it for the whole family. Matera felt that this was insensitive, and pulled Elsie Reynolds aside.

"This will be very difficult to hear," he said, referring to what is always a chilling account of the first anguished moments in a tragedy. "Are you sure you want to hear it?"

"Yes," she said.

Matera popped the tape into the small cassette recorder and punched the play button. Halfway through, we heard Charles Reynolds utter a sentence that nearly knocked us off our feet.

"Stop it!" I shouted. "Play that again."

Matera did as ordered. There was no mistake.

"Damn them. Damn them all," I raged. They had to know he was telling the truth. The cops, the prosecutor, the public defender. The state put an innocent man in jail. How the hell could they do this?

What we had heard was the final clue we needed to prove that Charles Reynolds hadn't murdered his girlfriend.

THE SUSSEX County medical examiner was a gray-haired woman with a demeanor as lifeless as her patients. Responding to Brady's direct examination, she identified the large belt as the "possible murder weapon," and said it had been used in a crisscrossed method of strangulation.

In her report, the medical examiner recorded that the wounds on Linda's neck were eight-tenths to one centimeter wide. On the stand, I had her measure the pink belt. It was more than two and a half centimeters wide.

I said nothing further on that subject, holding back until I could tie it all together in the summation.

The medical examiner offered some additional surprising testimony. Under my cross-examination, it was brought out that she had described Linda's "extremities," i.e., the hands and feet, as "unremarkable." The photos showed that her toes were bloody and bruised. The doctor also testified that she had found a considerable amount of brownish fluid in Linda's stomach. What was it? Coffee? Coke? Cyanide? Lighter fluid? Kerosene? Rat poison? Raid?

The M.E. didn't know. She didn't have it analyzed.

Before his second arrest, Charles told the police that Linda had taken triple the maximum dose of the nonprescription painkiller Advil in the twenty-four hours prior to her death. That amount was one-tenth of a milligram below the minimum lethal level. Linda had lingering pain from a past auto accident, and had been gobbling up Advil tablets in an attempt to wean herself from stronger, prescription analgesics. Charles showed the police the bottle of Advil that Linda had purchased the day before. He tipped it over and counted out how few of the fifty pills remained. Despite Charles's revelation, the medical examiner not only failed to check for the drug, she professed to know nothing about its properties or those of its main chemical ingredient, ibuprofen. That meant the doctor was unaware that even a regular dose of Advil can be dangerous to an asthmatic, which Linda was, or that an overdose can cause disorientation, mental confusion, constriction of the air passages, and other serious reactions.

The Advil overdose was critical because it was a major component in solving the mystery of Linda's death. Amid the botched police investigation and disputed ligature, one question remained. If Charles or a third person couldn't have strangled Linda with the string belt, how had she died? Matera and I were both almost certain we knew, but it was another tremendously risky play. We debated all week whether I should pursue the kinky subject. I had all but decided against it when the medical examiner took the stand. Then, as so often happens during trials, I abruptly changed course. I decided the jury needed the complete picture.

While claiming ignorance of Advil, the medical examiner did acknowledge that she was aware of a rare form of autoeroticism. At my request, she described a technique of nonfatally strangling oneself during masturbation to cut off the oxygen supply to the brain. This is done to heighten the intensity of the orgasm, or so practitioners claim, and can be fatal. About a decade ago, in Miami, the body of a Hare Krishna cult member was found hanging from a tree. The circumstances baffled police investigators until the sexual-asphyxiation angle surfaced. Matera was in the newsroom when a fellow *Miami News* reporter broke the story.

Linda had done time in an Arizona prison for trafficking in

heroin. That experience no doubt made her aware of all forms of masturbation, including the dangerous asphyxiation technique. In addition, Linda had been raped by five men when she was nineteen and had experienced vaginal pain ever since, especially during inter-course. Charles told both me and the police that in order for Linda to climax, he had to lie beside her and gently enter her from behind while she manually aroused herself.

Although the evidence pointed to the "three A's"—Advil, asthma, and autoeroticism—as being the deadly combination that led to Linda's demise, I suspected it would be a difficult theory to sell to a small-town jury. The judge felt Linda's prison record would prejudice the jurors, and ruled it inadmissible. Charles wasn't going to testify (since Brady was going to play the jury his taped state-ment), so he couldn't describe Linda's sexual peculiarities. And the medical examiner, as expected, refused even to consider sexual asphyxiation as the cause of Linda's death. She had already gone on record, testifying at the previous trial and at this one that it was a homicide.

My strategy was to touch upon the masturbation angle with the medical examiner, let the jury mull it over, then move on to other aspects of the case.

The autoeroticism revelation did, of course, create the biggest headlines of the trial.

TO CEMENT our case, we needed the crime-scene photo negatives in order to enlarge the photographs showing the ligature mark on Linda's neck. I requested the negatives from Brady and the lead police detective, but they refused to hand them over, claiming they were police property. I protested to Judge William Swain Lee. Lee felt the request was reasonable, and ordered Brady to cough them up. That made her sour face grow even more sour. Brady was quickly learning that she was a big fish in a small Delaware pond. Despite her local reputation, there were dozens of prosecutors I had tangled with in South Florida who were far superior—if only be-cause the range of experience is greater in "Miami Vice" land.

According to Matera's always perked ears, the chatter among the lawyers packing the courtroom was that I was giving her a good whipping. That was unfair. Most of the time, it's the facts of the case, not the skill of the attorneys, that determines who wins and who loses. In Brady's situation, she was being undermined by the weakness of the evidence the police had given her. Still, young prosecutors usually take cases quite personally, and Brady was being true to form. She was reacting like an undefeated fighter who has been knocked down for the first time in his career. The fighter finds himself in a totally unfamiliar position and doesn't know how to clinch, hold on, dance away, and give himself time to recover. This is one of the reasons I love to tangle with undefeated prosecutors. If you bat them around in the early rounds, they can come unglued. It's the old, defeat-scarred war-horses like me who are the toughest courtroom adversaries.

Even so, Brady remained smart and feisty, and still had a few tricks up her sleeve. A few hours after the judge issued the order to let us have the negatives, Brady called and informed us that they didn't have a police officer available to bring them to us. She said we would have to drive 50 miles to Dover and get them ourselves. It was a little after 3:00 P.M. when she called. She said the office in Dover would close at four.

"We'll get them Monday," I said.

Brady was also being suspiciously protective of the crime-scene photos. She had ordered only one set and refused to let us view them for more than an hour or so during the day. I had taken them that afternoon with the intent of studying them over the weekend. Brady wanted the photos back immediately. I called Judge Lee and received permission to keep them until Monday. We beat it out of Georgetown for our motel in Lewes, about fifteen miles away, before Brady could find out. That night we analyzed the pictures and picked the ones we needed.

The next morning, Saturday, Judge Lee was on the phone telling me that Brady had demanded that the photos be returned. Brady had them for eight months, and had already called the police photographer to the stand and placed the ones she wanted into evidence. Yet she was now insisting that she needed them that day at noon. I consented without argument. We returned the photos on schedule to a pair of stone-faced detectives at the Georgetown police station.

Dary and Doris were enraged, but I had expected such a maneuver and calmed them down. I had gotten up at five that morning and studied the photos further for six hours.

"We'll get the negatives Monday. It'll be a rush, but we'll get the blow-ups," I assured them.

On Monday, one of the detectives dutifully brought in the

negatives. Before the proceeding started, Matera and I sat at the defense table, held the film strips up into the ceiling lights, and located the ones that matched the photos we wanted blown up. Matera focused on the ligature mark, while I wanted specific shots of the scene. To confuse Brady, we chose a few extra photos that had no meaning. I dispatched Doris to a photo shop with instructions on which negatives to blow up. While Doris performed that mission, I cross-examined another detective.

At this point, everybody in Delaware knew the police had bungled the investigation. There was no need to jump all over this man. Instead, I took off my jacket, took the pink belt from the evidence table, and criss-crossed it around my neck. I then lay down on the courtroom floor and stuck my left leg into the air to mimic the position in which Linda's body was discovered. I had the detective lift me up from behind as Charles had lifted Linda, then point my limp body toward the jury.

The jurors could clearly see the thick, pink belt hanging in two strands down to my waist. I asked the detective how Elsie and Charles Reynolds could have missed seeing such a large belt draped across the body of a nude woman?

He couldn't even speculate.

The next witness Brady called was Elsie Reynolds.

For the prior two nights, Matera and I had bolstered Elsie's confidence. We told her not to be afraid to tell the truth. If the belt in evidence was not the one she saw that night, I wanted her to say so, and say it firmly, without fear.

After asking Elsie a few routine questions, M. Jane Brady walked to the evidence table and cuddled the pink belt in her arms. Watching Brady approach Elsie with it reminded Matera of those teenagers in all the horror movies. As they enter the dark basement where monsters like Freddy Krueger or Jason are hiding, someone in the audience invariably screams, "Watch out behind you!"

In the gallery, Matera nudged Doris.

"This is it," he whispered. "The fireworks are going to fly."

"Is this the sash you saw around Linda's neck that night?" Brady asked, verbally wandering into the dark basement.

"No," Elsie said.

Brady was clearly rattled. I could see her jaw quiver as she turned to get a transcript from the previous trial. She read the part where a frightened Elsie had testified that the belt could "possibly" be the one she saw.

Judge Lee was frowning. I was certain he believed Elsie was lying, and that I had instructed her to do so.

Elsie explained, as she had to us, that she was so shocked when presented with the belt at the previous trial that she didn't know what to say. She believed in the system and couldn't believe the state—the good guys—could have made such a mistake.

I took over for the cross-examination, and led Elsie through her story. I placed the long belt in my hands and had her repeat that it wasn't the right one. I leafed through the previous transcript and read the line following the one Brady had read. Elsie had clarified her statement about the belt by saying that it was the same color, but was wider than she remembered.

"Elsie, after you testified about the belt the last time, did you tell anybody that it was different?" I asked.

"Yes," Elsie said. "I told public defenders Haller and Hudson and Ms. Kitchen, Haller's assistant."

I glanced at Judge Lee again. He was still frowning, but it was different. I sensed that he now believed Elsie, and for the first time was beginning to understand what had happened in this case.

As if by magic, I pulled a pink fabric string tie from my pocket. Doris had purchased it a few days before, and Matera had cut and sized it to match Elsie's recollection. It came to about thirty inches—less than half the length and one-fifth the width of the pink cloth belt in evidence. I showed it to Elsie on the witness stand and had her identify it as being nearly identical to the string she saw on Linda's neck. I then doubled it and looped it around my neck in the choker knot and showed the jury how it was found on Linda's neck—a demonstration that clashed with the medical examiner's criss-crossed demonstration using the fat belt.

After I finished with Elsie, Brady stood and rested the state's case.

At that point, the seven men and five women of the jury had to be thoroughly confused.

THE PREVIOUS night, I decided to forgo all my planned witnesses and just call the "911" tape. Matera suggested that it would help to have the doctor from the clinic testify about the properties of Advil, a step that would set up the accident angle and also allow me to submit Linda's medical records. I agreed. The doctor, a Filipino woman from Dover, was extremely hostile because of the interruption in her schedule, and refused to testify about Advil. I let her go after a few questions. The record got in.

I then recalled one of the detectives. That was done solely for the purpose of having someone identify the "911" tape. The bailiff placed the tape into the courtroom recorder and pushed the button.

The first call was from Elsie, just as she had testified. She reported that a girl had "passed out" in her bathroom and requested an ambulance.

The next call was Elsie again. Her voice was trembling and she was nearing shock.

"Will you please send an ambulance quick, I believe this girl has done something. Please send an ambulance. I just called for one."

The dispatcher, the same man, assured her that an ambulance was on the way.

The third call was from Charles. He explained that something terrible had happened to his girlfriend and that he had tried to give her CPR.

"She's dead. Oh God. It's too late, man. It's too late," he cried.

As the tape rolled and Charles's crucial statement neared, his voice was drowned out by loud sobs coming from the courtroom audience. I turned and searched the gallery for the source. The sobs were coming from a blond woman clutching on to Matera—Doris Reynolds! The tough ex-cop who ramrodded the defense of her brother and had yet to show her first sign of emotion had suddenly cracked. From across the room, I could see that Matera instantly picked up on my fear; Doris was going to ruin the most important moment in Charles Reynolds's life. I gave Matera a "shut her up" look, but he was ahead of me.

"Damn it, Doris," he whispered. "You're going to kill him. They won't hear what he said."

As Doris tried to muffle her sobs, the dispatcher on the tape told Charles to hang on, that he would transfer him to a switchboard closer to Ellendale. The call, for some reason, had come in to the Dover switchboard. As the dispatcher transferred the call and Charles held on, Charles was heard to say:

"Mom, I didn't know it was even on her neck until I carried her into this room here."

The off-the-cuff comment to Elsie was picked up on the "911" master tape twenty-five miles away.

The jurors gave no sign that they understood the implications of Charles's statement. It was proof positive that neither he nor his mother had noticed the thin string around Linda's neck. They were telling the truth. The belt in evidence was not the murder weapon, and Charles was innocent of murder.

But instead of hearing the case-breaking utterance, the jurors' attention was probably diverted to Doris's breakdown in the gallery.

Fortunately, the alert dispatcher, Ed Marecki, picked up on what Charles said. He could be heard repeating it to the ambulance driver.

"He didn't say this directly to me, but as I was transferring the call down, I could still hear him. I don't know if he was talking to his mom or he talked to somebody and said, 'I didn't know it was around her neck.' I think we have a 91," Officer Marecki said, using the police code for "dead on arrival." The dispatcher repeated Charles's comment to another rescue officer, adding that it appeared to be a suicide, then repeated it a third time to the ambulance driver.

That repaired some of the damage caused by Doris's sobs, but without hearing it in Charles's own words, the moment might have been lost.

When the tape ended, I stood in court and said, "Your Honor, the defense rests."

There was a buzz in the courtroom. My sudden move caught everyone by surprise, especially M. Jane Brady. It was obvious she had a lot of points she needed to make during her cross-examinations of my listed witnesses, particularly with an ex-cop that Doris insisted was Charles's friend, but of whom I was extremely wary. It turned out that the officer had buried Charles with a bad character reference when the police came to question him, and no doubt planned to do the same on the witness stand.

The summations were set for the next day—exactly a year from the day Linda died. That evening I decided again to go easy on the police. I would outline all their mistakes, but blame them on the confusion surrounding the Riddleberger murder. Doris's disastrous timing for an emotional outburst could be further healed by repeating to the jury what Charles had said on the "911" tape, and by suggesting that the jurors listen to it again in the jury room. I would then finish by showing the blow-ups of the ligature marks on Linda's neck and revealing what Matera had discovered.

By nine on the morning of the summations, virtually every seat in the courtroom was taken. There were rows and rows of nervous police detectives and excited attorneys. Linda's friends and family as well as Charles's turned out in force. Even some of Brady's family came to see her beat the "famous Miami attorney." Despite my accomplishments during the trial, there was no reason to believe Brady wouldn't do just that. I was asking the jury to believe that Linda Palacios had died accidentally with a string twisted around her neck while performing some outlandish form of masturbation. And from what the area lawyers told me, a Sussex County, Delaware, murder trial jury had not spoken the words "not guilty" in three hundred years.

In the judge's chambers, Brady kept trying to persuade Judge Lee to offer murder in the second degree as an alternate selection. I refused, saying it had to be all or nothing, a position Charles supported. The judge agreed with me, saying that if Charles strangled his girlfriend, then went to sleep on the couch, that was as cold-blooded as murder gets. After some other details were dispensed with, Brady and I went and took our positions.

Brady had opening and closing summations. I had one shot in between.

Despite the lack of evidence and the terrible beating she had taken in the last rounds of the trial, Brady was surprisingly effective. Her theory was that Linda had been planning to leave Charles and he couldn't take it, so he killed her. In her version, it was boy meets girl, boy wins girl, boy is about to lose girl, so boy strangles girl and takes a nap from the fatiguing effort.

It's the presentation that sells, and Brady's was good. With her jaw set and ice-blue eyes flaring, she branded Charles a vicious murderer, emphasizing that it was "impossible" that anyone else could have killed Linda. She ridiculed my theories, especially the masturbation angle, and reminded the jury of the medical examiner's contrary testimony. She even attacked me personally, painting me as a self-aggrandizing city slicker who came to Delaware to accuse the locals of being backwoods idiots.

It looked bad. Charles's family was devastated.

"Just wait," Matera assured them. "Don't worry."

But *I* was worried. Brady was good. She had scored heavily.

During the break following Brady's first summation, I began feeling unusually nervous. I've given thousands of summations, but somehow this one was different. I had never represented anyone who was so completely innocent, but was nonetheless in such deep danger of being put away for life for a crime he didn't commit. While Brady was describing Charles as a savage beast, one of the jurors had placed her hand over her mouth. On her face was a look of absolute terror, an expression she shared with many of her cohorts.

It would be up to me to convince that woman, and her fellow jurors, that Charles Reynolds deserved to live among them again. If I failed, Charles's life and his family's would be destroyed forever.

I walked out into the foyer to burn off some nervous energy. My knees were weak, and almost gave out. The weight of the challenge before me bore down upon my neck and back. I couldn't believe it. I hadn't felt that nervous in forty years.

Matera rounded the corner.

"This is it, Ellis," he said. "You have a packed house. The whole state of Delaware will be listening. The pressure is on. This is the moment you exist for. You're Mr. Summation. Mr. Summation!"

"Like Mr. October," I said, aware that he was playing off the nickname given baseball great Reggie Jackson for his clutch performances in the World Series.

"You're the best," Matera continued. "You feed off the pressure. You can do it. Go get 'em, champ!"

I guess it seems silly, looking back on it, but Matera's cheerleading infused me with renewed confidence. My knees strengthened and the weight vanished from my shoulders. Three hundred years be damned!

I returned to the courtroom, greeted the jury, then started talking. I went over the entire case, step by step, pointing out all the flaws in the investigation. I finished by displaying the sensational blow-ups. The first showed a bloody bruise on Linda's neck, proving the the wide belt couldn't have killed her because the FBI hadn't found any blood on it. Then I demonstrated again how the small string tie had been doubled and looped around Linda's neck, and said that if that's what happened, there would be two lines, not one, circling her neck. I walked to the podium, took a blow-up photo of the neck, and slowly showed each juror the two distinct parallel furrows that Matera had discovered on a section of Linda's neck. The tiny furrows were the exact size of the string tie Elsie and Charles swore they had belatedly seen around Linda's neck that night.

In subsequent photographs taken later, the furrows had not only disappeared, they blended together into a single, larger bruise. This may have been what caused the medical examiner to reach her erroneous conclusion.

To complement these bombshells, I explained that a self-manipulated "choker knot" would have left a gap in the bruise lines on Linda's neck, while the medical examiner's criss-crossed "attacker" method would have produced a continuous, unbroken line. I returned to the podium, retrieved another blow-up, and showed the jury a distinguishable gap in the lines on the front of Linda's neck.

As dramatic as all of this was, I had one last revelation. The blow-up of the ligature bruises on Linda's neck clearly showed the direction in which the ends had been pulled through the loop. In trying to match the marks during our motel-room demonstrations, Matera and I kept getting it backward. We were instinctively positioning the loop to the left and pulling the ends through with our right hands. The photo showed it had been positioned the opposite way and pulled to the left.

Linda Palacios was left-handed.

Brady returned for her final words, continuing to maintain that the pink sash was the murder weapon.

THREE HOURS later, the bailiff announced that the jurors had reached a decision. The news traveled around the courthouse, down the stairs, out the doors, and into the nearby stores and luncheonettes. The courtroom went from empty to overflowing in minutes.

Doris clutched Matera's arm, bowed her head, and began sobbing the moment we entered the courtroom. Another relative was hanging on his other arm.

Charles, who had cried periodically throughout the trial, sat quavering between me and our local attorney, Benjamin F. Shaw III.

There's absolutely nothing that compares with the gut-wrenching drama of the last moments of a murder trial. The jury files in, and you know that in the next few seconds the foreman will say the words that will determine whether a man goes home or is to be locked in a savage prison for the rest of his life. If you have any stake at all in the verdict, be it as a relative, an attorney, or just a courthouse buff, the tension sits in your abdomen, the palms sweat, the body is nearly paralyzed.

"We, the jury, find the defendant, Charles Reynolds, not guilty."

The next thing I heard were the wailing prayers of Mabel Reynolds, Charles's grandmother. She was sitting in the gallery one person away from Doris and Dary. After Doris cracked, Mabel had been the last remaining rock-solid member of the family, staying cool and holding everyone else together. The pent-up emotion was now bursting out of her.

"Thank you, Jesus. Oh, thank you, Jesus," she screamed, standing with her hands raised in the air. "I knew it. I knew it. I knew he was innocent. Oh, thank you, my Lord Jesus," she continued to scream with the fervor of an evangelist.

Judge Lee was powerless to do anything. The bailiff came to the end of the row, but there was no way he was going to bodily remove an eighty-four-year-old grandmother. Charles's Aunt Catherine tried to put her hand over Mabel's mouth, but the little lady would have none of it. Finally she just wore out.

I could then hear that practically the entire courtroom was sobbing, either in joy or despair. By far the loudest sobs came from Charles's family, which indicates the tremendous suffering they had been put through.

When it dawned on him that he was free, Charles hugged me tightly in the center of the courtroom. The newspapers reported the next day that both he and I were crying.

Doris, her head still buried in Matera's chest, was unchanged. She was still sobbing violently.

"We won, Doris!" Matera said. "You did it. It was all you. He's free."

Nothing. Doris had hit the wall, and it was scary. She was unable to share the exhilaration that had swept over the rest of us. I suspect that aside from the incredible tension, it had something to do with the fact that the brotherhood of police officers she was once part of had fouled up so badly.

The crowd moved outside. One by one, everyone in Charles's family hugged Matera and me with all the thanks they could muster. Nearly all were alternately smiling, laughing, shouting for joy, raising their fists in the air, and sobbing.

I'll never forget the feeling.

Everyone was around but Elsie. In a daze, she had wandered off by herself. Ironically, her wandering took her to the lonely corner of the courthouse parking lot where Judge Lee had parked his car.

"Are you okay, Elsie?" Lee asked.

"Can you tell me how I can get my son?" she answered.

"Don't worry," he said with a warm smile. "Your lawyer will take care of it."

An hour later, Charles Reynolds walked out of the Sussex Correctional Institution a free man. He was swept into a crowd of family members and reporters. He was still missing his front tooth, but didn't seem too much the worse for wear. He held up a page from the Christian devotional booklet "Our Daily Bread" and announced that he had become a born-again Christian in prison. Later that night, at the big family celebration at the Blue and Gold Restaurant in Georgetown, he looked into a television camera and said, breaking down in tears, "I would have killed myself if we had lost. God bless the jury and Ellis Rubin."

EPILOGUE

Outside the restaurant, Elsie Reynolds came over to collect Charles's things from our rental car.

"Where's your car, Elsie?" I asked.

"I don't know."

"Did you drive here?"

"I don't know."

"Did you ride with someone?"

"I think so."

"Do you know who?"

"No."

I laughed. Matera didn't. He was too busy trying to put together the final pieces of the puzzle, the pieces that he felt Elsie Reynolds had just provided.

The acquittal of Charles Reynolds still left two questions unresolved. What happened to the original string tie? And why had the police erred so?

Everything else had fallen into place behind the "three A's." Even the cuts on Linda's face and the few bruises on her body indicated that she had simply fallen on the sink's faucet and handle, simultaneously producing the two wounds that perfectly matched the angle and distance between the sharp edge of the faucet and the sharp edge of its handle. Linda then must have fallen to the floor, seriously cut, disoriented, and choking from the string around her neck. She writhed and eventually curled herself under the toilet-paper holder and around the commode. She probably bruised her right arm and right side on the commode base when she wedged herself between it and the wall. Her final actions may have consisted of kicking the cabinet door and jerking up her head, twice banging it on the hard underside edge of the commode tank, causing injuries consistent with the medical examiner's report.

That was as far as I was willing to go. Speculation is not my game. Attorneys defend clients. They don't wrap cases up in a pretty bow for the television producers. I had done my job. It was time to go home. But Matera continued to search for answers, solutions, and a cohesive ending. He developed an intriguing theory that carried the case all the way through. He explained it as follows:

> After Elsie found Linda in the bathroom, the story happened exactly as Charles and his mother described—with one important exception. Following the discovery of the small string tie around Linda's neck, Charles went to make the third call to 911, leaving Elsie in the room with Linda's body. Placed on hold, Charles turned and saw his mother. Elsie Reynolds had wandered out of the bedroom and was standing in front of him with a shocked look on her face.
>
> In her hand was the thin, pink string tie.
>
> "Mom, I didn't even know it was on her neck until I carried her into this room here," Charles said, responding to his mother's questioning eyes and what he saw her holding.
>
> The 911 operator came back on the phone and instructed Charles to wait outside for the ambulance. Charles left the trailer and ran the hundred or so yards down to the end of the dirt driveway, as he stated.
>
> Elsie Reynolds, instinctively, without thought or memory, stuck the string belt in the pocket of her coat.

Presented with Matera's scenario, Charles brightened and said he remembered seeing his mother holding the pink string tie in the living room. Elsie however, insists that she wasn't.

If Charles's memory is correct, that still leaves the mystery of the police department's actions.

Matera had a theory for that, as well:

Faced with two cooperative witnesses and no "murder" weapon, they apparently were forced to improvise. The long pink belt could have been found in the dirty clothes hamper, in the closet, or lying across an end table, or it could have been on the bed to begin with. One of the officers may simply have spotted it somewhere else in the room and assumed it was the right one. As more officers arrived and it was pointed out to them, they were led to genuinely believe it was the death instrument. After all, there it was. And it was pink, just as Charles and Elsie described. The dilemma of placing the belt in its correct spot on the scene could explain the reason for the multiple photographs. The police took shots with it behind Linda's neck, next to her body, and not there at all. Wherever Charles and Elsie would eventually agree it had been left, the police would have the picture to prove it.

I should emphasize that this is a theory that springs from the imagination of an author. It is not intended to cast any aspersions upon the Delaware police force. Another view is that the police were dispatched to what was reported as a suicide and therefore didn't investigate it as thoroughly as a murder. That would explain the sloppy investigation, and explain why items were moved or kicked around and steps weren't taken to protect evidence and preserve the scene. When the medical examiner arrived and mistakenly designated it as a homicide, it was too late for a proper investigation. As one high-ranking officer testified, "The scene was already contaminated when I arrived."

Confronted with a routine suicide belatedly turning into a homicide, what else could the officers have done? In their eyes, Charles was the only credible suspect.

(Actually, even if it had been a murder, there are still a thousand variables. Someone could have quietly slipped into the house and killed Linda while Charles was in the shed or even while he was sleeping on the couch. Stranger things have happened.) Perhaps, as the police so often do, they took the path of least resistance. They arrested poor Charles, and Brady ran with it.

Whatever, all that really mattered was that Charles Reynolds's year-long nightmare had ended, thanks to his courageous sister Doris.

* * *

DORIS, BY the way, quickly recovered from the overdose of tension that caused her untimely sobbing. She eventually came to realize that she had literally saved her brother's life. That memory can never be taken away from her.

When she returned home, Doris discovered that her teenage daughter, until then an obedient A-student, had skipped school and spent the time partying with her friends along the famous "Spring Break" strip in Fort Lauderdale.

Life goes on.

22

VISUAL OBSERVATIONS

The defense is arguing that she committed suicide and
was murdered by an outsider.
—Delaware television anchorwoman

IF I may be so presumptuous as to assume that I've learned a thing
or two during my thirty-eight years on both sides of the bar, so to
speak, I'd like to offer a few suggestions regarding the future of
America's judicial system.

But first there's a little story that helps put all of us so-called
experts in our places.

In the midst of the Charles Reynolds trial, I had an FBI laboratory expert fly in to testify about being unable to find any printer's
ink on the cloth belt. The determination was crucial because the FBI
crime laboratory in Washington, D.C., represents the epitome of
police science. They have space-age instruments, tools, chemicals,
lie detectors, lasers, you name it. Operating these state-of-the-art

instruments are some of the world's most skilled polygraph examiners, serologists, pathologists, chemists, fiber experts, hair experts, handwriting experts, fingernail experts, saliva experts, fingerprint experts, and dozens of other highly trained specialists. Taking a tour through the FBI headquarters makes one wonder how anybody gets away with a crime anymore.

Naturally, I wanted this "super cop" to come to the trial and explain the ingenious electron microscopic technique he used to scour the belt for a single molecule of printer's ink. I wanted him to describe the chemical solution he coated the belt with that would have turned an atom of ink into a bright red mark for all the world to see.

When the agent arrived, Dary Matera and I met him in the witness room. I asked the agent to brief us on what brilliant FBI laboratory technique he had used, so that I could properly question him on the witness stand.

"I made a visual observation," he said.

I cast Matera an incredulous glance.

"You *what?*"

"I visually observed it for any signs of ink."

"That's it?"

"Yeah."

"You *looked* at it?"

"Yeah."

So much for space-age police science.

With that said, I'll offer my "visual observations" of what I feel are some problems in our legal system and how they might be corrected. These suggestions are not geared toward making a criminal defense attorney's life easier. To the contrary, they are mostly designed to correct the present imbalance that favors the criminal and his lawyer to the detriment of society. Many are also designed to give greater power to the citizen jurors.

1. Jury verdicts should be by a three-quarters majority vote rather than unanimous.

Although it's noble to insist that all twelve jurors (or all six) vote the same way, it's an unnecessary burden upon society. Currently, jurors render death penalty recommendations by majority. If juries are allowed to rule on the most critical issue of all—life or death—by a majority vote, then guilt or innocence should also be decided in a similar fashion. (The U.S. Supreme Court has approved non-unanimous verdicts and allows the individual states to decide whether to implement it.)

This is not to say there should be a single vote taken in the jury room. The jurors can still take sides, go through numerous preliminary votes, and hash it out for as long as they want. But when they lock into a consistent vote, that's the decision. The three-quarters rule would mean that instead of causing a hung jury, an 11–1, 10–2, or 9–3 verdict would be acceptable. (The minimum leeway for a six-member jury would be 5–1.)

Cynics may note that if this rule were in effect, two of my biggest victories would be erased. In 1986, a woman named Betty Evers was tried twice after confessing that she killed her husband eighteen years before. In the first trial, the jurors voted 11–1 that she was guilty. The final juror refused to budge for three days, resulting in a hung jury. We went to court again. This time, Betty Evers was acquitted. (The second trial made national news when I used psychic Micki Dahne to help select the new jury. Many court observers believe it was Dahne's presence in the gallery, and her open support of Evers, that convinced the jurors that Evers had confessed to protect someone else.) The early tabulation on Lisa Keller was 9–3 to convict. (The three Keller jurors eventually swayed the majority, since that was merely the initial vote.) Regardless of the above, mandatory unanimous decisions have enabled too many criminals to return to the streets to kill, rape, or rob again.

Unanimous verdicts also make it much easier to corrupt a jury. The defendant's cronies need only bribe, blackmail, or frighten one juror to avoid a conviction.

2. Judges and jurors should have three standard verdict options, not two. Along with "guilty" or "not guilty" they should have the option of ruling that the prosecution's case was "not proven."

One of society's greatest misunderstandings is the not-guilty verdict. While it may mean the jury felt the accused was innocent, more often than not it simply means the jurors felt the prosecution did not prove guilt beyond every reasonable doubt.

A "not proven" verdict would protect a person's legal rights, but it would prevent a criminal (and his or her attorneys) from smugly pronouncing that he or she has been vindicated by a not-guilty verdict. (This system is working well in Scotland.)

3. Jurors should be allowed to present questions to witnesses.

The legal system places the burden of deciding guilt or innocence on randomly selected citizens. Yet we force these same citizens to sit through trials figuratively bound and gagged.

After the direct and cross-examination of each witness, including the defendant, each individual juror should be allowed to submit written questions to the judge. The judge would then screen the questions to weed out those that are outside the rules of evidence (such as, "Come on, turkey, who you kiddin'? You did it. 'Fess up!"). The judge would then ask the witness or defendant the jurors' legitimate questions.

4. In capital cases, the first step in a trial should be to transport the jurors to the scene.

In most trials, everyone involved has been to the scene of the crime except the jurors. It helps the jurors picture what everyone is talking about if they too have been there. It also enables them to better sort out the differing scenarios that are presented by the prosecution and defense.

(Currently, a defense attorney can request that the jury be taken to the scene. The judge can grant the request or deny it. Even if the judge assents, the jurors usually aren't transported to the scene until the prosecution finishes its case and hands it over to the defense. That's often too late.)

5. Bring down the walls of the witness box.

If *The Caine Mutiny Court-Martial* took place today, in a modern courtroom, the result might be entirely different, The jury of military officers would never see Captain Queeg (Humphrey Bogart) roll the steel balls around in his hand as he ranted about the missing strawberries on his warship. The chilling body language that exposed the captain's unraveling mental state would have been hidden behind a wooden partition.

I don't know how or why the bare-bones witness stand inherited from England evolved into the enclosed witness box of today, but I do know that a lot has been lost in the transition. Often, the only tools a juror has to determine whether a witness or defendant is lying are the juror's own powers of observation.

People usually train themselves to keep a "straight face" when they lie. Less attention is paid to the rest of the body. If the person on the stand is clenching his hands, tapping his feet, squeezing his thighs, fidgeting, squirming, or rolling steel balls around in his fingers, the jury should know.

To accomplish this, the panel in front of the witness box should either be removed, constructed of clear glass, or replaced by a thin railing.

6. Potential jurors should be called from driver's license records, not from voter registration rolls.

In the 1988 presidential election, it was determined that half the people eligible to vote never bothered to register. (And of the half that did register, only half actually voted.) A common reason given for not registering was that the people didn't want to be called for jury duty. Let's kill two birds with one stone by having jurors selected from driver's license records. This might encourage more people to vote, and it would double the jury pool.

7. Jurors should be shown a film explaining the basic procedures of a court trial before they are seated on a jury.

According to the book *The American Jury on Trial,* more than three million Americans are called for jury duty every year. They are asked to decide more than 300,000 cases. Most enter the courtroom with little or no prior knowledge of what a jury trial is all about. Jurors often don't have a clue as to what the lawyers are talking about, why certain evidence isn't presented, what an "overruled" or "sustained" objection means, and hundreds of other seemingly baffling procedures that pop up during our increasingly complicated trials.

In contrast, potential jurors probably spend more hours languishing at the courthouse, twiddling their thumbs and waiting to be selected, than they do sitting on a jury. Let's make better use of this wasted waiting time by having the jurors watch a film or video that instructs them on the principles and procedures of a criminal or civil trial.

8. Judges and attorneys should wear traditional robes in court.

This is standard procedure in England and Canada, and has been adopted by Florida Circuit Court Judge Richard Feder. I found that it lends the proper respect, dignity, and decorum to the proceedings. (No wigs, though, like in England.)

9. Lawyers who willfully lie to a jury or aid another in lying should be disbarred.

For instance, in a publicized Miami case, the defense attorneys won a motion to suppress a confession to the police by their client. The accused had admitted that he had fired the gun that killed the victim "in self-defense" because the victim was bigger than he. The jury was not allowed to hear that confession; however, during their closing argument to the jury, the defense lawyers argued that their client was not guilty because he looked nothing like the killer and the whole prosecution was built on confused witnesses who had mistakenly identified their client as the killer.

10. Judges should be stripped of the power to order attorneys to knowingly present false witnesses or evidence, or to participate in any other form of dishonesty.

No ifs, ands, or buts. It's time to clean up the profession. If such rules were in effect, the courts would be cleansed overnight.

11. Capital punishment works.

I've looked into the eyes of hundreds of accused murderers. The electric chair is the only fear many of them harbor. At the very least, the threat of the chair brings about plea bargains that prompt the guilty to accept punishment without forcing an expensive and time-consuming trial.

12. Criminal appeals should be limited to one on the state level and one on the federal level, for a total of two. The first appellate decision should be rendered within six months of the jury verdict, the second within a year. And all grounds should be presented in both appeals. In death cases, a third and final appeal to the U.S. Supreme Court would be allowed.

In the present appellate court system, a case can be appealed more than two dozen times through different judicial tiers, with new grounds being dreamed up along the way. Wealthy crooks can sometimes dodge jail for a decade, waiting for all the appeals to clear. Even an indigent, convicted mass murderer can beat his death sentence by filing appeal after appeal.

The best deterrent to crime is the promise of swift and certain punishment. Our current appellate laws destroy this concept.

In civil cases, sick, injured, or defamed victims who win monetary verdicts are sometimes forced to wait as long as ten years to collect their first penny. More often than not, the amount is lowered or thrown out along the way. A swift and certain appellate system would aid in giving these victims the financial assistance the trial jury intended them to have.

13. The defense attorney who handled the original trial should not handle the appeal.

This mandatory switch would not only require the creation of a stronger body of appellate lawyers, but would allow the new attorney to raise the issue of ineffective assistance of trial counsel in the initial state and federal appeals. Such a charge against the former lawyer is most often the best and only chance a defendant has for a reversal.

14. All broadcast journalists should complete a training session before they are allowed to cover the courts.

Television is a powerful medium that persuades, educates, and sometimes prejudices the population. Throughout my thirty-eight years of dealing with the media, it has never ceased to amaze me how much misinformation goes out over the public airwaves. Television news operations usually don't have the resources or staff to allow their correspondents to specialize in any one area of expertise. Instead, the reporters rush from one scene to another and are forced to cover complicated stories in a limited amount of time. This results in confusion over the differences between federal, state, and county courts, the difference between a criminal proceeding and a civil one, and the function or ruling of a grand jury. I cringe every time I turn on the six-o'clock or eleven-o'clock news and hear that a grand jury has "convicted" someone. Grand juries don't convict anyone. They rule on whether there is enough evidence to charge a crime. But because it all sounds so "grand," the broadcasters feel some binding decision has been made. I suspect that a simple, two-hour workshop would help these influential journalists get a better handle on the law.

(Such a course might have prevented the Delaware anchorperson quoted at the top of this chapter from informing her viewers that I was arguing that Linda Palacios had committed suicide along with being murdered—quite a feat.)

I don't recommend this workshop for print (newspaper) journalists. Newspapers have larger staffs and generally assign beat reporters who are, or quickly become, well versed in the nuances of the legal system. They usually can be depended upon to get the facts straight.

15. There should be a course taught in law school called "Electronic Advocacy."

In this age of cable and satellite television, "trash TV," and modern newspapers, people are being "tried by the media" more often than they are being tried in courtrooms. The consequences, frequently the destruction of one's good name and reputation, may be worse than the eventual court decision. Today's defense attorneys need to know how to defend their clients against accusations in the media as well as in court. This would include instruction on how and when to grant interviews and hold press conferences, how the attorney should respond publicly to charges against a client, how the client should respond, the difference between broadcast and print journalists and how each faction should be handled, and preparing a community for a major trial. Simply put, as I often say: "If you're going to convict my client on the six o'clock news, I'm going to file his appeal and win his acquittal on the eleven o'clock news."

16. Eliminate plea bargaining.

This form of playing God is ruining the criminal justice system. It might be clearing the books and moving court dockets along, but at what price? It does not make punishment a deterrent. It trivializes the sense of being in court, ready to pay the price for criminal actions. When a prosecutor and a defense attorney can sit down in a morning and decide between them who goes to jail (and for how long) and who gets probation (or gets charges lowered or dropped all together), that is not justice. Only a judge or a jury should render punishment or mercy.

EPILOGUE

As the bitter memory of my jailing continues to fade, I've decided to keep practicing my brand of the law for as long as I can stand upright and talk. That is, if I can avoid being tossed in jail again for refusing to compromise my ethics.

And that may be the ultimate challenge.

AFTERWORD

*Everybody has to have a hometown. Binghamton's mine.
When I dig back through my memory cells, I get one
particular distinctive feeling—and that's one of warmth,
comfort, and well-being. For whatever else I may have
had, or lost, or will find—I've still got a hometown. This,
nobody's gonna take away from me.*
—Rod Serling

I RECENTLY returned to Binghamton for the second time since my
mother's funeral, in 1956. While planning the trip, I thought of my
high school teacher, Helen Foley. Miss Foley was a beautiful bru-
nette with a body that inspired a thousand schoolboy fantasies. She
came into my life at the precise time a boy begins having the
thoughts of a man. Rod and others were similarly captivated, and
we all fell instantly, hopelessly in love with Miss Foley. Rod was so
smitten that he would later use her as the inspiration for one of his

281

"Twilight Zone" episodes. The story revolved around a strange little girl named Markie, sitting on the stairway outside the apartment of a beautiful teacher named Helen Foley (played by Janice Rule). Markie turned out to be the teacher herself, as a child, and had materialized to warn the teacher that the man who murdered her mother two decades before had returned to kill her.

For me, the memory of the real Helen Foley perfumed my life even more deeply than Rod's fictional tribute. Despite my speech impediment, she showered me with the same attention she gave Rod and everyone else. Actually, I think she gave me more. It was the only time my handicap paid off.

While researching this book and hunting for old photographs, Dary Matera unknowingly tracked down Helen Foley. It wasn't difficult. She still lived in Binghamton. Matera had no idea of the significance of his find, as I had never mentioned her to him. Shortly before my return trip home, he handed me a note.

"By the way, this lady would like you to call her when you get there," he said.

When I saw the name on the note, my sixty-three-year-old heart started fluttering. Helen Foley wanted me to call! Those were the words of a young boy's dream.

I met with Miss Foley in Binghamton. Although she was in her seventies, she was vibrant, youthful, and nearly as alluring as ever. She had the same enchanting smile, the same kind voice, and same magical glint in her eyes that had driven Rod, and me crazy a half century before.

Miss Foley and I spent a wonderful afternoon together, driving around Binghamton and reliving the past. She took me to the high school and showed me the new additions, including a large auditorium—the Helen M. Foley Theatre. She blushed at the name, but I told her the honor was well deserved. That evening, we had dinner together.

Aside from my reunion with the lovely Miss Foley, Binghamton itself offered little nostalgic comfort. It had changed so much I could hardly recognize it. But there remained a few things that brought back the memories. Thomas Jefferson Grammar School was there and my old house was still standing at 98 Grand Boulevard. We lived on the second floor of the modest, two-story, red brick duplex. It had weathered the passing years remarkably well. I walked around back to see if the wooden stairway that led up to our quarters also remained. It did, but it appeared smaller than I recalled.

As I gazed up the stairway, frozen in my memories, hundreds of childhood scenes flashed through my mind. The one image that endured was that of my mother leaning out the hall window. I could almost see her black hair pulled back in a tight bun, and the wispy tendrils that always escaped and danced around her face in the morning breeze. She leaned out the window like that every time I left home, whether it was to join the wartime navy or to attend a distant law school. Many times it was snowing when I left for the train station. Often, it was so early that it was still dark. Sometimes my mother cried as she waved good-bye. Sometimes she smiled. Sometimes she did both.

She always said the same thing.

"Make us proud, Ellis. Make us proud."

I tried, Mom.

Pictured are Ellis Rubin, Mark Rubin, Kendall Truitt, Truitt's wife Carol, and Guy Rubin.

CONTINUING DEVELOPMENTS IN THE LIFE OF ELLIS RUBIN

ELLIS RUBIN AND THE FLORIDA BAR

FOLLOWING THE denial of all appeals in the contempt case, Ellis Rubin served his jail sentence. Then, The Florida Bar Association filed disciplinary charges against Rubin for his disobedience of a court order. A Grievance Committee of the Bar found him guilty and recommended a private reprimand, which the lawyer promptly refused, requesting a public appeal. The Florida Supreme Court appointed a Circuit Judge to decide the matter. Judge J. Cail Lee ruled after a lenghty hearing that under the circumstances, Rubin did not violate any ethical obligation by refusing to present perjury to a jury and that the charges against him should be dismissed. The Florida Bar then appealed that holding to the Florida Supreme Court where the matter is currently under consideration. Their ruling will make new law.

In the summer of 1989, the governing board of the Florida Bar, after a two-year study by several committees, decided to amend Florida's Code of Ethics for lawyers. They have asked the Florida Supreme Court to approve the change that would now command lawyers never to permit or introduce perjured testimony in court, including the narrative testimony of a criminal defendant. Of course, the Florida Bar is also recommending that if the trial judge orders the lawyer to allow perjured testimony from his client, then the lawyer must obey. Rubin promises never to obey such an order.

IN LATE May 1989, Ellis Rubin took the disturbing case of U.S. Navy Gunner's Mate Kendall Truitt, age twenty-one. Truitt was one of the eleven survivors of the gun turret explosion aboard the U.S.S. *Iowa* that had killed forty-seven sailors the previous month (April 19, 1989). Although Truitt had acted heroically in frantic moments following the blast, flooding the turret and possibly saving the ship, the navy later leaked a story that he might have caused the explosion to collect insurance from an alleged homosexual lover who died in the blast. Truitt, who is not a homosexual, a mass murderer or a bomber, was caught up in a media frenzy and saw his "reputation thoroughly trashed," as a sympathetic Ted Koppel explained on "Nightline." Rubin struck back against the damning allegations by holding impassioned press conferences defending Truitt in Miami, Norfolk, and Washington, D.C., and by appearing with Truitt on "Good Morning America," "The Today Show," "Larry King Live!" "Sonya Live," and Nightline." After Rubin's media blitz, fueled by countercharges that the navy was using the heroic sailor as a scapegoat to cover its own negligence, the navy unofficially cleared the young gunner's mate of any wrongdoing by announcing that he was no longer the target of any investigation. No criminal charges were filed. "Mr. Tuitt was lucky," Koppel added on "Nightline." "He found himself a good, tough, aggressive lawyer who forced the navy to back off."

Carol Truitt's father, Ray Smith, put it this way:

"The first night when the story broke I turned to my wife, Micki, and I said, 'He's got to get Ellis Rubin.' "

INDEX

Abramson, Barbara, 101–102, 104
Abramson, Erinn, 97–107, 111, 113, 121
Abramson, Herbert, 100–102, 104, 106, 121
Abramson, Scott, 101–102
Ackerman, Helen, 36–38, 52
Agrella, Darrell, 26–30, 33–34, 47, 53, 61, 63
Agrella, Linda, 53–54
Ali, Muhammad, 75, 130, 186–187
Allen, George, 177–178
Amabile, Philip, 197–203, 207–208, 222, 228, 240
Anderson, Dave, 174
Arnovitz, Abe, 16
Aykroyd, Billy, 160–161
Aziz, King Abdul, 80

Bailey, F. Lee, 191, 285
Baker, Paul, 49–55, 58–61, 63
Baretta (TV character), 43

Bass, Mike, 183
Batista, Fulgencio, 14
Bias, Len, 143
Bilanelli, Diane. See al-Fassi, Dena
Blake, Robert, 43
Book, Ronald, 170
Bradshaw, Terry, 182–183
Brando, Marlon, 87–88
Brady, M. Jane, 246–247, 253–254, 256–259, 261–264, 268
Brown, Johnny, 130–132, 192
Buchanan, Edna, 29–30
Buchanan, Jim, 39
Bundy, Ted, 148
Burger, Warren, 182

Cahill, Timothy, 27
Cahn, Burton, 210–211, 229, 232–233, 239
Campo, Johnny, 174
Carballosa, Al, 172–173
Carlson, Arthur, 18

Carson, S. O. "Kit," 18
Chambers, Whittaker, 140
Chica, Ron, 105–107, 110–111, 113
Conover, Richard, 102
Coppolino, Carl, 285
Corwin, William, 36, 57
Cosell, Howard, 168, 170
Cowan, Irving, 73
Cregan, Jim, 78
Cross, Pete, 225
Cunningham, Glenn, 165–166
Curran, John, 230
Curry, Pat, 201

Dahne, Micki, 273
Davis, Joe, 141–143
Demosthenes, 161
Dempsey, Robert, 125
Dershowitz, Alan M., 190–191
DiGregory, Kevin, 121
DiMaggio, Joe, 182
D'Orsio, Robert, 230
Drew, Mike, 64

Edwards, Edwin, 187
El-Amin, John, 134
Evans, Christine, 212–213
Evers, Betty, 273

Fahd, King, 67
al-Fassi, Aptisam, 77, 89, 91, 92
al-Fassi, Abdulaziz, 82
al-Fassi, Dena, 77–82, 85–88, 90–91, 93–94
al-Fassi, Hend. See Turki, Princess Hend
al-Fassi, Hessha, 82
al-Fassi, Hoda, 94
al-Fassi, Mohammed, 70–95
al-Fassi, Shamsuddin Abdulla, 80
al-Fassi, Tarek, 72
al-Fassi, Victoria, 77
Fawcett, Farah, 209
Feder, Richard, 91, 276
Feliz, Antonio, 13
Fichner, Henry, 239
Ficker, Robin, 178–182, 184
Firestone, Roy, 186
Fisten, Michael, 70
Flaherty, Pete, 180, 184
Foley, Helen, 281–282
Franza, Arthur, 172–174
Frumkes, Melvyn, 82–88

Fuqua, Frenchy, 182
Fuqua, Matt, 110–111, 114

Gardella, Kay, 64
Garvey, Ed, 182
Gerbner, George, 60
Gibb, Robert, 25–26
Gilbert, Michael, 32–33, 35, 41, 44, 46–48, 52, 55–58
Gilbert, Roswell, 219
Glick, Leonard, 142
Goetz, Bernhard, 240
Gordon, Fritz, 17–19
Greene, Cynthia, 86
Gross, Michael, 43

Haber, Leonard, 208–209, 214–218, 232–233
Haggart, Elinor, 24–29, 33–35, 44–45, 47–48, 54, 56, 63
Hall, Zell, 25–26
Hamlin, Harry, 120, 191
Hancock, Kelly, 205–206, 211–214, 218–220, 222–226, 231, 233, 235–237, 240
Harkins, James, 28
Harris, Franco, 183
Hart, Gary, 100
Hassan, King, 95
Headley, Thomas, 28, 46, 49, 51–55, 57–61
Henheghan, Delores, 179, 181
Herbst, Candace, 214, 220–221, 236, 239
Hiaasen, Carl, 137
Hicks, Odell, 127, 136–137, 143–146
Hiss, Alger, 140
Hollander, Xaviera, 91
Horner, Charles, 49
Horton, Mallory, 86–87
Houlihan, Richard, 108, 109
Hubbard, Don, 177, 187
Hubbart, Phillip, 147
Hudson, Catherine, 254, 265
Hyder, Shibley, 160

Jacobs, Jack, 26
Jamel, Ali, 73–75, 77, 90, 92
Johnson, Charles Wesley, 1–22, 192
Johnson, Don, 15
Jorge, Angel, 148

Kallet, Harry, 155–156, 158
Katz, Richard, 46, 49, 51–52, 57–58

Keaton, Steven (TV character), 43
Keller, Candace. *See* Herbst, Candace
Keller, Charlotte, 215, 236
Keller, Dorothea, 197–210, 215, 219–221, 222–226, 229–239
Keller, Lisa, 198–210, 213–228, 230–240, 273
Keller, Morris, 195–201, 203–204, 206–211, 213–219, 222–226, 230–239
Keller, Sam, 215, 236
Keller, Victoria. *See* Marron, Victoria
Kelly, Clifton, 285
Kilroy, John, 207
Kirk, Claude, 49
Kissinger, Henry, 182
Kleindienst, Richard, 179, 184
Kojak (TV character), 29, 35, 43, 53–55
Koppel, Ted, 285–286
Kortvese, Steve, 170
Kubik, Connie, 69
Kuzak, Michael (TV character), 120, 191

Lane, Mark, 284–285
Lansky, Meyer, 67
Larkin, Henry, 129
LeBlanc, Frank, 196
Lee, William Swain, 256–257, 259, 262, 265–266
Lehrman, Irving, 149
Leibowitz, Sam, 16, 164
Levine, Jay, 153
Lievano, Jorge, 32–33, 38, 47
Lindner, Alvin, 103

McGowan, Carl, 181
Mackinnon, George E., 181
McNeill, Joel, 9–10
MacPhail, Bill, 175
McRaney, Gerald, 43
"Maggot," 43
Malnik, Alvin, 67–68, 93, 94
Malnik, Mark, 94
Mandel, Howie, 43
Marecki, Ed, 261
Marino, Dan, 187
Marron, Eugene, 214
Marron, Victoria, 197, 203–207, 209, 215–217, 231–232, 234, 238
Marder, Teri, 195
Martinez, Bob, 285
Mastos, Ted, 151
Matera, Dary, 241, 246–251, 253–260, 262–268, 272, 282

Matera, Fran, 249
Means, Russell, 87–88
Mell, Jeff, 170
Menninger, Karl, 59
Mercado, Mary Jo, 104
Messerschmidt, Al, 86
Miller, Gene, 30
Mitchell, Martha, 91
Mitchelson, Marvin, 78, 82–88, 94
Morphonios, Ellen "Maximum," 137, 151
Musial, Stan, 77
Muskie, Edmund, 182
Mutter, Charles, 42

Neary, Robert, 226
Nixon, Richard, 140, 179–181, 183–184

O'Brien, William, 219, 227–228, 235
Orr, George, 84
Ortiz, Ana, 105
Osthoff, Sue, 239

Pacheco, Ferdie, 130
Palacios, Linda, 242–245, 247, 249–251, 254–256, 258, 260–262, 267–268, 278
Pastore, John, 177–178, 184
Pearson, Daniel, 149
Phillips, W. Keith, 167
Pierpont, Robert, 160
Pollock, Paul, 108
Price, Joe, 76
Prinze, Freddie, 44
Proxmire, William, 178, 184

Rasco, Russell, 16
Rasheed, Prentice, 127–128, 132–146, 148, 151, 192, 240
Reagan, Ronald, 90
Recio, Augustin A., 141–142
Reese, Betsy, 284
Reeves, Richard, 59
Reitmeyer, Joe, 172
Renick, Ralph, 5
Reno, Janet, 138, 141, 285
Reynolds, Charles, 241–251, 254–268
Reynolds, Doris, 245–247, 254, 257–261, 264–265, 268–269
Reynolds, Elsie, 242–245, 247, 250–251, 254, 258–264, 266–268
Reynolds, Mabel, 254, 265
Rice, Donna, 100
Richardson, Annie Mae, 284
Richardson, James, 283–285

Richardson, Marci, 206
Richter, Alvin, 7
Richter, Mr. & Mrs. Daniel, 6–10
Richter, Joseph, 7–8, 10–11
Richter, Ricky, 6–8, 11, 22
Riddleberger, Susan L., 244, 261
Ritter, John, 43–44
Robbie, Joe, 170, 185–188
Roberge, Aurelien, 12
Rodak, Michael, 181–182
Roosevelt, Franklin D., 140
Rothblatt, Henry, 91
Rozelle, Alvin Ray "Pete," 168–174,
    178–180, 183, 186
Rubin, Ellis
  childhood and youth of, 155–166,
    279–281
  al-Fassi family and, 67–95
  jailing of for contempt, 123–126,
    147–154, 189–192
  Johnson, Charlie, and, 1–22
  judicial system, thoughts about,
    271–278
  Keller murder trial and, 193–240
  NFL and, 167–188
  Rasheed, Prentice, and, 127–146
  Reynolds murder trial and, 241–269,
    271–272
  Richardson murder trial and, 283–285
  Sanborn murder trial and, 97–121,
    147
  Zamora murder trial (television
  intoxification defense) and, 23–63
Rubin, Guy, 77, 186
Rubin, Irene, 24, 89, 91–92, 95, 153, 165,
    169
Rubin, Kim, 23–24, 30–31, 48–49, 60, 92,
    186
Rubin, Mark, 77, 110, 118, 126, 135, 138,
    141, 144, 168, 186, 203
Rubin, Peri, 48, 98, 186
Runyon v. McCrary, 131

Sanborn, Holly, 98–99, 103–104, 107–109,
    114–115, 117, 121
Sanborn, Russell "Rusty," 98–121
Savalas, Telly, 43, 53
Schaub, Frank, 285
Scheff, Richard, 197–202, 207–208, 222,
    228, 240
Schwartz, Richard, 68
Seamans, Ike, 170
Sefedinoski, Scott, 36, 54–55

Serling, Rodman, 160–162, 281–282
Shafer, Harry T., 82
Shannon, Paul, 201
Shapiro, Sidney, 108–109, 116–121, 123,
    148–149, 153
Sharif, Omar, 75
Shaver, Kenny, 125
Shaw, Ben, 264
Shea, Joseph, 30
Shula, Don, 187
Simon, Rick (TV character), 43
Skomskie, Steve, 161–162
Smith, Ray, 286
Snickers, 193, 197
Sosa, Victoria. *See* al-Fassi, Victoria
Sotorrio, René, 108
Soul, David, 43
Spear, John, 134, 136, 145
Speiser, Mark, 200, 203–205, 213,
    219–220, 222–223
Spellman, Eugene, 62
Spinks, Leon, 186–187
Spitzer, Anne, 124
Starr, Bobbi, 68–69
Staubach, Roger, 183
Stein, Gary, 240
Stevens, Connie, 179, 181
Sturgis, Frank, 148
Surowiec, William, 98, 108

Tate, Larry, 195–196, 200, 225
Tatum, Jack, 183
Taunton, Earl, 9
Teriaca, Craig, 68
Teriaca, Vincent, 68
Thomas, Margaret Hanratty, 50–51
Thomas and Thomas, 76
Toledo, Paul, 24–25, 27
Tripper, Jack (TV character), 44
Truitt, Kendall, 285
Turki bin Abdul-Aziz, Prince, 67–70, 71,
    73, 80, 83, 94
Turki, Princess Hend, 68–69, 71, 80
Turner, Jack, 84–86, 88, 91–93
Turner, Roosevelt, 103–107
Tutti-Frutti, 142–144

Vinson, Steve, 134
Vlatofe, Elsie, 202

Waddy, Joseph, 179–181
Waksman, David, 119, 121
Walowitz, Bert, 7, 11, 16, 17

Warren, Fuller, 30
Weiss, Bryan, 54
Wells, Earl, 127, 134
West, John, 69–70
White, Marilyn, 195, 199
Whited, Charles, 149, 246
Wiggins, Marshall, 9
Wilbanks, William, 240
Wilke, Bob, 77
Wilkey, Malcolm R., 181
Willard, Ben, 2–4, 19–20, 129
Williams, Clarence, 129, 132
Williams, Edward Bennett, 180, 182
Woollcott, Alexander, 185

Wordsworth, William, 76
Wright, Dorothy, 140
Wyche, Charles, 20–22

Yahweh, Yahweh Ben, 151
Yepremian, Garo, 183
Young, Robert, 220

Zamora, Frank, 31, 36, 38,
    61
Zamora, Ronny, 23–63
Zamora, Yolanda, 25–28, 31, 35–38,
    54–55, 61
Zarowny, Michael, 19